Patterns of POWER

Inviting Young Writers into the Conventions of Language, Grades 1-5

JEFF ANDERSON with Whitney La Rocca

Stenhouse Publishers
Portland, Maine

Stenhouse Publishers
www.stenhouse.com

Library of Congress Cataloging-in-Publication Data
Names: Anderson, Jeff, 1966– author. | La Rocca, Whitney, author.
Title: Patterns of power : inviting young writers into the conventions of
    language, grades 1–5 / Jeff Anderson with Whitney La Rocca.
Description: Portland, Maine : Stenhouse Publishers, [2017] | Includes
    bibliographical references.
Identifiers: LCCN 2017023612 (print) | LCCN 2017039945 (ebook) | ISBN
    9781625311863 (ebook) | ISBN 9781625311856 (pbk. : alk. paper)
Subjects: LCSH: English language—Composition and exercises—Study and
    teaching (Elementary)
Classification: LCC LB1576 (ebook) | LCC LB 1576 .A543 2017 (print) |
    DDC 372.62/3—dc23
LC record available at https://lccn.loc.gov/2017023612

Cover design, interior design, and typesetting by Martha Drury

Manufactured in the United States of America

PRINTED ON 30% PCW
RECYCLED PAPER

23 22 21 20 19 18   9 8 7 6

For my mentors Candace Anderson and Dr. Nancy Roser

—JA

For my learning community

—WL

Contents

v

Acknowledgments

Jeff's Acknowledgments

Books happen because they are written, but it takes much more than that. It takes years of teaching and learning and working and thinking and reflecting and revising of thinking. It takes years of study and reading and experimentation. And most of all, it takes relationships. From an inspiring university professor like Dr. Nancy Roser to colleagues that modeled and prodded and encouraged me, like Candace Anderson. My relationships now span the United States and even New Zealand. I'm grateful to the people who come to my workshops, who ask questions, who invite me into their districts, schools, and classrooms. Thank you for helping me come to know what ended up in this project. I shared, but I also listened. Thank you especially to the teachers of Pattison Elementary, who shared their classrooms and their students' work, so we could provide a picture of what "it looks like."

A special thank-you to Jessie Miller, Nanette Raska, Kyle Warren, Lisa Thibodeaux, QEP books, and everyone else who helps me connect with teachers and students, all of which give me light and hope. Thank you to our editor, Bill Varner at Stenhouse, for allowing us to break molds and do what we thought you the reader needed. We appreciate the trust and allowance of our own creativity to go beyond "what has always been done." We thank everyone at Stenhouse. You're family! Thank you to the whole book team: Louisa, Jay, Chandra, Nate, Dan, Martha, and Drew and his tireless work to share our message with more and more people.

And most of all, a heartfelt thanks to my colleague Whitney La Rocca, who helped me with the hard parts on this project. I have a lot of good ideas that I am unable to make come to fruition. Whitney, you helped me close loops and add depth and ease and joy. She added more to this book than I could have ever hoped. She works hard and you will be hearing more from her, that I am sure of.

And as always thank you to my first editor and partner for life, who allowed me to work on this project on Thanksgiving Day, Christmas Eve, and Christmas Day—and other days we could've been at the park or doing something else. You are the perfect supportive and savvy partner. At the risk of sounding trite, you're a part of me and all I do.

Jeff

Whitney's Acknowledgments

It's awesome to witness what young writers can do when they've been using the patterns-of-power process for a while. Recently, I worked with a small group of fourth-grade writers, preparing for a high-stakes writing test. Before they crafted their introductions and conclusions, I shared a few techniques with a mentor for each. They drafted their own, automatically studying the mentors closely and imitating when they needed. These struggling writers were confident and ambitious. Their writing was incredible! I'd like to thank Jeff Anderson for introducing us to this powerful process. It truly changed the way our students involve themselves in writing.

I never thought I'd end up creating a resource for teachers with my mentor, Jeff Anderson, but here I am. I'm still in awe. Jeff, not only have I learned from you, but I also value our friendship and teamwork. Thank you, Jessie Miller, for bringing us together.

Thanks to everyone who supported me and cheered for me. Pennylane Lara, you heard it all. To the staff at Pattison Elementary, thank you for listening and working with new ideas. Because of you, our students enter junior high as writing risk-takers. Jeff and I appreciate all the student work samples submitted and the enthusiastic e-mails and phone calls to "come right away to see what my students are doing now!" Special thanks to Anna (Ghedi) Fleming, Rebekah Springer, Megan Mitcham, Gentry Bryan, Jill Hortness, Christi Elrod, Ashley Rice, Caroline Berg, Madeline Baker, and MaryLou Zeiders for opening your doors of your classrooms. To fourth-grade teachers Beth Andersen, Blake Mohnke, Lauren Niedzielski, Stephanie Rundell, and Mona Macias, who, in addition to providing work samples, collaboratively planned the interactive sentence wall for students referred to in this book. To Alice Cardner, thanks for suggesting a text when my brain was fried. Most of all, thanks to Debbie Barker, my principal, who supported me 100 percent. Your willingness to learn with the staff is an inspiration. To my future staff at Bryant Elementary and my new principal, Dr. Will Rhodes, I'm excited to see what we'll do together. To the teachers in Katy ISD, who use the invitational method in your classrooms, you are the legacy.

So many influenced and inspired me to take on new challenges and follow my dreams. To my teachers in Casper, Wyoming: I am who I am because of you. A huge thank-you to my Katy Instructional Coach group past, present, and future. Our time together is powerful. I leave each meeting with a brain full of ideas. To my book club, you are my cheerleaders, thought-provokers, instigators, and challengers.

A special thanks to everyone at Stenhouse for welcoming me. This process allowed me to see how much goes on behind the scenes. To Terry Thompson, you're brilliant. You pushed my thinking, caused me to reflect, and engaged Jeff and me in healthy conversations.

By looking at the stacks of books all over my home and office, you can see I have countless mentors. However, the two who raised me need special thanks. To my grammar nerd, Ed Daley, thanks for helping me edit my essays that I submitted in contests and assignments throughout my childhood. Because of you, I laugh hard at grammar jokes and read witty grammar books. And to my first writing teacher, Amy Daley, who never did the writing for me. Instead, you conferred with me and pulled a Lucy on me more times than I can count. Thank you for growing me as a writer.

Finally, I thank all who put up with me working odd hours and leaving town to write with Jeff. Tyler, you are an amazing writer. Never let go of your gift. John and Margie, you're awesome. Thanks for all the love and support you give every day. Emmeree, watching you develop as a writer is the best gift of all. Thank you for enjoying life and giving me a bright look into it. Keith, there is no way I could do this without your support. You light my path. I love you.

Whitney

Introduction

> *Out beyond ideas of wrongdoing*
> *and rightdoing there is a field.*
> *I'll meet you there.*
> —Rumi

Beyond ideas of absolute right and absolute wrong lives a classroom where writers thrive. They live in the questions and the wonders of language. Here, instead of avoiding errors, young writers make choices based on thinking and purpose. To these writers, the conventions of language are patterns of power they use to shape meaning. This classroom is built on the knowledge that brains naturally seek patterns to make sense of the world (Cunningham 2016). And after all, writing is about making sense, isn't it? Patterns attract our attention. They draw us in with familiarity and beauty and meaning. And like all patterns, language conventions can be counted on to repeat over time.

Instead of showing young writers the mistakes to avoid, we argue for illuminating the patterns of language that mold meaning and have powerful effects on readers. Creating a classroom in which the special-effects devices of grammar and conventions are studied in authentic texts (real books and student writing) generates writers who naturally come to know the conventions of the English language. They come to know them as the patterns of power. Without much work, they'll note that the most effective patterns are repeated more often because they get the job done.

We call the conventions of language *patterns of power* instead of *rules*, because we think that phrase better represents them. Rules allude to absolute right and wrong. Like laws, rules are expected to be followed—or else. Patterns are created, noticed, and repeated because they happen naturally, like cycles in nature. Patterns show and rely on purpose rather than an outside authority. Would you rather face down rules burdened with confusing exceptions or turn toward attractive, meaningful patterns that repeat often to communicate meaning?

Figure 0.1
Often students think author's purpose is as easy as PIE (Persuade, Inform, Entertain). Author's purpose is much more than that. Author's purpose is the reason behind why authors make certain craft moves in their prose to telegraph certain meanings.

Take capitalization, for example. When most of us think of capitalization, correctness and rules come to mind. What if we thought about conventions—even as simple as capitalization—as author's purpose and craft? What if we considered capitalization as a pattern of power that telegraphs meaning to our readers with purpose?

When Mo Willems capitalizes a word in his beloved Elephant and Piggie series, he does so for a reason. It can be as simple as capitalizing Gerald and Piggie, the main characters' names. Writers and readers know the pattern of capitalizing names. When they use the capitalization pattern, writers give their readers an additional detail about a word. When they don't, their readers squeal to a stop and wonder, "Is *piggie* a name or not?" We only capitalize words for a reason. In *There Is a Bird on Your Head*, Piggie asks Gerald where he wants the birds, which are hatching eggs on his head, to be. Gerald replies

"SOMEWHERE ELSE!"

The reader knows exactly how to read aloud Gerald's reply. Willems's choices of capitalization or "all caps" and the end punctuation ensure that. Knowing and using these patterns empowers readers to read and writers to write.

In the patterns-of-power philosophy, young writers explore the conventions as special-effects devices for the words they read and write. They experiment and grapple with the power of meaning that conventions create—moving, pausing, stopping, speaking, yelling, comparing, timing, identifying, emphasizing.

Conventions activate meaning, showing us how to read the text: words, punctuation, and syntax unfold before us, triggering meaning, sentence by sentence, paragraph by paragraph. These conventions live in the books sitting on young students' desks and are modeled in the overstuffed bookshelves in the corner. These patterns inhabit the words and punctuation young writers scratch down on paper, expressing meaning.

No quick fix exists. Worksheets and workbooks aren't a necessary evil. We don't need pages of fill-in-the-blank exercises designed to cram language into a tidy black-and-white package tied up with a chevron bow. We use messy, glorious writing and reading. Workbooks and worksheets don't

Life is unpredictable but patterns form.
    –Adam J. Kurtz

As we learn, we recognize the patterns that support our ways of knowing. This process occurs much the same way that the brain seeks to organize information, and the formation of patterns enables us to recall what has been learned.
    –Larry C. Holt and Marcella Kysilka

explore the real application of language. They are designed for limitation, not possibility. Worksheets avoid the gray areas of usage. They stick to absolute right and wrong. If there is only one answer, you know it's a worksheet. When children write and read, learning is orchestrated, composed, and notated. They are busy mucking about with conventions, experimenting and approximating and discovering. Expression and meaning dance across the pages in this classroom as students talk about the patterns they notice and try them out in their own compositions.

Messy wall charts drip with examples, and students' noticings fill every nook and cranny of this classroom, capturing learning for future reference and application. The classroom is abuzz with meaning-making and interaction: talking and listening, and reading and writing, not filling in blanks.

How Do Young Writers Often See the Conventions of Language?

Sadly, not all young writers experience the joy of language in this way. They don't see grammar as an invitation to play with patterns of power, to make their own kind of meaning. They don't see that language is like squishing wet mud through their hands to see what happens, making shapes and remaking them. The act of doing transforms. Instead of this kind of play, often a right-or-wrong attitude seeps into their minds, permeating and hardening beliefs: there is only one choice—the right one, which they'll never make. Anything they come up with is inept and incorrect. To them, the distinction between right and wrong feels arbitrary and lacks any meaning they can grasp. Abstract grammar edicts are less appealing than trying out the moves writers make and exploring the special effects they create. And no matter how often these vague edicts are repeated, they fail to improve writing:

- Write in complete sentences.
- Avoid run-on sentences.
- Avoid fragments.

Sure, many students can parrot this well-worn advice, but do they have any idea what the words *mean*? When Jeff taught sixth grade, many students would ask, "Does this have to be in complete sentences?"

"What's a complete sentence?" Jeff would ask.

"Do we have to or not?" they'd snap.

"How will you know?" Jeff stepped closer, curious.

Eyes would roll. "Never mind."

Jeff wanted to see where their understanding of a complete sentence led. Students could spout terms, but they didn't understand what they meant or how they could best use them in their writing. They wanted to avoid errors; they wanted to avoid the rabid red pen. They thought complete sentences were the holy grail. But they only knew the label; they didn't understand what it meant.

"That's just the way it is in English," students may be told.

But that's not true, is it? There is a reason behind every convention, and each choice a writer makes has an effect. That's author's purpose and craft. The purpose is why, and the craft is how. These are the patterns of power.

Students don't often see grammar as choices they craft to create. Instead they glean that conventions are valued only if they're "right." This fear of missing the mark causes young students to act like zombies, eyes glazed over, slowly trudging toward us, holding out their papers, chanting, "Is this right? Is this right? Is this right?"

That's not power.

That's dependence.

That's saying, "I can't. You can, so do it for me." If we truly want to move our conventions instruction from a right-and-wrong tango to conversations about meaning, we must approach errors differently. So what *do* we do when a developing writer inevitably makes a mistake along the way? How can we deal with that in a positive, empowering way?

In a third-grade classroom, Jeff notices Aaron using language at his growing edge. Jeff kneels beside Aaron and recognizes that the young writer is taking a risk, reaching into possibility, so he responds carefully. Jeff's aware that how he responds to these first attempts will affect Aaron's attitudes toward future risk-taking and growth. Aaron has written this:

When I woke up this morning. My stomach hurt.

The error is right on the surface. But beneath the surface error, a writer is moving toward correctness and complexity. His attempt at a complex sentence—starting with a subordinate clause (*When I woke up this morning*)—reaches toward more complex writing, which matches the way he speaks. He intuitively chunked his sentence into two parts to be understood. But instead of using a comma to set off the opening dependent clause, he used a period. An approximation. But consider how close he's gotten to a complex sentence.

"Wow! I'm impressed, Aaron."

"Huh?" He looks up, confused.

"Read this aloud to me," Jeff says, pointing to Aaron's paper.

As Aaron reads his sentences aloud, he pauses after morning. "How did you know to pause after *morning*?" Jeff asks.

"I can hear it."

"And you just reached out and tried something to show that pause." Jeff high-fives Aaron. "That's what writers do. They show their reader what to do."

Aaron smiles.

"Do you want to know a writer's secret?" Jeff asks, smiling back.

Aaron nods.

"See how when you say, 'When I woke up this morning . . .'" Jeff leans in, silent, exaggerating that he's waiting for the rest of the sentence to come. "See how it doesn't feel complete?"

Aaron squints.

"The writer's secret is when you start a sentence with the word *when*, you're probably going to need a comma. So, instead of a period, you put a comma after *morning* to show that both of these things go together. What was the period doing?"

"Telling us to stop?" Aaron doesn't seem sure.

"Yes, a period was telling us to stop, that the sentence is over." Jeff smiles. "And the comma says pause. More is coming. It's not over yet."

Aaron changes his period to a comma, but he leaves the possessive pronoun *My* capitalized. Jeff could correct him, but he resists the reflex. He's building confidence and competence, not drowning a writer in a deluge of doubt and discouragement. Sometimes we just need to let a mistake go.

Writing is a process. The most important thing we can do when teaching the patterns of power is to refrain from compulsively addressing everything at once. We resist the urge to fix it all. We know in our hearts that fixing everything unintentionally causes the writer to shrink and learn nothing, except perhaps that there are endless ways to be wrong.

Aaron won't suddenly become an expert at crafting complex sentences and eradicating fragments. But his risk has been honored, and he'll keep reaching. When students stop reaching and risking, they stop growing. Period.

In the patterns-of-power lessons, we want elementary writers to stretch and to apply the conventions to their reading and writing. That is the point, after all, isn't it? We steward primary and intermediate writers into the lifelong journey toward meaning.

The Patterns of Power in the Classroom

Somewhere, there are people who haven't heard the music.
—Laurel Snyder, *Swan: The Life and Dance of Anna Pavlova*

Somewhere, young writers wait to hear the musical patterns conventions can give their words. Somewhere, teachers are curious and hungry for a better way to teach the conventions of language. This book is an invitation to anyone who desires to move young writers beyond right and wrong and into an open world of taking risks, experimenting, and creating meaning with the patterns of power.

Young writers can confidently move through a process of digging into meaning through use and application. Working with grammar and conventions is much more than avoiding a boring barrage of mistakes they might make. Conventions are discovery and power. Mistakes demonstrate growth, a moving beyond what is currently known. Ask any writer. These *mis*-takes are part of the writing process as we reach out and grapple with and approximate meaning. Our classrooms can be about progress rather than perfection, moving toward both correctness and meaning. Conventions are ready-made patterns writers can learn and use naturally as their words and marks spill onto the page.

A patterns-of-power classroom cultivates curiosity and nurtures noticing. In our classroom, the books and articles we read become a continual conventions curriculum. Every sentence holds a truth about writing, if only we pay attention. In classrooms where writers flourish, students engage with the world around them, noticing things that not everyone else sees. In this same way, young writers notice things about the conventions writers use. The narrator of Sara Pennypacker's *Clementine* explains how paying attention to the world benefits any endeavor:

> Every sentence holds a truth about writing, if only we pay attention.

My dad says I am excellent at noticing interesting things. In fact, he says if noticing interesting things were a sport, I would have a neckful of gold medals. He says that's a Very Good Sign for My Future. He says I could be a good detective, of course, but that noticing things is good for any career.

My mom says that means I could be a good artist, too.

Or a writer. Last year, a writer came to my school, and said, *Pay Attention!* But she didn't mean to the teacher, she meant pay attention to what's going on around you, so you can write about it. Then she looked exactly at me and said to notice the good stuff and write it down so you don't forget it.

We want students to become expert at the sport of noticing the "good stuff" writers do. Our continual question, "What do you notice?" (Chambers 1985) develops students' observational cognitive structures (Garner 2007), inviting them to slow down, look closely, talk and question freely, and pay attention to the language moves writers make in new ways.

The thinking and observation skills students will gain in the patterns-of-power lessons will not only directly apply to the reading and writing they do, but affect their ability to reason and draw connections between style, attitude, tone, and any author's purpose or craft. It will affect how they read math problems and see patterns in science and social studies. As Clementine observes, this concentration, this observation that literacy requires, bolsters anything we do, academic or otherwise.

Creating Space for Young Writers

The author and reader know each other;
they meet in the bridge of words.
—Madeline L'Engle

Our youngest writers can fulfill what language and convention standards ask of them while they are building a link between writing and reading workshop. After all, meaning is made when reading and writing meet. We can also think of grammar and conventions as the meaning-making bridge that joins comprehension and composition. This bridge transports the natural, reciprocal flow of literacy (see Figure 0.2). The grammar bridge is undergirded with meaning. Conventions and grammar activate meaning in the writing and reading processes, linking effect and purpose for writers and readers. The conventions aren't separate. They are, in fact, the meaning-making element, binding reading and writing with meaning.

How Do We Fit This into Our Tight Schedule?

What if we took five minutes from our reading workshop and five minutes from our writing workshop to study how reading and writing connect in the conventions? A ten-minute daily dose of attention would create miraculous

Figure 0.2
The grammar bridge links composition and comprehension. The bridge is undergirded or supported by meaning. The grammar bridge activates meaning and purpose, which operate between the acts of reading and writing.

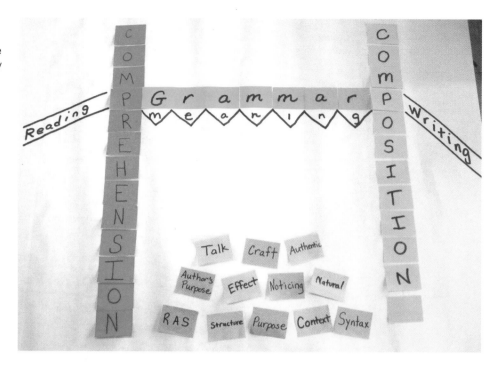

effects on students' understanding of how language works to create meaning, benefiting both reading and writing workshop directly.

So what do we do with those ten minutes a day? We suggest using the patterns-of-power process, which is based on the invitational process (see Figure 0.3) introduced in Jeff's book *Everyday Editing* (2007). Here, we've adapted this process for grade levels 1–5, tweaking it for the primary grade levels for the first time. Additional support for planning and application are included in Part 1 and within each lesson.

We know that foundational attitudes about the wonder of language and all its power are formed in elementary school, especially the primary grades, so we didn't take on this task lightly. Whitney, a K–5 literacy coach, is on board to make sure the primary grade levels are represented. Jeff has worked in first- through fifth-grade classrooms along with Whitney to discover the adaptations we need to make for our youngest writers.

The basic idea of the invitational process is that it is driven by students' natural curiosity about language. We step in and share the patterns of power in bite-sized, digestible chunks. We invite literacy learners to experiment and play with these patterns with loads of talk, support, and modeling. Instead of drowning writers in sentences flooded with errors or lists of *nevers* or skills or rules, we soak them in beautiful sentences found in the literature already in our classrooms. These experiences occur over a series of days in ten-minute increments. (The process is explained fully in Chapter 2.)

The teacher displays a sentence. Students notice a move the writer has made in the sentence, such as adding dialogue or using commas in a list. They study the move and talk about it. Then they try it out with the teacher or a partner. Just one move. It's doable for the teacher and the students. Then we celebrate the move we are learning, creating new possibilities for students to reach toward. Finally, they are nudged to apply the move to their individual compositions.

Figure 0.3
The invitational process for teaching
conventions in 10-minute daily doses.

Invitational Process

- Invitation to **NOTICE**
  A sentence from literature is displayed to model a pattern of power. Discussion begins with the question, "What do you notice?"

- Invitation to **COMPARE AND CONTRAST**
  An imitation is studied as it sits below the original. Discussion begins with the question, "How are they alike and different?"

- Invitation to **IMITATE**
  Using the sentences they've been studying for inspiration, writers "try out" the pattern of power through shared, interactive, or paired writing. When appropriate students try on their own to use the pattern.

- Invitation to **CELEBRATE**
  Young writers share their work with an appreciative audience.

- Invitation to **APPLY**
  The pattern is used to respond, revise, or used in some other purposeful way.

- Invitation to **EDIT**
  Students study four versions of the original sentence, including three variations to illuminate how small changes affect meaning.

Nudging writers toward the application of the patterns of power permeates our planning and instruction. This is the best way we've found to create a space where young writers experiment and play with meaning. This shows them how to learn from authentic reading and writing processes. To put it in simple terms, learning deepens as they see these moves repeated, driving meaning into everything they read and write. We intentionally accelerate this process by inviting our students into the patterns-of-power process.

If you're new to the invitational process, this book is arranged so you can easily access all that an elementary teacher needs to teach the convention lessons. If you've already had experience with invitations, you'll notice we've made some adjustments to the process, keeping our youngest writers in mind. Even if you feel familiar with the invitation process, we suggest you begin with the overview in Part 1, because revisiting the *why* behind your instructional moves is essential to teaching the lessons that follow.

How Do I Work with This Book?

You could jump right to Part 2's lessons, but we try to give you brief "just what you need at the moment" material in the lessons for ease of use. The important background and connective tissue is in Part 1, which sets up a way of thinking, so we highly recommend you read it first and return to it whenever clarification is needed. Here's a peek.

Part 1

Getting Started with the Patterns-of-Power Process

In Part 1, we explore intentional planning, instruction, and application that push students to participate as meaning makers rather than error avoiders. Our first three chapters give an overview of this adapted invitation process, offering foundational support to implement the lessons.

Chapter 1: **Into Planning: What Do You Need to Do Before Teaching the Invitations?**

The value of spending a few minutes talking about what we actually want students to do with a convention at our grade level and how the convention connects to craft is the crux of successfully implementing the patterns-of-power process. Thus, this chapter explores a step-by-step process for effectively planning and thinking through conventions instruction.

Chapter 2: **Into the Classroom: How Do You Teach Conventions with the Invitations Process?**

Displaying a powerful piece of writing is only the beginning of the process in the classroom. The talk, the moves that we make in each phase of the invitational process, is explained in depth through a model lesson on capitalization for first or second graders.

Chapter 3: **Into Application: How Do You Ensure Writers Apply What They Know?**

Once the pattern has been taught, teachers need ways to nudge authentic use. This chapter includes a menu of options to ensure the patterns are applied multiple times across multiple contexts.

Part 2

Into the Patterns-of-Power Lessons

Part 2—the largest part of the book—brings readers ready-made lessons designed for classroom use. These lessons are broken into bite-sized, digestible chunks grouped by writer's craft and author's purpose. The range of lessons is specifically designed for primary and intermediate grades to step through the invitation process. We include content, texts, and lessons based in the state and national standards for grade levels 1–5. Within each section or grouping of lessons, multiple chapters move from beginning concepts to more advanced lessons toward the end of each chapter. Lessons aren't labeled by grade level, so you can start in any chapter based on your students' needs. We've also included classroom-ready support materials alongside each lesson, so you'll have everything you need at your fingertips—no need to flip to the appendix.

The Power of Sentences

The Power of Pairs

The Power of Details

The Power of Combining

Whether you teach first or fifth grade, struggling or advanced writers, you can find the right lesson at the right level for your class. Tip boxes, thoughtful quotes, and power notes hang out on the pages of the lessons and chapters for you to go deeper or pause and think.

Writing is a process of approximations, moving us closer to clarity of image and message.

Part 1

GETTING STARTED with the

Patterns of POWER PROCESS

It's amazing what you can see when you just sit quietly and look.
—Jacqueline Kelly, *The Evolution of Calpurnia Tate*

Getting Started with the Patterns-of-Power Process

"How am I supposed to get kids to edit stuff if they don't know the rules in the first place?" an elementary teacher wondered aloud at a recent staff development session.

That's a good question.

No matter how closely students look at their writing, they can't correct a convention if they don't understand its purpose. Asking novice writers to practice editing before they've learned the meaning behind a convention is useless. We have to teach the conventions—actually *teach* them. Editing *practice* comes only after editing *instruction*, not before or instead of it.

We don't expect kids to multiply before they've been taught how to do it. Why is it acceptable to have young writers practice editing over and over when we haven't taught the meaning behind the conventions in a deep way?

Not covered.

Taught.

We build understanding through instruction. That means inviting our students to apply the patterns of power to their own writing, so they can understand their effect on their readers. If they're not applying the conventions, we still have some teaching to do.

To get to the point where they can fluently edit their own writing, students need to slow down and pay close attention. In fact, they need to gaze at sentences as intensely as a dog stares at a squirrel. But rather than paying attention to errors or fixing mistakes, young writers home in on *how* writers' moves activate meaning. They slow down and observe the special-effects devices writers use in literature. They investigate the way conventions breathe life into sentences. We link them to author's purpose and craft, inviting students to talk about what they see and wonder about in an author's sentences.

Part of understanding the invitation process is identifying how it differs from the grammar and conventions work commonly done with young writers. The invitations let go of traditional grammar instruction: reliance on labels and definitions, a right-or-wrong stance, and a lack of connectedness to what writers really do. Students don't feel invited into lessons flooded with abstract terms that sound impossible to them: *auxiliary modals, correlative conjunctions, past perfect versus past progressive, determiners* (or do we call them *articles*?). It's all too much even for most adults, much less six- and seven-year-olds.

With invitations, we take a step back. Instead, we study the conventions authors use to communicate meaning clearly to their readers. We read a selected sentence for meaning first, and then investigate it, discussing what we notice and see and wonder about. We make conventions and grammar accessible. We invite students into the possible, into what they *can* do rather than what they *shouldn't* do.

Books, talk, and curiosity naturally drive the invitational process.

The hallmark of the invitational process, then, is beginning with a beautiful sentence to study and learn from, rather than one filled to the brim with errors. We share the effective sentence with students and ask, "What do you notice?" The worst-case scenario is that students will burn an accurate, well-written sentence into their visual stores.

And students speak first.

As teachers, our responses and teaching flow from the font of children's noticings. We are careful not to weigh down the discussion with abstract labels and laundry lists of exceptions. Instead we explore the sentence and live in the possibility of the meaning-making that writers and readers do.

Certainly just looking at strong writing won't necessarily change writers, but when we investigate a sentence and talk about the moves writers make to support meaning—the conventions and grammar—we begin transforming what students know. Since student talk drives the invitations, we cultivate curiosity and delve into discovery in a student-centered way as learners process how conventions work together to communicate meaning in the model sentence. Young writers come to know correctness rather than run from wrongness.

To help you get ready to explore conventions as a process of invitations, Part 1 will walk you through the three stages you'll need to work through to get started.

Let the Process Begin

If you want people to become passionate, engaged in a field, transformed by an experience—you don't test or lecture them and you don't force them. Instead, you create an environment where willing and caring individuals can find an experience that changes them.

—Seth Godin

Part 1 serves as an overview of the patterns-of-power process. It will take you by the hand and guide you through the steps you will use to teach the lessons in Part 2. All the information you need to begin teaching conventions with the invitation process is in these blue pages. You can return to this section for review as needed while planning, teaching, or applying the convention lessons of Part 2.

Learning Conventions Is Not a One-Time Event

Absorbing how to use conventions and grammar effectively is a lifelong pursuit.

Learning conventions is not a one-time event. It's a process. Absorbing how to use conventions and grammar effectively is a lifelong pursuit. We will continue to make decisions about the effects of a convention's use for as long as we write.

May the joy of learning grammar become a part of the meaning-making fabric of your classroom. May your young writers thrive.

A voice comes to your soul saying
Lift your foot. Cross over.

—Rumi

Into Planning: What Do You Need to Do Before Teaching the Invitations?

> *When we raise our planning to [a] conscious level, we are able to make clear, informed decisions about exactly where we want to take our learners. Our aim must be calculated and precise.*
>
> —Terry Thompson, *The Construction Zone*

Both the most challenging and the most beneficial aspect of teaching conventions through invitations is the work we do *before* teaching the lessons. To teach the patterns of power in a way that sticks, planning is essential: we think deeply about what students actually need to know and be able to do before designing our lesson.

Teachers have told us that discussing and clarifying the learning target or standard beforehand has a direct effect on how successfully they nudge students to use the convention in their writing over time. Planning gives us insight into how intertwined author's purpose and craft are with conventions. In each lesson in Part 2, we briefly share the results of our planning process. Though this work has been prepared for you, knowing *how* and *why* the lessons are organized and progress as they do will inform the depth and flexibility with which you move through the invitational process.

> Planning gives us insight into how intertwined author's purpose and craft are with conventions.

With this in mind, we begin by giving you a closer look at our planning process summarized in Figure 1.1.

The Patterns-of-Power Planning Process

Select a Standard and Uncover What It Asks Students to Do

Selecting a convention or language standard is an obvious place to begin, but how do you decide which one to start with? Or more importantly, how do you deconstruct it into a teachable chunk?

You could review your students' writing and see what they need right now, or reflect on common struggles you have observed at your grade level over the years. You could also refer to

Figure 1.1
Planning Process

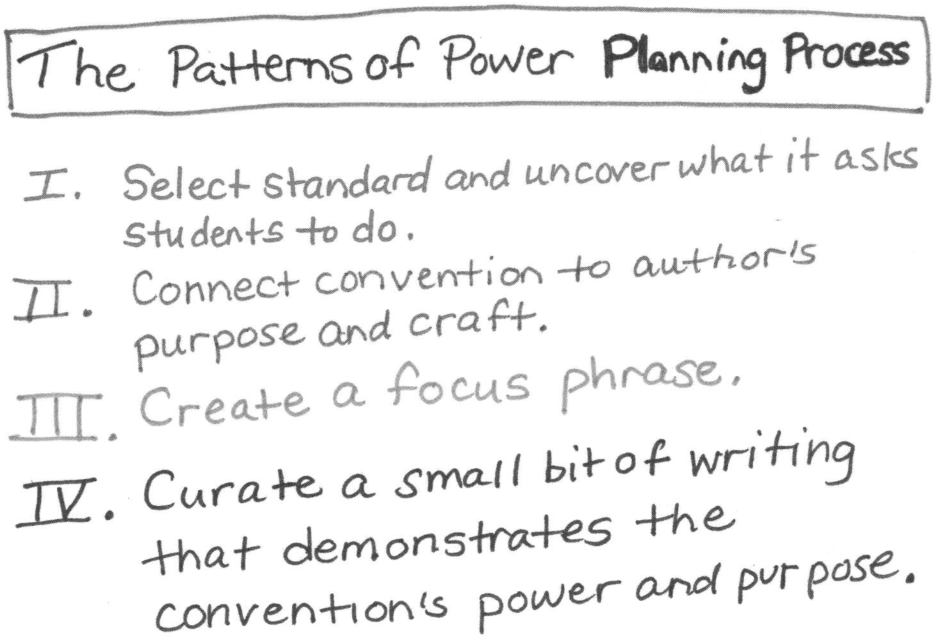

The Patterns of Power **Planning Process**

I. Select standard and uncover what it asks students to do.

II. Connect convention to author's purpose and craft.

III. Create a focus phrase.

IV. Curate a small bit of writing that demonstrates the convention's power and purpose.

local, state, or national standards documents, which guide what is to be taught and when.

Though you'd think a standard would be fairly straightforward and classroom-ready, one standard may encompass multiple teaching goals. To illustrate, consider first-grade standards on nouns through the lens of a first-grade teacher. Multiple standard sources address this convention in various related but different ways:

- Capitalize names.
- Use common, proper, and possessive nouns.
- Understand and use nouns (singular, plural, common, and proper) in the context of reading and writing and speaking.

As you can see, one standard can be stacked with multiple concepts. Even though you've selected a standard, you still may not be have decoded what the standard actually asks an elementary student to know and do. If we don't have a clearly defined learning target, how on earth will we know when our writers hit it? What a standard really asks may not be clear on a first or second reading. To highlight particular patterns of power for instruction, we delve into each standard and sort out its smallest developmentally appropriate chunk. With this in mind, we begin by pondering the following questions, knowing we'll build on a convention's concept over time:

- What's a digestible chunk for our grade level?
- What do our writers need to know *first*?
- What will our students need to know about the convention to gain meaning from it as both readers and writers?

Let's walk through these questions with our example of teaching first graders nouns, looking closely at the standards' intent and purpose.

What's a digestible chunk for our grade level?

When we look at the noun standards for first grade, we see, as noted earlier, that other skills are embedded. Too many related but different skills would not be digestible for first graders. We start small. All of them mention proper nouns or names. But we also note that none of the standards say, "Teach nouns." The standards refer to particular uses of nouns. For now we will leave possessive, singular, and plural for later.

We settle on beginning with the difference between common and proper nouns, because this skill is foundational for the basics of detail and helping students understand specific ideas, people, places, and things versus general ones. Later, we can build on this learning by including possessive nouns, singular nouns, plural nouns, and more.

What do our writers need to know *first*?

For our focus on common and proper nouns with first graders, we decide on beginning with the feature that distinguishes common from proper nouns (names of people, places, and things): the fact that we *capitalize proper nouns*. Beginning with capitalization of proper nouns helps readers see what function they serve (specifics and names) as opposed to common nouns. It's a manageable instructional target.

What will our students need to know about the convention to gain meaning from it as readers and writers?

When we uncovered the identifiable distinguishing feature of the capitalization of proper nouns, we began down the path to usage. Writers capitalize names—or proper nouns. Proper nouns, in fact, *are* names. We now ask ourselves if the standard is pointing writers toward memorization of terms and definitions or steering us toward the convention's use and function.

Making a plan also requires us to discern how students will later apply our chosen standard to their reading and writing. If we lose focus on the convention's connection to author's craft and purpose, we may drown children in meaningless abstract terminology and definitions that hold no meaning or purpose for the learner. With this in mind, we'll make sure our instruction encourages writers to consider how they can use common and proper nouns with an eye toward craft and meaning. In other words, we want our lesson to leave kids thinking less about what common and proper nouns are *called* and more about the job they actually *do*.

Generally, standards ask students to apply skills in their own writing, not label or diagram sentences or complete a fill-in-the-blank or multiple-choice worksheet. Deep down, we already know that memorizing terms and definitions isn't a higher-order thinking task.

Instead we tap into young writers' natural curiosity about what conventions do—especially when translating standards for young writers' eyes and ears.

They want to know.

Unpacking a standard takes conversation and an understanding of the purpose and craft of a convention, which define its usage. This inquiry into the learning target's intent and our first steps takes thought and collaboration and continues in the next planning step.

Linking the conventions of language to the art and craft of what authors do isn't always easy, but it is essential for real grammar instruction to occur over time. We continually connect the convention to craft and clarification of meaning. In the next section, we'll explore moving conventions from *correctness* to a skill of *communication*, connecting these important patterns more deeply to author's craft and purpose—the *how* and the *why*.

Connect Convention to Author's Purpose and Craft

Author's purpose informs *why* writers do what they do, and writer's craft is *how* they do it. Writers craft their compositions in certain ways for clarity. They don't use ellipsis points because they think they're pretty polka dots all in a line. They have a meaning-based reason for a convention's use. And writers need to know what effect conventions will have on a reader—a question mark and question words (*who, what, when, where, why,* and *how*) affect the pitch of how a reader reads their sentence. The voice goes up at the end, doesn't it?

Authors are powerful. They can make us do most anything they want. They can choose any pattern of power: periods, question marks, exclamation marks, conjunctions, commas, compound sentences, complex sentences. All these moves affect how writing is read and how the reader makes and infers meaning. Conventions direct our reader on a path: these ideas go together, these don't.

In the end, the whole purpose of grammar and conventions instruction is to elevate writing. When determining what a standard is asking, we think about how writers use it as a craft move. Aren't noun standards asking first graders to know that the world is made up of *people, places, things,* and *ideas* that they already use in their writing? Try writing without nouns. It's impossible. Nouns are the stuff that writing is made of. Nouns ground your reader in the material of the world, including ideas. And young writers come to understand this by writing and reading.

To narrow the common and proper noun standard to a bite-sized chunk for first graders, consider the craft difference and purpose between common and proper nouns when writing (Figure 1.2).

Even if the reader doesn't know the particular park, person, car, class, or museum, they know the writer does. They know this writer pays attention.

Figure 1.2
The craft of proper nouns

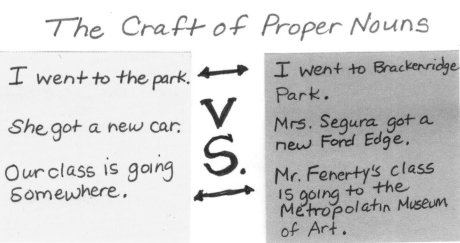

The Craft of Proper Nouns

I went to the park. ⟷ I went to Brackenridge Park.

She got a new car. **VS.** Mrs. Segura got a new Ford Edge.

Our class is going somewhere. Mr. Fenerty's class is going to the Metropolatin Museum of Art.

Writers know and show the particular. Since first graders often write about siblings, pets, toys, and friends, this is a good place to begin. It makes their writing more visible to the reader when they use names.

Writers show readers that a noun is proper by capitalizing it. For a first grader, proper nouns elevate writing with concrete detail and specificity. To speak about proper nouns at this level, we pivot from proper nouns to capitalization. We do this because capitalization is a digestible, concrete action that moves writers to understand the difference between proper and common nouns on a basic level that's meaningful to young writers.

Pondering a convention's intended effect on a reader can unlock the *why*. And when students know *why* a convention is used—its purpose—they will be able to comprehend its meaning while reading and create meaningful effects while writing—that is, they'll be able to practice the craft. They'll also gain the knowledge needed to edit for the convention's correct usage when they make a mistake in their own compositions, which invariably happens. In short, once they understand a convention's purpose and craft, they know how to use it. It's not just some rule to prattle off with no understanding. It's a part of what they do to write.

Next, we'll explore focus phrases, which shape our young writers' understandings by making the planning we've done thus far accessible to our elementary students.

Create a Focus Phrase

Once we've uncovered what we want to teach young writers and understand why and how authors use it, we create a focus phrase. The term *focus phrase* comes from Terry Thompson's book *The Construction Zone* (2015). A focus phrase helps teachers and students commit to a concise and manageable learning target, such as *I capitalize proper nouns*. The focus phrase needs to be brief, so students will be able to say it and internalize it. Kid-friendly language states a clearly defined learning goal, making instruction intentional and effective. Additional benefits of the focus phrase become evident throughout the writing and teaching process because the statement

- keeps the teacher focused on the instructional goal during planning and delivery,
- maintains student focus on the goal throughout the instruction, and
- becomes a source for students' self-talk when they are working independently and eventually becomes their independent thought.

Although a long-term goal might be "I use capital letters only when I need them," students in the early stages of learning capitalization will need to investigate why we capitalize proper nouns. For this instructional goal, depending on students' needs, the focus phrase could be something like one of these:

- "I use proper nouns to name particular people, places, and things."
- "I capitalize the names of people, places, and things."
- "I show important people, places, and things by using a capital letter."
- "I capitalize names."

We share several focus phrases for multiple reasons. We need to generate more than one so that we can choose which is best for our particular situation. Since the focus phrase can look different based on the needs of your students, we include suggestions, but encourage you to shape, revise, and allow them to evolve in your classroom.

But focus phrases will mean nothing to students unless they see the convention used in the context of authentic writing. So, we suggest you share the focus phrase only after a mentor or model text has been displayed and students in some way notice the focus convention within the sentence. Since we teach by responding to students' noticings, finding a model sentence that demonstrates the focus convention is essential.

Curate a Small Bit of Writing That Demonstrates the Convention's Power and Purpose

After we've defined our focus phrase, the next planning component is to find model text that shows the convention in action. Remember, making the lesson narrow directs students' attention to a particular convention. Often one sentence is adequate to demonstrate a skill or standard in context, but from time to time, more than one sentence may be needed to model a particular skill or give sufficient context. For example, teaching the conventions of dialogue may require three or four paragraphs to show multiple conventions in action.

When selecting a sentence that demonstrates the accurate use of the skill, identify the author's purpose and craft for yourself. Consider the sentence's length and level of difficulty as you search for a model of the learning target. We've found that using sentences in literature near or just above your group's appropriate reading level usually works most effectively. It will also be important to consider the ease with which your students will be able to imitate the sentence later.

Many primary students enjoy titles from Kate DiCamillo's Mercy Watson series as read-alouds or early chapter books, so lifting a sentence from *Mercy Watson to the Rescue* to help first graders focus on proper nouns is a good choice.

Mr. and Mrs. Watson have a pig named Mercy.

We chose this sentence because of the multiple uses of proper nouns, both first and last names. However, because we're using DiCamillo's authentic writing, young readers and writers will likely notice more than the focus skill. And that's okay. The additional conventions may not be the focus of the lesson, but teaching in context is about showing how language works together to create meaning. At a minimum, seeds are planted or awareness is activated about a future focus or we can spiral back to previous learnings. We'll explore this idea of flexibility more in the actual teaching of the example lesson in the next chapter.

Even though each lesson in this book includes possible sentences, craft connections, and focus phrases, we still strongly recommend talking through the author's purpose and craft links with colleagues before jumping into instruction. You'll find your lessons are more flexible and effective when you take the time for this important step of planning and clarifying the learning target, focus phrase, and model text.

The Power of the Plan Is Activated

Once the plan is in place, we confidently step into the next part of the patterns-of-power process, teaching and interacting with students through a set of invitations. Now that we've deepened our awareness of what we're teaching, we've also bolstered our trust in ourselves, students, and the process. The process will unfold easily as we invite students to interact with a mentor text in various ways.

We stand back and wait for their reactions, and then we build upon their noticings. Students will guide us to the next place instructionally. We'll never be prepared for all their noticings, but as long as we honor their attempts at making meaning, together we can learn how language's complexity unfolds in both predictable and unpredictable patterns.

Patterns-of-Power Planning Process for Invitational Grammar and Editing	
Standard/Skill	Review your students' writing samples, reflect on common struggles you see each year, or refer to standards or skills. Choose a standard or skill and break it down by uncovering what it asks the writer to do.
Author's Purpose/Craft	Connect the convention to the author's purpose (*why* writers do what they do) and craft (*how* they do it).
Focus Phrase	Create a focus phrase: kid-friendly language that states a clearly defined learning goal. Ex: *I start sentences with a capital letter.*
Mentor Sentence/ Invitation to Notice	Curate a small bit of writing that demonstrates the convention's power and purpose by searching your read-aloud, favorite mentor texts, or texts that are popular with your students.
Invitation to Compare and Contrast	Create an imitation of the mentor so that students can compare and contrast the two.
Invitation to Imitate Together	Decide if this imitation will be through shared writing, interactive writing, or paired writing.
Invitation to Imitate Independently	Decide how the students will imitate independently: Notebook? Sentence strips? Notecards? Class book page?
Invitation to Celebrate	Decide how the imitations will be celebrated while bringing back the focus phrase: Class book? Hang on wall? Document camera? Graffiti wall?
Invitation to Apply	Decide how you will extend the work throughout the day in other areas. What opportunities will the writer have to apply the skill?
Invitation to Edit	Copy and paste the sentence three times beneath the original sentence. Change one thing in each of the pasted sentences to lead a discussion about how the author's message is changed or affected by the change.

Patterns-of-Power Planning Process for Invitational Grammar and Editing	
Standard/Skill	
Author's Purpose/Craft	
Focus Phrase	
Mentor Sentence/ Invitation to Notice	
Invitation to Compare and Contrast	
Invitation to Imitate Together	
Invitation to Imitate Independently	
Invitation to Celebrate	
Invitation to Apply	
Invitation to Edit	

Be notorious. I have tried prudent planning long enough.
From now on I'll be mad.

—Rumi

Into the Classroom: How Do You Teach Conventions with the Invitations Process?

Writing is not a fill-in-the-blank exercise.
—Arthur Applebee, National Council of Teachers of English session, 2012

The plan is in place, we've winnowed a standard down to a manageable skill, refined a focus phrase, and chosen a model sentence that shows the convention or pattern in action. We're ready to walk into the classroom and move through the invitations process (see Figure 2.1). And you won't even need a fill-in-the-blank worksheet.

Figure 2.1
The invitation process

Invitation	Process
Invitation to Notice	"What do you notice?"
Invitation to Compare and Contrast	"How are they alike and different?"
Invitation to Imitate	"Try it out."
Invitation to Celebrate and Connect	"Share."
Invitation to Edit	"What changed?" "What effect does that change have?"

The author's sentence and our conversations around it will begin to teach grammar and conventions—and more. Though this process can be done in different ways, we've found it most effective to start by scheduling each step of the invitation process in approximately ten-minute time slots across a week or so. We've also found it beneficial to share these lessons early in the day, so our young writers will have ample opportunity to apply the lesson focus across the day and curriculum. Since reading and writing skills meet in the meaning-activating conventions, writer's craft, and author's purpose, some teachers capture five minutes from both reading and writing workshop to create the ten-minute space in their day. On the chart, "Possible Schedule for Daily 10-Minute Invitations," is an example of how one convention might proceed over a few weeks. Of course, there is no set formula, just a pattern of invitations that start young writers on the path of discovery. Responsively adjusting by extending, accelerating, or deleting ten-minute blocks may be necessary, depending on the complexity of the convention and student readiness.

Possible Schedule for Daily 10-Minute Invitations	
Day	**Invitation to . . .**
1	Notice
2	Compare and Contrast
3	Imitate with Interactive or Shared Writing
4	Imitate as a Pair
5	Celebrate (Celebrating can be as simple as students reading their sentences aloud or displaying them on a document camera.)
6	Imitate Independently
7	Celebrate (Sharing on wall charts or class books could go on for more than a day.)
8	Edit

Invitation to Notice in Action

In the classroom, the invitational process commences when we display the selected sentence. At this point, we still haven't written the focus phrase on the board or shared it with students. Not yet. Instead, students discover the pattern within the context of the sentence. Student curiosity drives the invitation process. The focus phrase remains in our back pocket, until we respond to and extend students' noticings.

What Do You Notice?

Once the sentence is displayed, we establish that it's correct so that young writers won't immediately try to fix it. "This year we're going to look at great sentences and talk about what authors do to create beautiful meaning with their words and punctuation. We'll learn how do it ourselves." Then we ask a question that opens magical discovery (Chambers 1985; Garner 2007): "What do you notice?" We love the gamble of this question. You never know quite what kids will say or notice—or in what order.

In a classroom of first graders, Jeff displays DiCamillo's sentence (see Figure 2.2).

Figure 2.2
Kate DiCamillo's sentence about Mercy

> Mr. Watson and Mrs. Watson have a pig named Mercy.
>
> ~ Kate DiCamillo, <u>Mercy Watson to the Rescue</u>

He reads the sentence aloud twice, inviting students to join on the second reading. After reading the excerpt, Jeff asks, "What do you notice?"

And he waits.

You may want students at the rug or at their desks to partner up and tell each other what they notice. You can listen in as the pairs talk.

Allow the time to follow students' lead, even when they don't notice what you want. Fifteen seconds wait time after the question is the minimum. If you're chatty like we are, count silently in your head. We'll get to the focus eventually. For now it's all about what readers notice.

Squinting, one boy asks, "Why are there three periods in the sentence?"

To be honest, Jeff isn't prepared for that question. At some point you won't be ready for something your kids say or ask either. Learning to write is messy. Nonetheless, whatever a student shares, we work with it. We simply honor, name, and extend students' responses as they come. It's important to first acknowledge something positive, or students won't take risks to share their noticings. We look for ways in which their comments point toward craft or the principle in action. You might have to thread the needle at times, but it becomes easier over time.

In this case, Jeff desperately flips through his brain for his next teaching move. Needing time to think, he vamps by honoring what he can. "It does *look* like three periods. That's a great eye. I hadn't thought about that." (He really hadn't. At all.)

"Let's count the periods together: one, two, three. Let's look at the last one first." Jeff touches the period at the end of the sentence. Starting with what's easy is a good rule of thumb. "What is *this* period doing? What's it telling the reader?"

"To stop," Destiny says.

Jeff throws his hand up, like a school crossing guard halting a speeding minivan. "Stop!" Jeff invites kids to stand and mimic his stance. "What's the period say?"

"Stop!"

"One more time: the period says . . ."

"Stop!"

"Now calm down—our shouting has ended." Jeff smiles. "Period. What else does the period tell a reader?"

Silence.

"Does it tell us the sentence is *over*?" Jeff clarifies.

"Yes!"

Jeff reflects what the students noted. "This period," he says, tapping on the end of the sentence, "tells us this sentence is over and we can begin a new one."

Is Riding the Curiosity Wave Okay?

There's an instructional choice to make now. Do we say, "We'll deal with the other two periods tomorrow," or do we dive in and show kids how we might figure it out? That's the power of the invitations. Teaching is always a gamble, but you are likely to win when kids are curious. So Jeff dives in, even though he isn't sure where it will go.

"Now let's look at these other two periods, one after *Mr.* and one after *Mrs.*" Jeff writes *Mister* and *Mr.* on a piece of chart paper (see Figure 2.3). "How do you say this word? How about this one?"

Figure 2.3
Students discuss how the two versions of *mister* are alike and different.

Students say both words are pronounced *mister*.

"How else are they the same?"

Students note that both *misters* start with an *m* and end with an *r*.

"How are they different?" Jeff asks.

"One is longer and one is shorter," Lizzie says.

"The bottom one has a period after it," another student observes.

"That's the thing. The shorter one has a period, because when we shorten words like *mister*"—Jeff points to *mister*—"to *Mr.*, we need to put a period to show we shortened it. It's called an abbreviation. We do that with some words we use all the time. We shorten—or abbreviate them. And when we shorten them, we show that we shortened them with a . . ."

"Period!" The class responds.

Don't be afraid of what kids may notice or wonder. Eventually you'll learn to use whatever they say with ease to drive forward their curiosity and engagement. You manage how much time is spent on what: you decide the focus phrase and pick the sentence. In planning, you've set everything up for the young writers to discover and learn. Let them share what they notice or wonder about the sentence or sentences displayed—questions, punctuation identification, or whatever they observe. They'll surprise you.

Even though capitalizing titles used with last names and their abbreviations aren't the targeted standard, we allow for the organic process to unfold. This detour actually lends itself to our focus on capitalizing proper nouns, when a title is used *with* a proper noun, it's capitalized (*Dr. Jones*). When the title is used *without* a proper noun, it's lowercase (*doctor*). Plus, when kids are curious about meaning, we follow that interest, engaging them deeply, our explanations springing forth from their wonderings.

What Else?

We've discussed how important wait time is for responses to the question "What do you notice?" But it's equally vital when you follow up with "What else?" Good therapists know this trick. If you keep asking, "What else?" eventually whatever needs saying will be said. Allow a generous amount of time for the analysis and thinking that students need. If you don't give the time, you'll be the one driving the lesson. Trust the invitational process.

After waiting fifteen seconds, we *might* prompt with other questions:

- "Does anyone know what this mark does?"
- "What are some other ways we could describe what Darren just noticed?"
- "Is there anything else you see or wonder about or know?"

In the *Mercy Watson to the Rescue* sentence, a first grader points out the presence of capital letters, so Jeff asks, "Which letters are capital letters?"

Several students come up and point to the capital letters in the sentence.

"How do we know those are capital letters?" Jeff asks, leaning over the chart stand.

"They're bigger?" a student offers.

"Let's look at each one to test that theory." Jeff touches each capital in the sentence. "Okay, they are bigger."

"Plus, we learned how upper- and lowercase letters are buddies, like over there." Adriana points to a chart of the upper- and lowercase letters on the wall.

"Oh, Adriana remembered that the charts on our wall can help us."

If a convention that a student notices has a function (for example, a capital letter, an end mark, a comma, or a conjunction), we extend the conversation by asking students to collaboratively answer two essential questions about the convention's function.

How Do You Talk About Function?

Research supports this focus on function during grammar instruction (Graham and Perin 2007), but how do we make talking about a convention's function accessible to our youngest writers?

Two simple questions can push students back to function when we put any punctuation mark or word in the blank (Figure 2.4).

Figure 2.4
What's the function?

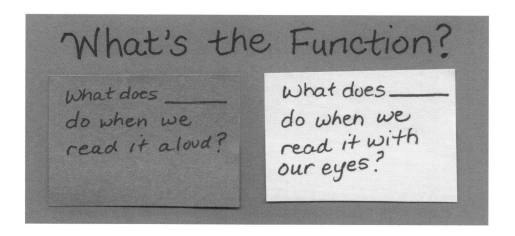

As students answer the two questions (What do _____ do when we read them aloud? What do _____ do when we read them with our eyes?), reading the model aloud and silently, they build a theory about the function of the convention. We listen in on their thoughts. We highlight, extend, and connect to them, adding explicit information when needed, and in doing so, enrich their understanding of the convention's function.

"What do capital, or uppercase, letters *do* when you read them aloud?" Jeff scans puzzled faces.

After about fifteen seconds, Jeff rereads the *Mercy Watson to the Rescue* sentence aloud and comments. "Well, the capital letters don't really *do* anything when we read it aloud, do they? When we read capital letters aloud, they don't make us stop, or take a breath, or change our voice, or anything. Hmm . . ."

The kids stare at DiCamillo's sentence.

"What about when we read the capital letters with just our eyes?" Jeff puts his hand over his lips and points to each word in the sentence in a left-to-right sweep.

"Well . . . ," Vanessa begins, pointing at the sentence, "the capital letters look like they're standing up, and the lowercase letters look like they're sitting down."

"Oh, so the capital letters stand up or stand *out*—look more *important*," Jeff says. "And writers only capitalize letters for a reason, so let's look at the capital letters in this sentence."

Pointing to the first word of the sentence, he says, "Why is this word capitalized?"

"It's the first word," a student says.

"Of a what?" Jeff prompts. "First word of a what?"

"A sentence."

"So one reason writers capitalize a word is if it's the . . ."

"First word of a sentence," several students respond.

"But this one also has another reason." Jeff quiets.

"It goes with a name," Trenice says.

"Yes, writers always capitalize names," Jeff says. "*Writers capitalize names.* Say that with me."

The class repeats it with him.

Now Jeff writes the focus phrase on chart paper. "I capitalize names." The class repeats, "I capitalize names." The focus phrase patiently waits in his back pocket until the students' noticing of the standard bobs to the surface to be named. "So when we put a title like *Mr.* or *Mrs.* with a last name, it is capitalized. But we also do that with any title used with a last name."

After the focus convention is discovered, we work in the focus phrase as much as possible throughout the lesson, the day, and the week. "What other words are capitalized by the author?"

"*Watson* is capitalized twice because it's two names," Chandra says.

"*Mercy* is the name of the pet," Darren adds.

"So, writers capitalize names of people *and* pets," Jeff affirms.

"And *Mr.* and *Mrs.*"

"And the first word of a sentence."

The funny thing is, if we ask, "What do you notice?" followed by "What else?" several times, students usually do notice most things, at least enough to begin a conversation. But what if students hadn't pointed out the capital letters? We could quickly draw attention to them, saying something like, "Hey, did anybody else notice that there are several capital letters in this sentence?"

How Do You Wrap Up the Noticings?

At the end of our invitation to notice, we restate what students discovered about the text—crediting the students who noticed them when possible— and provide explicit information about the convention, calling attention to its function and use (i.e., the focus phrase). We send students off with an invitation to continue noting the conventions we've discussed as they read and write that day, encouraging them to point them out when they see and use them in context—and of course *why* (author's purpose, function, and meaning).

We'll return to the same sentence the next day with an invitation to compare and contrast.

Tip: Do You Mark Up Sentences as Students Notice?

We don't mark up model sentences during this process because it can be distracting to learners, looking like some sort of abstract syntax surgery. Is it okay sometimes? Yes. However, keep in mind that overmarking could actually hinder students' ability to observe how the author has woven meaningful conventions together, merely making it next-generation sentence diagramming.

Invitation to Compare and Contrast in Action

The next day, we continue to invite students to notice our focus convention by calling on the power of comparison and contrast, a practice deemed a successful research-based teaching method across all areas of the curriculum (Dean et al. 2012).

To begin, we display the original sentence we explored during the invitation-to-notice lesson and pair it with an imitation we've crafted during planning.

Mr. and Mrs. Watson have a pig named Mercy.
Dr. Gonzalez has a cat named Aristotle.

Our imitation sentence closely follows the original sentence in terms of pattern and structure while demonstrating how the pattern of power can be applied to other situations and content.

"How are these sentences alike and different?" Jeff asks.

In pairs, students analyze the mentor text and its imitation—orally, in writing, or both. This collaborative conversation deepens students' consciousness of the standard and its effect, laying the groundwork for later application. As they do so, we repeat our focus phrase, "I capitalize names."

Once the focus phrase has been named, we refer to it frequently to expand students' understanding of the convention's function and use.

We discuss how the imitation and original are alike and different. Anything students note is a place to start. We're building observational skills and concentration by allowing our young writers the time to take the sentences apart, chunking them and comparing and contrasting them. If students say, "*Mr.* starts with an *M* and *Dr.* starts with a *D*," we ask, "How else are *Mr.* and *Dr.* alike or different?"

"They both end in a period."

"And why do *Dr., Mrs.,* and *Mr.* end in a period?"

"They were shortened!" Hector says.

"What else is alike and different?" Jeff asks.

"At the beginning, there are two *Watsons* and there's only one *Dr. Gonzalez.*" Harmony says.

"True." Jeff smiles. "How else are the *Watsons* and *Dr. Gonzalez* alike?"

"They're capitalized."

Jeff mouths the word *why* and several kids jump in and shout, "Whyyyyy?"

"We capitalize people's names!"

"Brilliant." Jeff walks over to the board. "Let's repeat, 'I capitalize names.'"

Tip: To Capitalize or Not to Capitalize: That's the Question About Titles with and Without Names

You may want to expand the discussion on titles of people to include more than abbreviations. In the proper nouns lesson, we used *Mr.* and *Mrs. Watson* and *Dr. Gonzalez* as examples of titles with last names. The titles were abbreviated and capitalized *because* they were used with last names. When these titles appear without last names, they are neither capitalized nor abbreviated: *mister, mistress,* and *doctor.* Depending on your standards and your student interest, you'll decide how much energy to spend here. To keep things manageable and appropriate for first graders, we didn't delve into all of this. Had we been working with fifth graders, we would have.

The capitalization of nonabbreviated titles is consistent with this pattern, though. When the title is used with a name, it is capitalized. When the title stands alone—without a proper noun—it isn't. So *governor, senator,* or *president* (not attached to a name) aren't capitalized. However, when we use any title with a name, it is always capitalized: *Governor Jackson, Senator Delacruz,* and *President Miller.*

Kinship names, like *aunt* and *uncle,* which describe how people are related, are capitalized when they precede a name or are used as their name as well.(*Aunt Allie and Uncle Jerry visit us often.*) However, when a possessive precedes a kinship name, it isn't capitalized. (*Carl's aunt Allie visited last week. His uncle Jerry couldn't get off work.*) See more on kinship names in Chapter 6.

Student conversation is paramount as they compare and contrast the two sentences. Conversation deepens understandings of structure and the choices that go into them. Conversations bring ideas to a conscious level of awareness (Eagleman 2011). Exploring another example is crucial to highlight patterns. Using a shared language to talk about patterns of authors' choices creates writers who own, understand, and use the concepts.

In addition, pairing the teacher's imitation sentences with the original sentence models how students can imitate it. The next day, writers will use the author's pattern as a lens through which they express ideas about their experiences as they try out the pattern.

Invitation to Imitate in Action

To this point, writers have explored a model sentence, discovered its pattern of power, connected it to a focus phrase, and compared and contrasted it with an imitation. It's time to apply the convention by composing. This is the practical application that grammar research supports (Graham and Perin 2007). Imitation provides a natural way to bring best-practice and research-based methods to convention and grammar instruction.

For this stage in the patterns-of-power process, you have several options for imitating the model sentence:

- Shared writing
- Interactive writing
- Paired writing
- Independent writing

This menu of imitation choices ranges from most-teacher-supported (shared writing) to least-teacher-supported (independent writing). You may choose to do all of these variations in order over a few days or choose just the ones appropriate for your students' needs or at the right level of complexity. Imitation can take more than one ten-minute block over more than one day if you choose. Let the complexity or the skill and student needs dictate that decision.

In general, when imitating a pattern, we follow the steps shown in Figure 2.5.

As writers, it's crucial that we build a habit of rereading our writing. Quite often we need to make adjustments. That's revision. That's editing. That's writing. Writers read and reread their own writing, even when it's just a sentence, and most of the time they tinker with it. (See Figure 2.6.)

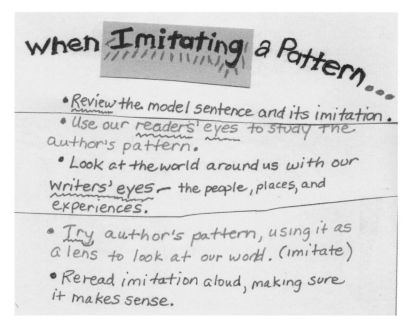

Figure 2.5
When imitating a pattern . . .

Figure 2.6
Reader's and writer's eyes

Shared Imitation

At this point, early in the year with first graders, we select the most-supported imitation choice to begin: shared imitation. In shared writing, we model, holding the pen (the blueberry-scented marker, in this case). Young writers share ideas, and the teacher manages the recording of the sentence. This way, students can witness meaning coming together.

"Okay, use your reader's eyes to look at Kate DiCamillo's sentence pattern. What does she do?"

"She uses capital letters," Monica says.

"Why does she use capital letters?" Jeff waits.

"We capitalize names," several students say.

"Let's say that again," Jeff encourages.

"I capitalize names."

Jeff walks over to the chart paper with the *Mercy Watson* sentence. "She uses names to tell us about what?"

"The Watsons have a pet."

"So our reader's eyes tell us we're going to use names to describe someone who has something. That's Kate DiCamillo's pattern. But we also use our writer's eyes. Our writer's eyes look at the world around us. Who could we write about from home or school?"

"Mrs. Chavez!" a student suggests.

"Way to use your writer's eyes," Jeff praises. "Mrs. Chavez is right next door—a part of your world."

"And she has a pet," Zander says, "and it's got a name."

Listening, Jeff records students' ideas, careful to remind students that it's okay if their idea isn't used. They'll be able to write their own imitation soon enough.

Mrs. Chavez and her class have a hamster named Winifred.

As appropriate, we revisit the focus phrase in our discussion. After you've worked through this imitation in shared writing, you may choose to use interactive, paired, or independent writing the next day. Decide based on the complexity of the task, student engagement, and need.

Interactive Imitation

Another choice that turns over a bit more responsibility to young writers is interactive imitation. It's close to shared writing, but in this option we share the marker with students as they assist us in composing the imitation. A student may come to the chart and write a capital letter or sight word or add a period or whatever they volunteer to do. Interactive writing takes more time, but its engagement has a high payoff. (See Figure 2.7.)

We choose to move to paired writing the next day and skip the interactive option on this one. It's up to you and your time limits whether you do or don't do the paired or independent imitation, depending on the decisions you make about how to scaffold and share.

Figure 2.7
Watson interactive writing

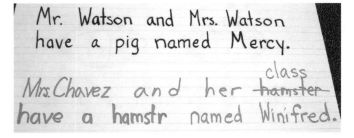

Paired Imitation

In the paired imitation option, students collaborate on an imitation with one other student. This is the last scaffold before independence. Sometimes you may skip straight to independent imitation, but we've found it to be a valuable addition to the flexibility of the invitation process.

In early first grade, you may choose not to do this or the independent option at first, but don't wait too long, because it's where the learning really blasts off. Second through fifth graders say they appreciate the process of negotiating with another person as a way to imitate the pattern of power. Writing is problem solving, and it's nice to have someone else's ideas to bounce against ours, creating something neither of us would have come up with on our own. (See Figures 2.8 and 2.9.)

Figures 2.8 and 2.9
Paired writing

Mr. Watson and Mrs. Watson have a pig named Mercy.

With your partner, imitate this mentor sentence.

My mommy and dad have a dog Iko.

But sometimes students prefer to do the imitation on their own. This can be allowed, but we remind them that they can use their idea the next day, when all students will be imitating independently. "It's really a good chance to make sure you understand the pattern," you can say. "Having someone to discuss your writing with is a gift many writers hunger for. Take advantage. You'll have plenty of time to write on your own."

Independent Imitation

The independent imitation option gives the students the most responsibility. (See Figures 2.10 and 2.11.) In some cases, you may skip right to this step.

Now write your own sentence, using the pattern of power from the mentor sentence.

Mr. Watson and Mrs. Watson have a pig named Mercy.

My friend has a pet hermit crab named Sandy.

Figure 2.10
First-grade independent imitation example

Now write your own sentence, using the pattern of power from the mentor sentence.

Mr. Watson and Mrs. Watson have a pig named Mercy.

Mrs. Rice and Miss Thomas ee have dogs named Parker and Blair.

Figure 2.11
Third-grade independent imitation example

Until further notice, celebrate everything.
–David Wolfe

If you do and it's not working, you can always go back a step, but we often find students are raring to go with their own sentences, some doing them even before they're asked, which of course we don't mind. The important thing here is for students to try the convention, reaching into possibility.

Once paired or independent writing is completed, it begs to be shared. This is one of the most important components of the process: celebration. It can happen the same day the imitation sentences are written or the next day, depending on the timing in your classroom.

Invitation to Celebrate and Connect in Action

After students have had a chance to imitate our original sentence in pairs or independently, it's time for some celebration! Debbie Miller says, "What is celebrated gets repeated." And how often do we celebrate grammar moves? Young writers are more likely to hear correction than clapping, and if that's what we model, that's what students will do as well.

We want to imbue positive feelings and associations in our writers' experiences with conventions. We focus on the illumination of the pattern rather than the eradication of error. Their experiences are anchored in what writers do rather than mistakes they could make. To move in this direction, we make time to share students' imitations with an audience and celebrate their efforts. As writing process teachers, we know the importance of sharing and audience, so we allow as many kids to share as we reasonably can.

To start off, students share their imitations.

"'My neighbor Raul has a pit bull named Rocko,'" Michael shares.

As part of the celebrating and connecting routine, we read our imitations twice. On the first listen, we hear the ideas; on the second, we hear how those ideas fit into the pattern of power.

Michael reads his sentence again, and the class applauds. Michael nods, smiling. Writing is hard work; it's nice to be appreciated.

"Why didn't he capitalize *pit bull*?" LaShawn asks, peering over Michael's shoulder. "That's the name of a dog."

We always try to honor what kids say. "That's a good question, LaShawn," Jeff affirms, and then he reviews the students' learning. "Michael didn't capitalize *pit bull* because we don't capitalize types of animals. We didn't capitalize *pig*, but we did capitalize *Mercy*. The word *dog* and individual dog breeds aren't capitalized. So *pit bull* isn't capitalized."

LaShawn isn't happy, but this whole language thing is complicated. It's a process. Jeff admits when he started teaching, he probably couldn't have answered LaShawn's question. What do we do when students ask tough questions?

We say, "That's a good question," and we look up the answer. Or we say, "That's such a good question, we're going to talk about it tomorrow," and then explain the next day—after we've done some research. Conventions are a lifelong process for you as a teacher as well. (See Figure 2.12.)

Figure 2.12
We-capitalize-names wall chart

During these discussions and celebrations, we deepen our understanding of the convention's use and see how the pattern connects across topics. As we hear others' sentences, we hear possibility. We hear the choices writers make. When celebration is skipped because of time, or we've forgotten the power behind sharing in various ways, we miss a perfect opportunity for writers to honor risks and inspire each other.

How Do We Continue the Celebration?

Of course, the celebration can continue. Student creations may be posted on a wall chart or anywhere to encourage the convention's use. We write the focus phrase across the top of the wall chart, allowing it to grow organically as students encounter the particular convention in action across texts and curriculum. (See Figure 2.13.)

Figure 2.13
Growing wall chart

We make books (see Figures 2.14 and 2.15). We partner with a teacher in the grade below, and our kids share what they know about the convention with the younger students (Figure 2.16). We share our sentences with others in other classes through the use of technology (Figure 2.17). We cover our doors with student imitations, communicating that conventions are fun and worthy of celebration, not something to dread (Figure 2.18).

Don't skip the celebration part of the process, and constantly search for ways to praise. Dull your need to correct every little thing. Don't be a party pooper. It's a progression, moving forward and honoring the work of risking and stretching.

When we celebrate our use of conventions, positive attitudes seep into our young writers' minds. Taking time to celebrate creates literate beings,

Figure 2.14
First graders create class books with each child's imitation as a page.

Figure 2.15
First graders read a class book together during buddy reading.

Figure 2.18
A-DOOR-able: Fourth graders celebrate by covering the classroom door with their imitations of complex sentences.

Figure 2.16
A third grader shares his writing with a second grader, pointing out the conventions he used.

Give it a Go!! Share your sentence with Pattison's fourth grade classes!

All sentences need a verb to show what the subject in the sentence is doing. We can use past tense verbs and irregular verbs as well.

Alexander
Ms. Macias ran into the room, slammed the door, and yelled like a howler monkey!!!

Sara
My brother shivered and ran outa my room because I put a prank ghost in there!

Aadit
I ran into my room, slammed the door, and slept in the bed.

Alina
My Marsh-Mellows fell into the fire and hissed at me as if I had just "killed" it.

Mason
"Go away " J she ran away dog.

iseon
seong feels the drops streaming ugh her arms, and she surprised.

Grayson
I stormed up the stairs with anger as Mom yelled at me for not doing my chores!

YOHAN
A bumblebee buzzed like an angry rhino behind me.

Talia
She pounded at the door like she was a bull.

**Sarah wa her backy suddenly

Daniel
Dark shapes rose before me,but I had to figure out what the actual address was or else I would die like everyone else.

Sakina
She was so tall,yet so pretty like her mother, and could run as fast as a agary leopard

Miles
I slammed my door and locked it an then I said to my little brother "You're going to get beat up",then I

Thomas
Thomas was run bob is swimming pool.

Cheryn

was going to punch him an then my mom said "no",but I still punched him pow

Jackson
Miles walked i store and he co decide so he b whole store

e
to the ice cream as fast as I could.

Mallory
I ran in my room, and I slammed the door

Jonah
My eyes stung like a roasting hotdog for

Morgan
Layla got so excited she

Figure 2.17
Fourth graders share their imitations and collections with each other via Padlet.com.

lifelong writers and readers—all because you took the time to value their voices and acknowledge and celebrate their attempts to grasp meaning and the written word. Instead of negative associations with conventions, we build positive ones.

Conventions do that—if you let them. Celebrations are actually just an invitation to apply what we've learned, covered in joy. Application is an essential part of the process in and of itself, so we'll explore it in detail in Chapter 3.

All this best practice is the best test practice you can get, but the next invitation builds a bridge between good teaching and how it may look on the test.

Invitation to Edit in Action

Editing their own writing is the main skill we want young writers to master, but like it or not, they will also face standardized tests, benchmarks, and other situations with multiple-choice editing and grammar questions. As stated earlier, practice comes only after instruction—we believe we should err on the side of building concepts and deep understanding of the patterns of power in authentic literacy instruction.

Although the invitation process has been preparing writers for this hurdle of test questions through sound instruction, we can also more explicitly reinforce students' ability to transfer what they know to testing. How do we sharpen students' editing eyes, helping them spot how little changes affect meaning?

On tests, students have to spot minuscule errors sometimes as small as a comma, and to help them do that, we first build a store of what the powerful patterns look like and mean. Then we can, from time to time, practice in a format aligned to how they'll be questioned on standardized tests.

On most standardized tests, a highlighted sentence or section of text is presented in four ways as a multiple-choice question. Three of the four versions contain an error. The fourth has no error. Writers are asked to choose the most correct one of the four. Yes, we want students to figure out the best way to express themselves and correct errors in their own writing, and the next chapter on application spends an ample amount of time on the meaningful practice of editing one's own writing. However, the invitation to edit can bolster that as well, building a bridge between *best* practice and *test* practice.

There is a place for test practice, but it's a very thin slice of the instructional pie. In fact, overreliance on test preparation actually weakens performance. We are weary of *test* practice replacing the *best*-practice instruction that makes students successful. We are attempting to meet somewhere in the middle. We are not ignoring the importance of testing, but instead showing how easily and quickly we can make a practical, well-aligned connection to the assessments students face. If they know a convention well, they will be able to spot meaning problems in sentences and choose the best answers.

Thus far in the invitation process, we have emphasized investigating effective and correct sentences. In fact, we go to great lengths to avoid the study of incorrect writing. We still don't overwhelm students with errors at

> The invitation to edit can bolster that as well, building a bridge between *best* practice and *test* practice.

this point. For the bulk of this process, students have been soaked in correct-ness and effectiveness and beauty. They know and understand the concepts behind the conventions' moves, and have applied them to their own compo-sitions. In addition to the best practice, we can, at certain marker points such as nearing the end of our formal study of a convention, give young writers multiple versions of the same section of text, some of which will have one error. This type of practice should in no way replace or crowd out the actual teaching of conventions. For far too long, practice has passed for instruction. And they're not the same. Here's our suggestion for a way to link to tests.

What Did We Learn About Writing from the Author?

In the invitation-to-edit part of the process, we start by showing the correct, effective version of the sentence we studied. We know the correct sentence won't always be first on the test. But we're teaching, not testing.

We'll investigate these editing sentences one at a time. In the first-grade classroom, Jeff uncovers the correct version of the sentence from *Mercy Watson to the Rescue*:

Mr. Watson and Mrs. Watson have a pig named Mercy.

"What did we learn about writing from Kate DiCamillo?" Jeff asks. The correct sentence is presented first to give us an opportunity to review and restate what we have learned from the particular pattern of power or mentor sentence. Students generate recollections of what they specifically learned about writing from the author, telling what they know about the conventions and grammar they've been studying. As this occurs, Jeff emphasizes the focus phrase: "I capitalize names."

"We learned that you capitalize *Mercy*."

"All of the letters in *Mercy*?" he asks.

"No!" several students chime in.

"Which letter do you capitalize?"

"The first one," the first graders say in a chorus.

"Maybe," Jeff says, standing back and looking at the sentence. "Maybe we should change our focus phrase to 'I capitalize *the first letter of* names.'"

"Everybody knows that!" Marco says.

"Show me, then. Because writers only capitalize letters for a reason."

They discuss the fact that abbreviated titles used with last names are capitalized, too, just as the first word of a sentence is, and we end this section repeating the focus phrase, "I capitalize names."

The Other Three Sentences: Students Identify What Changed and Consider the Effect of the Change

We look at the sentences one at a time, much as one would on a standard-ized test. It takes careful, close reading. Jeff covers the correct sentence and uncovers the second sentence, which has one change:

Mr. watson and Mrs. Watson have a pig named Mercy.

After revealing the second version of the sentence, Jeff asks, "What changed?"

We don't ask kids to find the mistake or error. We ask them to find what changed.

A student notices that *Watson* isn't capitalized.

"Why does it matter?" Jeff looks out at the class. The editing eyes first notice differences, and then they consider how the meaning is affected by the change. Writing isn't about right and wrong; it's about communicating meaning and effect. If appropriate, after the change is identified, ask something along these lines: "What is the effect of the change?"

The hope is that young writers will return to the focus phrase, but if they don't, Jeff will keep nudging it in. "Repeat it with me: 'I capitalize names.'"

We may even go through every word in the sentence, asking if it should or shouldn't be capitalized. Each time we ask, "How do you know?" We do it till we feel the momentum dropping, and then we're off to the next version of the sentence. This one is covered and the next version is revealed:

Mr. Watson and Mrs. Watson have a Pig named Mercy.

"What changed?" Jeff asks.

"*Pig* is capitalized." Michael stands up and starts pacing.

"So what?" Jeff says. "I like the capital *P*."

"I like it too," said Patricia.

"It doesn't matter if you like it or not," Michael chides. "You capitalize names." He walks over to the focus phrase on the wall and points to each word of the focus phrase as he says it: "'I. Capitalize. Names.'" He turns around and shrugs.

"Michael, you're right," Jeff says. "We only capitalize letters for a reason. And *pig* or other types of animals aren't capitalized."

"Unless we give them a name," Alexis says.

And together we all say, "I capitalize names!"

"One more sentence. Can you handle it?" Jeff covers the sentence we've been working on, then displays the last of the four versions of the sentence:

Mr. and Mrs. Watson have a pig named MercY.

The students sit quietly, studying the sentence.

"You only capitalize *M* in *Mercy*, not the *y*," Lizzie says.

"Why don't you capitalize the letter *y*?"

"You don't," one student offers.

"Can anybody think of a reason you do not capitalize the *y* in *Mercy*?"

"Well, it's a name, but . . ."

"We capitalize only the first letter of names," Arianna announces.

"Ah!" Jeff repeats, "We capitalize only the first letter of names."

As Jeff closes the discussion to transition into writing workshop, he encourages writers to keep noting the capitalization of names the rest of the day and week. As we've discussed earlier, we invite students to reread their writer's notebook or journal entries, scrounging for words that need to be capitalized or shouldn't be capitalized. We only use capital letters for a reason.

At some point, students need to own the concept as we move on to others. To own the convention, they need to take on the responsibility for using it in drafts, and when they don't, for making adjustments. In small doses, invitations to edit move writers in that direction.

How Do You Make an Invitation to Edit?

Though we already created invitations to edit for each lesson, they're easy to make for new sentences from the class's reading or writing you may want to highlight.

- Type the sentence or sentences studied throughout the invitational process.
- Copy the sentence.
- Paste the copy of the sentence three times beneath the correct one for four versions total.
- Leave the first sentence as it is—correct.
- Change one convention in each of the three sentences beneath the correct one. What kinds of conventions do you change? Of course, we can change the convention the lesson focused upon. To follow our invitations on capitalizing proper nouns, we could change a capital letter to lowercase, or change a lowercase letter to a capital. We also use our students' common errors to drive the editing items. For instance, if several students continually use a capital *y* within words without purpose, we'd use one of the sentences to incorrectly capitalize the letter *y* in a word.

We may change conventions other than the one we're focusing on if it would be beneficial for students to build on or deepen their awareness about another type of error. Young writers develop an editing eye, deepening an awareness of how minor changes affect meaning. This is what they need to be prepared for as test takers, and it just so happens to help them clean up their own writing as well.

The Invitations Were a Beginning

Now that we've given instruction on a convention through the invitation process, explicitly introducing the purpose of the convention and its craft, we consider multiple ways to continue application of the pattern of power across the curriculum and day to ensure its usage over time. This brings the conventions front and center and into the world of meaning in any reading or writing students do, regardless of the subject area. Let's look at some ways we can keep the conventions alive through meaningful application.

Into Application: How Do You Ensure Writers Apply What They Know?

Writing is an act of faith, not a trick of grammar.
—E. B. White

"My kids don't apply the conventions I've taught to their writing." Has this exasperating thought ever crossed your mind? Is it easy to believe it's a common complaint? But let's ask another question: how many conventions are writers actually applying effectively? Grammar is customarily viewed from a deficit stance, identifying what writers are doing incorrectly. But it's important that we also consider the things they are doing well. If students aren't applying a convention in their writing, we have to ask ourselves the following:

- What are we doing to facilitate our students' application of this convention?
- Are we merely expecting application without showing young writers how to use the convention in various contexts, with little or no scaffolding?

Writers must be nudged. Although the invitations to imitate and edit are the beginnings of application, students need more opportunities to apply their learning and gain fluency. We can do several concrete things to ensure application happens over time. Not tricks, but writing. Acquiring a convention isn't an event; it's a process, a process that takes place over time, slowly and cumulatively.

In our experience, to become fluent at editing their own work, students need to apply a skill in multiple contexts. When we show them a convention's use in context across the curriculum, we're grounding them in understanding and use, giving them the foundation they need to catch their own errors later.

We don't teach division once, in one way, and expect kids to divide perfectly from that point forward. Division is a complex, multistep, foundational process. We'd argue that applying grammar skills to writing is even more difficult because division solutions are outcome determinate. In other words, there's one answer to the division problem, no matter how you get there. With division, you get the correct answer or you don't. But a student can write without using punctuation or capital letters correctly. The student has still completed a piece of writing. Sure, the writing would be enhanced if the conventions were followed in the standard way. But it's still writing. Writing isn't outcome determinate. There isn't one right answer. Writers make choices—consciously or unconsciously—that affect their message.

Perfecting writing is a lifelong process, ever-spiraling onward and upward, gaining accuracy as our exposure and experimentation grow. An error-free piece of writing is a destination we move toward—a goal—but the cost of meeting this goal with exacting precision is much higher than its benefits would merit. The writer will move forward through the years. The essay will not. We teach writers, not the writing.

If you're like us, you still make plenty of mistakes while drafting and still miss others while editing—as most professional writers do. It's a process of moving toward a standard of correctness. We're better at conventions than we were when we were seven, fourteen, twenty-one, even thirty-nine years old. Children need a chance to apply language conventions, and authentic use is the best way.

Once we've taught the focus convention through the invitational process, we explore ways to extend the work throughout the instructional day, discussing the importance of connections across curricular settings. That is what we'll explore in this chapter.

We prod the application of the convention, keeping in mind that doing so is a process continued over time in varying situations. Here's a menu of application choices.

Invitations-to-Apply Menu

- Use the convention as a tool to respond to reading.
- Apply the convention to think through or summarize content.
- Find the convention in reading and writing and start a collection.
- Nudge students to reenter their own writing to revise or edit for the convention.
- Confer with students to encourage continual, thoughtful application.
- Invite students to add the convention to a shared editing checklist.

Let's step through these application possibilities to give student writers opportunities to intentionally and regularly use the conventions we teach.

Use the Convention as a Tool to Respond to Reading

Using the convention to respond to reading is a quick, practical application of the learning students grapple with through the invitational process. After a read-aloud, guided reading group, or any reading task, students write a response, using the convention at least once. For example, in the invitation process where we focused on capitalizing names, Jeff reads aloud *Knuffle Bunny* by Mo Willems, one of his favorites: "Write a sentence about the book we just read."

Jeff distributes slips of lined paper. "Here's a challenge. Try to include some names in whatever you write."

"Like about Trixie." Lisa offers.

"Yep." Jeff pauses. "And what do writers know about names?"

Several students respond. "I capitalize names." The students affirm the focus phrase, framing it as something they can do.

This was our favorite response because it made us laugh:

Elephant and Piggie aren't in Knuffle Bunny.

Besides offering additional practice in using the convention you're studying with writers, responses serve as an informal assessment. A quick look at the responses gives an idea where to go next.

- Do we need to shore up any angle?
- Do we need to reteach to a small group?
- How can we display successful responses and celebrate them?
- Is there another way to display the student models? A book? A bulletin board?

Responding to reading throughout the day supports students' need to see the convention living in the world beyond grammar lessons, increasing its importance and value. But we can respond to other things besides reading.

Apply the Convention to Think Through or Summarize Content

A science lab
A tough math lesson
A social students unit
A field trip

Figure 3.1
Conjunctions connect words and ideas.

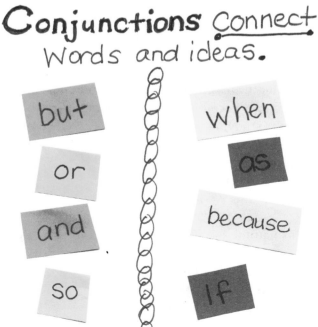

All these experiences are ripe for writing. In these instances, we select an appropriate situation or experience for which students can use a convention we're studying. In this type of response, we widen the scope beyond reading response, moving the convention out into the world of reflection on experiences in another content area. As they did when responding to reading, students reflect on the event or lesson and think through an issue or summarize it.

If the class is studying the use of common conjunctions, we might point to our collection of conjunctions (see Figure 3.1) and ask them to use at least one in their response to a social studies lesson.

Whatever the convention—conjunctions, verb tense, nouns, or compound sentences—perhaps students summarize a science lab in a few sentences or write about one aspect of the lab they're thinking through. Maybe after a field trip to a museum, students write a sentence or two about the field trip, focusing on using verb tense intentionally for effect. Or they exchange sentences and rewrite them in another tense, followed by conversation about the effects of the changes. As a bonus, we've debriefed the field trip as well. Purposeful. Since we've been exploring the capitalization of names, after a social studies lesson on a historical figure or place, students write a response, using at least one name. When exploring measurement in math, young writers can report about measuring a classmate's arm or arm span or some other form of measurement:

> *I measured Elisiah's arm and it was three inches longer than mine.*
> *My Doritos weigh the same as Michele's Lay's Kettle Chips.*

Composing a quick response offers students a reflective opportunity to think through the experience and the power of the convention's pattern to express meaning. When we simply add the goal of using a particular convention in short reflections on learning experiences outside the writing and reading classroom, we reinforce that literacy is everywhere and ever present. And as a bonus, we add to the goal of using the convention to communicate clearly.

Find the Convention in Reading and Writing, and Start a Collection

In the previous section, the focus was on *using* the convention to reflect on experiences. Here the focus is on *noticing* the convention in action in other contexts. Young writers' continual noticing of a convention's pattern deepens and expands their visual stores, so that when the time comes to apply it in their own writing or on a test, they have a strong connection to it. This phenomenon is borne out of the brain's reticular activating system, or RAS, which functions as a brain filter. This filter works automatically. For instance, when a good friend gets a new red pickup truck, have you ever noticed you suddenly start seeing red trucks every where you go? That's the reticular activating system. Once we've become conscious of something, like capital letters or other conventions, they stand out more in our reading encounters, increasing the attention paid, which leads to more consistent use.

Across the day, across subject areas, students create and consume the written word, and as they do, we encourage them to note where they or others use the convention we're studying (or have previously studied or will study). Once young writers tune in to the conventions, they'll encounter them everywhere and be excited to share their findings, deepening every-one's engagement with text. This extends writing lessons and encourages students to see how the conventions we learn are used all around them to make meaning.

To take advantage of this natural discovery and enthusiasm, start a class collection on a wall chart. Beneath the convention's focus phrase, post sentence strips with what students find or create. Older writers can dedicate a page in their writer's notebooks to collect examples of the convention they find in their reading and writing. The power of collecting personalizes our noticing, deepening the patterns of power concepts. (See Figures 3.2–3.5.)

I use collective nouns to name groups of
People, Places, and things as one.

I Pulled an ace out of diamonds
from the thick deck.

The soccer team came out as the
crowd was watching, and everyone
started cheering.

Figure 3.2
A fifth-grade student has started imitating and collecting
sentences that use collective nouns in her writer's notebook.

It had a tin cover,
and was filled with
paintings of their town
in Vermont.

I survived the Battle
of Gettysburg, 1863.

By: Lauren Tarishis.

Lauren probably made the
word paintings plural because
if she hadn't it
wouldn't have made sence.
Also there are many
paintings, not just one.

Figure 3.3
A fourth grader reflects on the author's choice to use plural nouns.

Figure 3.4
Class collections wall

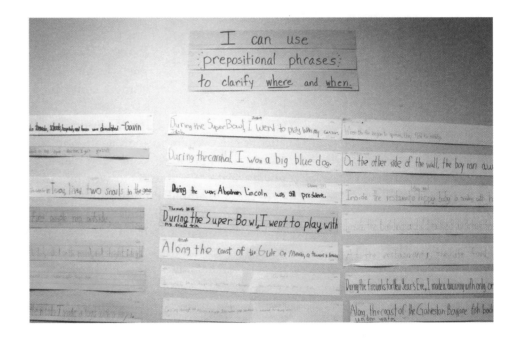

Figure 3.5
Class collections hang below a chalk
rail in this classroom that is tight on
space.

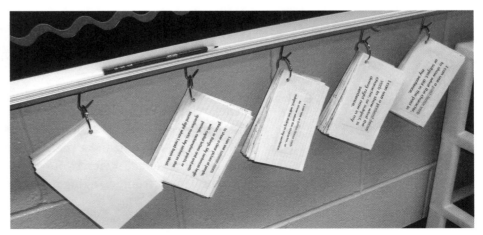

Nudge Students to Reenter Their Own Writing to Revise *or* Edit for the Convention

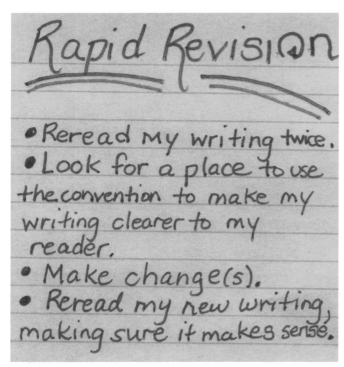

Figure 3.6
Rapid Revision

Writers read.

Writers reread.

Some of the most powerful reading writers ever do is reading their own writing. The most authentic way to apply a convention is to revise and edit for it. Writers look again at their own drafts, at their own words, at their own conventions. That's the writing process in action. Students authentically revise or edit with a focus on one convention. This is not a generalized direction to merely revise or edit. That doesn't get results. Instead students run through a quick, teacher-directed, tightly focused *Rapid Revision* or *Quick Edit*. This narrow focus eases and increases young writers' direct application of convention. (See Figure 3.6.)

Rapid Revision

We'll tackle Rapid Revision first (see Figure 3.6). Using a convention to revise relies on the convention as a craft. Rapid Revision is not correcting capital letters used incorrectly. Instead, Rapid Revision encourages writers to look again and see how the craft of proper nouns—names we capitalize—could add clarity and detail to their writing. In first-grade words, "We reread our writing to see if there is something we can make better. For example, if I write 'my dog,' maybe I could add my dog's name and it would make my sentence more detailed for my reader."

To demonstrate, Jeff chooses this sentence to revise:

For the holiday, I went on vacation with my dog.

"As I reread my sentence," Jeff explains, "I decided that this was a sentence with some spots where I could change a few common nouns to names—a specific holiday name, the city name, and my dog's name." Jeff writes his revision beneath his original:

On Memorial Day, I traveled to Austin with my dog Paisley.

"I capitalize names," Jeff says. We're always looking for opportunities for students to repeat the focus phrase in the context of our writing and revising.

As Jeff directs students to look back at a piece of their writing, he asks, "Is there a place where using a specific name of a person or place could give the reader more detail? Reread your piece of writing twice. Look for a spot that might benefit from changing a common noun to a name."

Jeff continues, "Make a change and we'll share our changes in six minutes. First, we'll have three minutes of silence and then we'll have three minutes when you can talk, if you choose. Even if you think you don't need to make a change, give it a try. Writers try things even when they're not sure they want to. Taking risks and trying is how we grow."

Remind your young writers that they won't have to keep the change, but that the practice of experimenting will help them develop as writers, even if it doesn't end up in their piece. Students realize it's their choice whether to keep the change, but it's not a choice to try it out.

Quick Edit

I read my writing twice so my reader only has to read it once.

Using another lens to reread, students apply their editing eye to accuracy—saying what you mean. To apply editing, students reenter a piece of writing—a freewrite, a draft, a response, a journal or writer's notebook entry. A Quick Edit is different from Rapid Revision because the focus is on the correct use of the convention in the writing as it is. Students change surface errors. The goal in a Quick Edit is to make sure that what we leave on the page is what we mean to leave on the page. Quick Edits ensure that we habitually reread our writing, presenting it as clearly as possible.

Later in the week, Whitney talks to the first graders. "Look for a place where you haven't capitalized a name, and capitalize it. Maybe you capitalized a word or letter for no reason. We can fix that as well. Let's do a Quick Edit."

- Read my writing twice.
- Highlight my correct use of focus skill.
- Make changes as needed.
- Read one more time.

As the students do a Quick Edit, Whitney walks around and confers. She stops the class at one point. "I see you're ready to learn the first mark that older writers use. Usually first graders aren't ready at this point in the year, but I think you are. Do you want me to show you?"

Of course they do.

Figure 3.7
Editing mark for capitalization

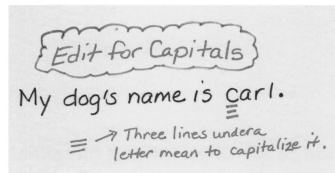

Whitney teaches them how to put three lines under a letter to show that it needs to be capitalized (see Figure 3.7). "This way you don't have to stop to erase. You underline the letter that should have been capitalized. Your three lines informs readers that word is meant to be capitalized because it's a name, or the first word of a sentence, or the pronoun *I*."

"I capitalize names," the class says without prompting. They own the concept, and that's the point of the patterns of power process.

Rapid Revisions and Quick Edits cue young writers to return to their own writing—rereading and refining for clarity and meaning. The more students revise and edit their words, the more we ensure the direct application of skills and the more we cultivate a habit or rereading. Rereading and rewriting are constant threads in the fabric of a literacy community.

Confer with Students to Encourage Continual, Thoughtful Application

To help students feel supported in reaching toward and using new conventions, we gently coach them through those risks. The way we respond matters: sometimes we correct errors; sometimes we don't.

How we respond depends on where a writer is and what he or she needs most at that moment. Correcting a child's error may actually hinder more than help. We always react to the error in a way that honors writers but also nudges them forward as they journey toward meaning. Here are a few guidelines to consider when conferring with a student who makes a mistake with a convention we've taught or are teaching.

Encouraging Conferring	
Possible Conferring Stems	**Extensions**
"Talk to me about your choice or decision to . . ."	"Tell me about your choice to not use end marks." If writers respond with "Oh, I wasn't thinking," we follow up with, "Okay, so what can you do now?"
"I notice you _____. Tell me about your thinking."	"When you read that aloud to me, I notice you stopped for a breath here. How could you show your reader to pause there, like you did?"
"Do you need that _____? Why?"	There might be an answer you're not aware of. You also send a clear message that you are not the arbitrator of right and wrong. Writers do things for a reason.
"Tell me something you're doing as a writer to help a reader understand your message."	Bringing it back to why we use conventions and craft to send messages to our readers is the crux of what we are trying to do when conferring within the patterns-of-power process.

How we respond matters. We don't want dependent writers; we want independent ones. We want them to take responsibility for their words and how they shape meaning. When we confer with this in mind, we encourage needed experimentation and connection to a convention's thoughtful purpose. To continue building fluent editors, we ask students to take on more responsibility by creating a shared editing checklist.

Invite Students to Add the Convention to a Shared Editing Checklist

According to the *Oxford English Dictionary*, the word *convention* finds its origins in this definition: "An agreement or covenant between parties" (2009).

That's really what the conventions of English are—agreements or covenants between the writer and the reader. And because of these agreements, certain situations require writers to use punctuation such as commas and question marks, or capital letters. For instance, over time we've collectively decided that we join two sentences with a comma and a coordinating conjunction to create a compound sentence. Verbs indicate action and time. Prepositions situate a reader in time and space. Adverbs show intensity. We agree as writers and readers that these shared patterns of power communicate accurately.

Figure 3.8
Class writing checklist

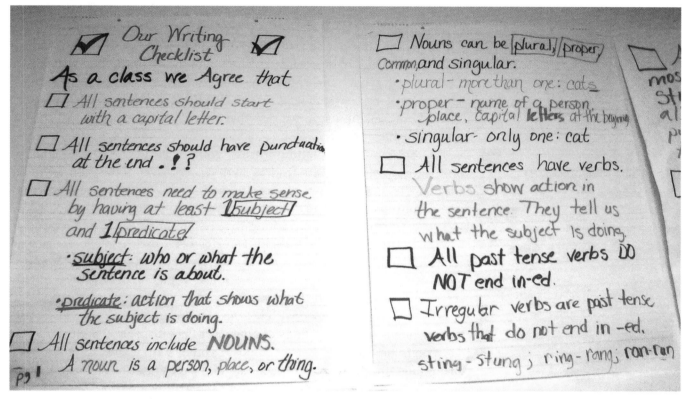

Often after teaching a standard, teachers add the convention to an editing checklist and expect it to become law. This assumption leads to frustration when writers don't apply the rules. But what if adding an item to a class-generated editing checklist was a community decision? (See Figure 3.8.) What if instead of being the arbiters of right and wrong, we instead ask, "Do you think we're all ready to add this to the editor's checklist?" We remind students that once we agree that a convention appears on our classroom editing list, they become responsible for rereading their writing and double-checking that they used the convention correctly—or at least intentionally. We're inviting ownership of the agreement.

Instead of expecting students to use a convention once it's on a checklist, the class chooses when they're ready to add it. If students are not in agreement yet, we ask, "What will help you be ready to add it to the list?"

In our first-grade process of capitalizing common nouns, Whitney continued the lesson. At the beginning of the year, she had set up the editing checklist with the class, explaining that whatever they put on the list would be a class decision. "By putting a convention on the editing checklist, as a community, as a class, we are saying we agree to be responsible for rereading our writing and making sure we use the convention correctly."

After reminding the class of the editing checklist, Whitney continues, "For the last few weeks, we've been working on the idea of capitalizing names."

"I capitalize names," several students blurt out without prompting.

"Yes," Whitney says, smiling. "Do you think we're ready to add that to our editing checklist?"

"I think we should put it up there," Khea offers, nodding.

"Okay." Whitney looks at the faces of the first graders. "What do the rest of you think?"

After some conversation, the class decides they are ready to be responsible for capitalizing names when they write. Whitney says, "As writers, we always reread. That's the cool thing about writing: we can always make changes. We can always make it better. This list helps us remember what we already know, making sure we do what writers do. We're writers, and we capitalize names."

We continue the invitation process, going back to the core of conventions: agreements between readers and writers. Approximation is to be expected. It's a natural part of concept attainment. Becoming strong, effective, and purposeful editors of their own work takes time and practice, so we can expect to continue giving young writers reminders for a long while.

We continue to provide scaffolds and slowly release them, we nudge, and we reteach in different contexts to keep the patterns of power alive. We trust the process—the writing process—and know young writers will eventually become independent with their learning.

> Let's open the door wide with lessons that inspire wonder, curiosity, and meaning about the conventions of language.

Let's open the door wide with lessons that inspire wonder, curiosity, and meaning about the conventions of language. Let's discover the patterns that give writers power. But keep in mind, if young writers aren't applying the conventions, think of ways to facilitate and accelerate that application. As you get into the lessons, you are given application options, but we hope you'll return to this chapter for even more options. Applying a convention once won't be enough, but this chapter gives us what we need to apply the skill multiple ways.

Our teaching of the patterns of power is not complete until students use those patterns in their own writing to make meaning for their audiences. It's a windy road, but it's worth the trek.

Part 2

INTO the Patterns of POWER

LESSON SETS

The journey is the reward.
—Chinese proverb

Into the Lessons: How Are the Lessons Formatted?

ow that you have an overview of the invitational process, how to plan for it, and what it looks like in the classroom, let's take a closer look at how the lessons that follow in Part 2 will be structured. In these lessons, you can easily access color-coded, organized plans for a span of conventions. Lessons include a focus phrase, teacher "power notes," and materials for classroom use.

For implementation support, two-page spreads of use-now resources accompany each lesson. You can project the half-page invitations, one at a time, on a document camera or other device. Or you can scan and drag the lesson images into a slideshow presentation. If you prefer that young writers hold these materials in their hands, photocopy the two-page lesson spreads, cut them in half to separate each lesson, then distribute them one at a time to students. This way, writers can study lessons up close, and then paste them into their writer's notebooks. We use a combination of these choices, depending on the needs of students and technology available.

The lesson that follows is based on the conversation about capitalizing names from Chapters 1–3 and serves as an example of how the rest of the lessons in Chapters 4–20 are formatted. The yellow boxes will give additional explanation on each part of the lesson. You'll notice that the lesson is presented with minimal narrative discussion and that the use-now support materials are within the lesson itself rather than in an appendix—so you'll have everything you need, where and when you need it.

4.1   Mercy Me! Capitalizing Names

Standard

Look at your standards and find the ones that are similar. The wording of standard varies, but most core ideas remain the same.

Capitalize names of people. (Distinguish between proper and common nouns.)
Capitalize titles with last names.

Focus Phrase

A student-friendly phrase that names the learning target contained within the standard. Focus phrases are written and said in the first person or *I* voice.

"I capitalize names."

Invitation to Notice

Mr. and Mrs. Watson have a pig named Mercy.
  —Kate DiCamillo, *Mercy Watson to the Rescue*

Power Note

We include this section in addition to the use-now teacher resources with each lesson. These Power Notes give the teacher tips, added information, and direction if desired.

Additional skills that might arise during student discussion: irregular verbs (have for plural present, and had for both plural and singular past) as well as the fact that we capitalize all names—even those of pets. Some students will note the "extra" periods. Say, "We already know what the period at the end of a sentence does, right? Who can remind us?" Then explain that the periods on Mr. and Mrs. help us abbreviate or shorten titles. Mister is shortened to Mr. and Mistress is shortened to Mrs. (See a fuller explanation in Chapter 2.)

Invitation to Compare and Contrast

Mr. and Mrs. Watson have a pig named Mercy.
Dr. Gonzalez has a cat named Aristotle.

Power Note

This is also in your use-now teacher resources, but the Power Notes continue to be a helpful guide to the important learning that happens when students talk about similarities and differences.

When you ask students to identify how the two sentences are alike and different, they may note how the irregular verb have changes to has when the subject is singular. Doctor is abbreviated to Dr., but like Mr. and Mrs., it can be abbreviated only when it is used with a last name.

Invitation to Imitate

When students imitate, we give several options with different levels of scaffolding. Choose one or all of the options, depending upon student need or the complexity of the pattern.

Imitate Together: Invite students to write a sentence with you, using interactive writing.

> Mr. and Mrs. Thibodeaux have a dog named Daisy.

Imitate Independently: Students use the model sentence and sentences created by the class to compose their own sentences, capitalizing names and titles with last names.

Invitation to Celebrate

Celebration is sharing. Students reading aloud their new creations will always be enough, but we also offer other options to teachers. Use what works for you, but don't skip the celebration because it is an essential part of the invitation process.

After students orally share their sentences, as a class, make a celebration-of-capitalization chart. Across the top write the focus phrase, "We Capitalize Names." Underneath the focus phrase, post capitalized names from your reading or writing as well as your sentences.

We Capitalize
~ Names ~

Mr. Watson
Mrs. Chavez
Miss Smith
Dr. Jones
Aunt Allie
Uncle Jerry
Governor Jackson

Mercy
Monica
America
South Elm Street
Crest Hill Elementary School

Capitalize names celebration chart

Invitation to Apply

Options are offered with every lesson. Remember, you can always go to Chapter 3 for more specific information and options for applying the patterns of power.

Respond to Reading: Students write about a character from read-aloud, shared, or independent reading time. They make sure to capitalize the characters' or people's names. We add that we capitalize the names of schools, parks, cities, and countries. Maybe it's time to start a list of names we capitalize in our reading and writing.

Invitation to Edit

The invitation to edit gives us the words to say or the support we need with the use-now teacher-support material for the invitation to edit. The first question you always ask for each invitation-to-edit lesson is here.

What did we learn about writing from Kate DiCamillo?	
Mr. Watson and Mrs. Watson have a pig named Mercy.	
What changed? What is the effect of the change?	
Mr. watson and Mrs. Watson have a pig named Mercy.	Watson *starts with a lowercase letter. When we don't capitalize a name, it's not a name, according to the convention pattern.* "I capitalize names."
Mr. Watson and Mrs. Watson had a Pig named Mercy.	*The irregular verb* have *has been changed to its past-tense form,* had. *This changes the meaning, because when the verb is in the past tense, it communicates the idea that the Watsons no longer have Mercy.*
Mr. and Mrs. Watson have a pig named MercY.	*The lowercase y has been changed to a capital Y.* "We only capitalize letters for a reason. We capitalize only the first letter of a name. Using capitals in unexpected places calls the readers' attention away from our message."

What Do You Notice?

Mr. and Mrs. Watson have a pig named Mercy.

—Kate DiCamillo, *Mercy Watson to the Rescue*

Here are the use-now teacher-support materials that are found within each lesson in this book. Remember, the use-now spreads are explained in the Power Notes or within each stage of the process.

How are they alike and different?

Mr. and Mrs. Watson have a pig named Mercy.

Dr. Gonzalez has a cat named Aristotle.

It's important that young writers have an opportunity to see another example and actively process it through talking. This stage of the invitation helps them clarify and deepen their understanding of the pattern.

Let's try it out.

Mr. and Mrs. Watson have a pig named Mercy.

Dr. Gonzalez has a cat named Aristotle.

Note that we left enough space for the option of imitating through shared or interactive writing.

Mr. Watson and Mrs. Watson have a pig named Mercy.

What changed? What is the effect of the change?

Mr. watson and Mrs. Watson have a pig named Mercy.

Mr. Watson and Mrs. Watson had a Pig named Mercy.

Mr. Watson and Mrs. Watson have a pig named MercY.

The first question and other possible responses for this use-now lesson are in the chart earlier in the lesson. This test practice comes only after the best-practice instruction.

The Patterns-of-Power Lesson Sets

The following acts as a quick guide to finding the lessons you need.

The Power of Sentences

The Power of Pairs

The Power of Details

Every time you are tempted to react in the same old way, ask yourself if you want to be a prisoner of the past or a pioneer of the future.

—Deepak Chopra

The Power of Sentences

We immerse ourselves in texts, we dive into their words, which make up sentences and pages that call out to us to be turned and then mysteriously unfold into ideas, touching us and impacting our lives. This process matters.
—Dorothy Barnhouse, *Readers Front and Center*

Words are our primary foundation in language, and even our youngest writers are expected to sew them together to express thoughts and feelings about the world around them. Sentences are a primary way for writers to string together words. Sentences are how we comment on the world and read to find out about it. In the hope of teaching this most basic unit of language, schoolchildren are often given this common but unclear reminder in endless loops: "Write in complete sentences."

"What?" Students tilt their heads and squint. Most of them still wonder how to know whether a sentence is a sentence or not: "It's some words that start with a capital and end with a period, right?"

"Sure, but to be a complete sentence, it has to be a complete thought," they are reminded. "What's *complete* mean?"

And when they're still unsure, they're instructed once again, perhaps more loudly this time, that *complete* sentences contain a *complete* subject, a *complete* predicate, and a *complete* thought. To young writers, this feels like a *complete*-tition!

Emphatically repeating a progression of abstract labels or smacking the adjective *complete* in front of a bunch of nouns over and over, more and more loudly, is not the answer. And insisting that our students memorize the seven parts of speech won't build strong writers either. Instead, an excessive focus on complete sentences creates glassy-eyed children lost in the abstraction of labels. At best, they'll avoid making mistakes. But that means they'll also avoid taking risks—and growing. Avoiding errors will not grow writers.

Avoiding errors will not grow writers.

So what do we do?

Young writers do need to learn about sentences; however, demanding complete sentences and labeling their parts is not the goal. Once we remind students of the real purpose of writing—expression, discovery, and mutual understanding—they will

There's a differences between the goals of students noticing what they observe and teachers waiting for students to label the parts of speech.

approximate and grow toward the sentence correctness we desire. And even though we will explore nouns and verbs, we won't memorize them in isolation. We'll discover them in the context of a sentence, connected in the authentic web of meaning.

Students do need a strong understanding of sentences at their foundational roots, especially if our young writers are to eventually craft even stronger, more detailed sentences. But what are the basic roots of a sentence? Nouns and verbs.

Nouns often dutifully serve as the subjects of sentences: the *who* or the *what*. And nouns would just lie around doing nothing if it weren't for verbs spurring them into action or linking them to an adjective. Verbs drive the action (*Jeff jumps*) or use the states of being (*is, are, was, were, be, been, am*) to link nouns to adjectives (*Whitney is smart*). Verbs, along with the noun, in fact, often complete our sentences, giving us the compulsory component of that complete predicate grammar cops always insist upon.

But where do we *begin* with young writers? Why not look at the components of a sentence within the context of sentences before tackling the definition of a sentence? Focus first on a bite-sized, digestible chunk they can manage and master. Why not explore concrete things, one at a time first, not because they're more important, but because they will always be a part of this important basic unit—the sentence. Sentences are the big-deal goal, but we found that introducing grammar study with simple sentences at any grade level was a curiosity killer. Instead, in Part 2, we get our hands dirty with basic conventions before we tackle the big question of what makes a sentence a sentence.

The lessons under each convention chapter go from the most primary ideas to the most complex, giving teachers an opportunity to follow a thread of lessons within each chapter that addresses the needs of their students and the required curriculum.

When a standard asks us to teach declarative, interrogative, and exclamatory sentences, we argue for using the terms writers and children do: *sentences, questions,* and *exclamations*. No more worksheets identifying sentence types as declarative, interrogative, or exclamatory. Instead, students study models, read, write, revise, and edit sentences, questions, and occasional exclamations.

By the time we get to what it takes to make a sentence, students have been using sentences all along. Rather than start with the mechanics of what a sentence is, we look at capitalization within sentences first. Then we investigate nouns, and then verbs. After we've become acquainted with both nouns and verbs, we talk about their necessity in forming a simple sentence. Just the guts. We study simple sentences as units of a noun and a verb. Then, since all good things must come to an end, we explore the end marks that help our readers create declarative, interrogative, and exclamatory sentences. Did you just throw up in your mouth a little? Never fear: reasonable terminology is here.

Abstract Grammar Converter: What Those Sentence Terms Actually Mean			
Abstract Term	**Actual Word Writers Use**	**End Punctuation**	**End Mark's Name**
Declarative	Sentence	.	Period
Interrogative	Question	?	Question Mark
Exclamatory	Exclamation	!	Exclamation Mark

If I waited for perfection, I would never write a word.

—Margaret Atwood

4

What Do Capital Letters Do?

C hildren often know the difference between capital and lowercase letters, but they don't always know why or how to use either with intention. From the first-person identifier of the self—the pronoun *I*—to helping a reader see proper nouns, capital letters are used for a purpose. We only use capital letters for a reason.

Students will need several focus phrases to meet specific capitalization goals. Like the capital cities in each state of our nation, capital letters are used to signify importance and emphasis. The *Oxford English Dictionary* defines *capital* as "related to head or top" (2009). And when capitalization is used haphazardly, emphasis is lost and confusion reigns.

As author's craft, capitalization makes a word stand out to a reader, which reveals something about it. For example, capital letters have the important job of kicking off a sentence, letting a reader know when a new one starts. In addition to shaping our sentences, capital letters show that proper nouns, or names and titles, are being used rather than common nouns: not book, but *Knuffle Bunny*; not author, but Mo Willems; not character, but Trixi.

Lesson Sets:

What Do Capital Letters Do?

4.2   I Am Capitalization Worthy: Capitalizing the Pronoun *I*

Standard Capitalize the pronoun *I*.

Focus Phrase "I always capitalize the pronoun *I* (no matter where it is)."

Invitation to Notice I'm Emily Elizabeth, and I have a dog.
  —Norman Bridwell, *Clifford the Big Red Dog*

Power Note *When students note that* Emily Elizabeth *is capitalized, ask why. "We capitalize names." This pattern shows how important each person in the room is. Go around the room saying, "Gavin, your first name is capitalized, and so is your last name. What about yours, Hillary? Both first and last?" At that point, we could say something like, "When we use the first-person point of view, the* I *voice, it's our name. That was also a compound sentence that used a contraction, in case you didn't notice."*

Invitation to Compare and Contrast I'm Emily Elizabeth, and I have a dog.
I am six years old, and I have two sisters.

Power Note *Since our focus is capitalizing the pronoun I, we chose not to include a name like* Emily Elizabeth *in our imitation.*

Invitation to Imitate *Imitate Together*: Invite writers to use interactive, shared, or paired writing to compose a sentence with you. (See Figure 4.1.)

Figure 4.1
This first-grade sentence was created during interactive writing.

Imitate Independently: Students use the model to create their own sentences, capitalizing the pronoun *I*.

Invitation to Celebrate Students share their sentences aloud. If you like, play "You're the Top" sung by Sutton Foster and Colin Donnell in the background and at transition times throughout the day and week. The song emphasizes one of the original meanings of the word *capital*: "the top." Share with students the association between what they are learning and what the singers are saying: Say something like, "You're the top; you deserve to be capitalized because *I* is your name when you write through your own eyes (first-person point of view)."

Invitation to Apply Use the convention as a tool to respond to a read-aloud or a shared or independent reading. Writers may use these stems. We purposely didn't start the stem with the letter *I* so that we could highlight *I*'s capitalization.

One thing I wonder is . . .
One thing I know is . . .
One thing I want to know more about is . . .

Invitation to Edit

What did we learn about writing from Norman Bridwell?	
I'm Emily Elizabeth, and I have a dog.	
What changed? What is the effect of the change?	
I'm Emily elizabeth, and I have a dog.	Elizabeth *starts with a lowercase letter. When we don't capitalize a name, it's not a name according to the convention pattern. Spiral back to the previous focus phrase, "I capitalize names."*
I'm Emily Elizabeth, and i have a dog.	*The pronoun* I *has changed to lowercase, which may confuse or distract our reader from what we are trying to say. "I always capitalize the pronoun* I.*"*
I am Emily Elizabeth, and I have a dog.	*The contraction* I'm *has been changed to* I am. *Both the contraction and the written-out form have the same meaning, but contractions are less formal.*

Tip: Why! Oh, Why Do We Capitalize the Pronoun *I*?

[I]n English, the solitary "I" towers above "he," "she," "it," and the royal "we."
—Caroline Winter, "Me, Myself, and I," *New York Times Magazine*, August 3, 2008

Interestingly enough, the pronoun *I*'s capitalization has nothing to do with grammatical principle, though a grammarian might freak if you didn't follow the accepted convention. In truth, the word origin of the pronoun *I* was a word with more letters (*ich* or *ic*). Once the word shrank to a lone letter, a problem with transcription and typography arose: the small letter *i* looked lost and unimportant and puny. Graphically, it needed to be taller; hence, it was capitalized as it in Standard English today (Winter 2008).

What do you notice?

I'm Emily Elizabeth, and I have a dog.
—Norman Bridwell, *Clifford the Big Red Dog*

How are they alike and different?

I'm Emily Elizabeth, and I have a dog.

I am six years old, and I have two sisters.

Let's try it out.

I'm Emily Elizabeth, and I have a dog.

I am six years old, and I have two sisters.

I'm Emily Elizabeth, and I have a dog.

What changed? What is the effect of the change?

I'm Emily elizabeth, and I have a dog.

I'm Emily Elizabeth, and i have a dog.

I am Emily Elizabeth, and I have a dog.

4.3   Time of Your Life: Capitalizing Months and Days

Standard   Capitalize months and days of the week.

Focus Phrase   "I capitalize months and days."

Invitation to Notice   On Saturday, D.W. and her family went out to eat.
 —Marc Brown, *D.W. the Picky Eater*

Power Note   *When students note the comma, remember to ask table groups to formulate a theory about what the comma is doing when we read it aloud and when we read it with our eyes. (It's setting off a time marker, prepositional phrase, or introductory element. You choose which terminology best fits your students.)*

Invitation to Compare and Contrast   On Saturday, D.W. and her family went out to eat.
On Monday nights, my mom goes bowling.
In October, I'm ready for a holiday.

Power Note   *We chose to have three sentences in this case so we could see how prepositions change, depending on the time referenced—in this case, months versus days. For a more in-depth explanation, see Chapter 16, "What Do Prepositions Do?"*

Invitation to Imitate   *Imitate Together*: Invite writers to use interactive, shared, or paired writing to compose a sentence with you. (See Figure 4.2.)

Figure 4.2
Second graders work together to create an imitation sentence during interactive writing.

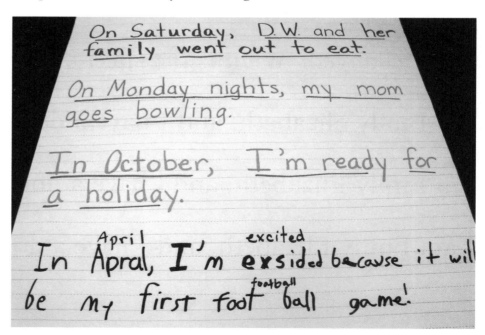

Imitate Independently: Students use the model to create their own sentences, capitalizing days or months.

Invitation to Celebrate   Volunteers post their sentences beneath the focus phrase on a wall chart. (See Figure 4.3.)

Figure 4.3
Days-and-months wall chart

Invitation to Edit

What did we learn about writing from Marc Brown?	
On Saturday, D.W. and her family went out to eat.	
What changed? What is the effect of the change?	
On saturday, D.W. and her family went out to eat.	The day—Saturday—begins with a lowercase letter. Since the agreement between writers and readers is the we capitalize days of the week, our readers may be confused. Cycle through the focus phrase several times: "I capitalize months and days."
On Saturday, D.w. and her family went out to eat.	The second letter of Dora Winifred's initials is lowercase. The pattern is that when two or more initials go together, all the initials are capitalized. When the pattern of power isn't followed, our reader has to pause to figure out what we meant.
On Saturday, D.W. and her family went out two eat.	The homophone in the infinitive to eat (this to is not a preposition because it is followed by a verb) has been changed to the adjective form of two. The word two describes how many. Using the wrong homophone muddles meaning.

Tip: Literally Capital Letters: Initials and Acronyms

Americans love turning long names into shorter ones. By using initials, acronyms, or abbreviations, a series of words becomes fewer letters, often using only the initial consonant of each word. Here's the lowdown:

- *Initials:* In the popular Arthur series, Dora Winifred doesn't like her name, so she goes by her initials D.W. instead. Sometimes we monogram our possessions with our initials or sign them to say we've read something and agreed to it.
- *Initialisms:* NBA is short for the National Basketball Association, which is an initialism. We call them initialisms when we say out each letter or initial instead of pronouncing them as a word. Other initialisms include *FBI*, or Federal Bureau of Investigation, and *NBC*, the National Broadcasting Company.
- *Acronyms*: NASA is short for the National Aeronautics and Space Administration, but we don't say out each letter like an initialism. We create a new word with the initials. Other examples of acronyms include AWOL, LASER, and SCUBA.

What do you notice?

On Saturday, D.W. and her family went out to eat.

—Marc Brown, *D.W. the Picky Eater*

How are they alike and different?

On Saturday, D.W. and her family went out to eat.

On Monday nights, my mom goes bowling.

Let's try it out.

On Saturday, D.W. and her family went out to eat.

On Monday nights, my mom goes bowling.

On Saturday, D.W. and her family went out to eat.

What changed? What is the effect of the change?

On saturday, D.W. and her family went out to eat.

On Saturday, D.w. and her family went out to eat.

On Saturday, D.W. and her family went out two eat.

4.4   Entitled to Be Capitalized: Capitalizing Titles

Standard   Capitalize the titles of written works.

Focus Phrase   "I capitalize titles."

Invitation to Notice   He had ledges full of *Star Wars* miniatures, and a huge *Empire Strikes Back* poster hung on his wall.
—R. J. Palacio, *Wonder*

Power Note   *As students share their noticings and mention the titles of books and movies, ask, "What's the pattern for capitalizing titles? Anything you know for sure?" Use the tip box if you're unsure how to help them fill in the pattern for titles. Students may also notice this is a compound sentence, because there is subject and a verb on both sides of the comma and coordinating conjunction. It's not the focus, but it is a very important sentence pattern discussed in Chapter 18.*

Invitation to Compare and Contrast   He had ledges full of *Star Wars* miniatures, and a huge *Empire Strikes Back* poster hung on his wall.
She had shelves full of Dyamonde Daniel books, and a copy of *Where the Wild Things Are* stood on the top shelf, facing out.

Power Note   *First and last words as well as verbs and nouns are always capitalized in titles. Short words such as articles (a, an, the) and prepositions (of, on, in) aren't capitalized . . . unless they are the first or last word of a title. See the tip box, "Do You Capitalize ALL Words in a Title?"*

Invitation to Imitate   *Imitate Together*: Invite writers to use interactive or shared writing to compose a sentence with you using movie, book, or TV show titles.

Imitate Independently: Students use the model to create their own sentences, capitalizing titles of written works and movies. Remember, when we're writing by hand, we can't italicize, but drawing a line under the title means to italicize it. No quotation marks are necessary for large written works (titles of books, TV shows, magazines, newspapers, movies).

Invitation to Celebrate   Start a collection of titles under the focus phrase "I capitalize titles." Students love this activity. Sharing titles is a social activity. (See Figure 4.4.)

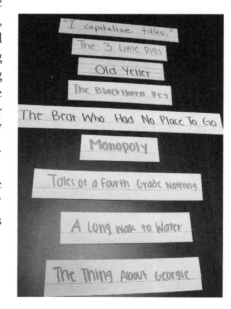

Figure 4.4
"I Capitalize Titles" celebration wall chart

Invitation to Apply   Write a sentence answering this question: What is your favorite book, movie, or TV show? Find a way to display favorites together. How about a class book, with each student writing and illustrating a page? If it's written by hand, underline the title. If it's written on a computer, italicize it. Don't do both.

Invitation to Edit

What did we learn about writing from R. J. Palacio?	
He had ledges full of *Star Wars* miniatures, and a huge *Empire Strikes Back* poster hung on his wall.	
What changed? What is the effect of the change?	
He had ledges full of *Star wars* miniatures, and a huge *Empire Strikes Back* poster hung on his wall.	*Wars isn't capitalized. The pattern is that first and last words of titles are always capitalized, so when a writer doesn't do it, readers are distracted from the writer's message.*
He had ledges full of *Star Wars* miniatures, and a huge Empire Strikes Back poster hung on his wall.	*Empire Strikes Back is not italicized. The title either needs to be either underlined or in italics to show it's a book or movie title. The effect is that it doesn't have the emphasis titles are supposed to have, which could slow a reader down.*
He has ledges full of *Star Wars* miniatures, and a huge *Empire Strikes Back* poster hung on his wall.	*The past tense verb had was changed to the present tense has. Now the first half of the sentence is in the present tense. In this sentence, the action is happening now. In the original, the action happened in the past. Talk to students about the effects of tense beyond time. (Present tense may seem more immediate.)*

Tip: Do You Capitalize ALL Words in a Title?

Reread the title of this tip box. Did we capitalize all the words?

Nope.

So which words are capitalized? The general rule of thumb is to capitalize all of the important words, leaving short words such as articles (*a, an, the*) lowercase. Although this advice is mostly true, a few caveats exist. If any word is positioned as the first or last word of a title, it is always capitalized—always.

In Matt de la Peña's *Last Stop on Market Street*, every word is capitalized except the short word *on*, which is a preposition. Prepositions and conjunctions aren't usually capitalized, unless they are five or more letters or the first or last word. In Joseph Marshall's *In the Footsteps of Crazy Horse* or Guadalupe Garcia McCall's *Under the Mesquite*, the preposition *of* and the article *the* are not capitalized because they are *not* the first or last words of a title. But *in* and *under* are capitalized because they are the first word of the title (plus, *under* has five or more letters).

This chart will help you identify other words that are capitalized in titles, even when they are not in the first or last position:

Beyond First and Last Words: What Other Words Do I Capitalize in a Title?	
Nouns/Pronouns	• *A Big* **Guy** *Took* **My Ball!** by Mo Willems • **Penny** *and* **Her Marble** by Kevin Henkes • **Zack Delacruz**: *Just* **My Luck** by Jeff Anderson (Possessive pronouns are capitalized, too.)
Verbs	• *Hippos* **Are** *Huge!* by Jonathan London • *How to* **Outrun** *a Crocodile When Your Shoes* **Are** *Untied* by Jess Keating.
Adjectives	• *A* **Sick** *Day for Amos McGee* by Philip Stead • *One* **Crazy** *Summer* by Rita Williams-Garcia • *The* **Right** *Word: Roget and His Thesaurus* by Jen Bryant
Adverbs	• *Separate Is* **Never** *Equal: Sylvia Mendez and Her Family's Fight for Desegregation* by Duncan Tonatiuh • *"***Slowly, Slowly, Slowly***," Said the Sloth* by Eric Carle • **Now** *One Foot,* **Now** *the Other* by Tomie dePaola
Conjunctions and **Prepositions** *Only* When Five or More Letters	• *Over and* **Under** *the Snow* by Kate Messner • *No Passengers* **Beyond** *this Point* by Gennifer Choldenko • *I Love You* **Because** *You're You* by Liza Baker

Sometimes words can function as more than one part of speech. Don't fret. In titles, capitalize all prepositions of five letters or more in every case. It's about use, not labels.

What do you notice?

He had ledges full of *Star Wars* miniatures, and a huge *Empire Strikes Back* poster hung on his wall.

—R. J. Palacio, *Wonder*

How are they alike and different?

He had ledges full of *Star Wars* miniatures, and a huge *Empire Strikes Back* poster hung on his wall.

She had shelves full of Dyamonde Daniel books, and a copy of *Where the Wild Things Are* stood on the top shelf, facing out.

Let's try it out.

He had ledges full of *Star Wars* miniatures, and a huge *Empire Strikes Back* poster hung on his wall.

She had shelves full of Dyamonde Daniel books, and a copy of *Where the Wild Things Are* stood on the top shelf, facing out.

He had ledges full of *Star Wars* miniatures, and a huge *Empire Strikes Back* poster hung on his wall.

What changed? What is the effect of the change?

He had ledges full of *Star wars* miniatures, and a huge *Empire Strikes Back* poster hung on his wall.

He had ledges full of *Star Wars* miniatures, and a huge Empire Strikes Back poster hung on his wall.

He has ledges full of *Star Wars* miniatures, and a huge *Empire Strikes Back* poster hung on his wall.

4.5   A Crayon Has Reasons: Capitalization in Letter Openings and Closings

Standard	Use capitalization for the salutation and closing of a letter.
Focus Phrase	"I capitalize the first letter of a letter greeting and closing."
Invitation to Notice	Dear Duncan,

As Green Crayon, I am writing for two reasons. One is to say that I like my workloads of crocodiles, trees, dinosaurs, and frogs. I have no problems and wish to congratulate you on a very successful "coloring things green" career so far.

The second reason I write is for my friends, Yellow Crayon and Orange Crayon, who are no longer speaking to each other. Both crayons feel THEY should be the color of the sun. Please settle this soon because they're driving the rest of us CRAZY!

Your happy friend,
Green Crayon
        —Drew Daywalt, *The Day the Crayons Quit*

Power Note   *Our focus is on the salutation (letter opening or greeting) and closing of the letter. However, students will notice quite a few craft moves within the body of the letter (using reasons to support the argument, capitalizing names, and using all caps). (See the tip box.) Honor what they notice in the body, but also guide them to focus upon the salutation and closing and their particular conventions: "I capitalize the first letter of a letter greeting and a closing."*

Tip: The Rare Craft of Using ALL CAPS

Young writers need to know that putting a word in all caps (short for *all capital letters*) connotes yelling in an email or a loud sound or shout in prose.

We may be tempted to say NEVER use all caps. But instead of stifling a child's convention use for a purpose, we could say, "*Rarely* use all caps." Wouldn't that do the trick? The word *rarely* implies that a writer chooses and considers the meaning and effect. If we use all caps too often, they have no emphasis or effect. Writers use capitalization only for a purpose, so *rarely* is a better adverb than *never*.

Invitation to Compare and Contrast	Dear Duncan,

As Green Crayon, I am writing for two reasons. One is to say that I like my workloads of crocodiles, trees, dinosaurs, and frogs. I have no problems and wish to congratulate you on a very successful "coloring things green" career so far.

The second reason I write is for my friends, Yellow Crayon and Orange Crayon, who are no longer speaking to each other. Both crayons feel THEY should be the color of the sun. Please settle this soon because they're driving the rest of us CRAZY!

Your happy friend,
Green Crayon

Dear Aunt Norma,

As your niece, I am writing for two reasons. One is to say that I like the meals you make for me when I come to visit. I have no problems and wish to continue having this delicious food.

The second reason I write is for my sisters, Kyra and Tammy, who want more meal choices. Both girls feel they should have extra desserts with their dinner. Please do something about this because they are driving me CRAZY talking about it all the time.

Your grateful niece,
Amy

Power Note   *These letters are in block style. In block style you skip lines between elements, including paragraphs. You do not, however, indent.*

Invitation to Imitate   *Imitate Together*: Invite writers to use interactive, shared, or paired writing to compose a letter with you. (See Figure 4.5.)

Figure 4.5 (left)
Interactive writing to principal
Figure 4.6 (right)
A second grader writes a letter to her teacher using the conventions of capitalization in the salutation and closing.

Imitate Independently: Students use the model to create their own letters, capitalizing the first word in the salutation and the closing, as well as the names. (See Figure 4.6.)

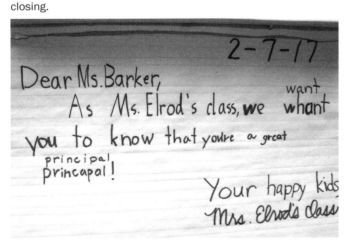
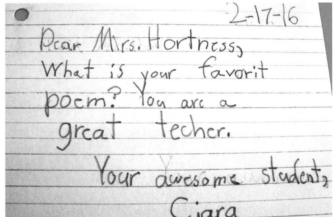

Invitation to Celebrate   Share the letters aloud and have the students mail or give the letters to the people they wrote them to if appropriate. This celebration can also turn into a lesson on how to address an envelope.

Invitation to Apply   Develop a list of different ways to open and close a letter. Have the students write a letter to their favorite author, choosing the best way to open and close it. Mail the letters to the authors. They will most likely respond!

Invitation to Edit

What did we learn about writing from Drew Daywalt?	
Both crayons feel THEY should be the color of the sun. Please settle this soon because they're driving the rest of us CRAZY! Your happy friend, Green Crayon	
What changed? What is the effect of the change?	
Your Happy friend, Green Crayon	*Happy is capitalized in the letter closing. Since only the first word of the letter closing need to be capitalized, the reader may think the letter wasn't written with much care.*
Your, happy friend Green Crayon	*A comma has been inserted after the word your instead of at the end of the closing line. The change causes the reader to pause in the middle of the closing, which doesn't make sense. Letter writers need only one comma at the end of the closing line.*
Your Happy Friend, Green Crayon	*Happy and friend are capitalized. The effect is that the name has less emphasis. And our names are too important to be overshadowed. Only the first word of a letter closing needs to be capitalized.*

What do you notice?

Dear Duncan,

As Green Crayon, I am writing for two reasons. One is to say that I like my workloads of crocodiles, trees, dinosaurs, and frogs. I have no problems and wish to congratulate you on a very successful "coloring things green" career so far.

The second reason I write is for my friends, Yellow Crayon and Orange Crayon, who are no longer speaking to each other. Both crayons feel THEY should be the color of the sun. Please settle this soon because they're driving the rest of us CRAZY!

Your happy friend,
Green Crayon

— Drew Daywalt, *The Day the Crayons Quit*

How are they alike and different?

Dear Duncan,
As Green Crayon, I am writing for two reasons. One is to say that I like my workloads of crocodiles, trees, dinosaurs, and frogs. I have no problems and wish to congratulate you on a very successful "coloring things green" career so far.
The second reason I write is for my friends, Yellow Crayon and Orange Crayon, who are no longer speaking to each other. Both crayons feel THEY should be the color of the sun. Please settle this soon because they're driving the rest of us CRAZY!
Your happy friend,
Green Crayon

Dear Aunt Norma,
As your niece, I am writing for two reasons. One is to say that I like the meals you make for me when I come to visit. I have no problems and wish to continue having this delicious food.

The second reason I write is for my sisters, Kyra and Tammy, who want more meal choices. Both girls feel they should have extra desserts with their dinner. Please do something about this because they are driving me CRAZY talking about it all the time.

Your grateful niece,
Amy

Let's try it out.

Dear Duncan,

As Green Crayon, I am writing for two reasons. One is to say that I like my workloads of crocodiles, trees, dinosaurs, and frogs. I have no problems and wish to congratulate you on a very successful "coloring things green" career so far.

The second reason I write is for my friends, Yellow Crayon and Orange Crayon, who are no longer speaking to each other. Both crayons feel THEY should be the color of the sun. Please settle this soon because they're driving the rest of us CRAZY!

Your happy friend,
Green Crayon

Your happy friend,
Green Crayon

What changed in the letter closing? What is the effect of the change?

Your Happy friend,
Green Crayon

Your, happy friend
Green Crayon

Your Happy Friend,
Green Crayon

4.6 History Is of Capital Importance: Capitalizing Historical Periods and Events

Standard	Capitalize historical periods and events.
Focus Phrase	"I capitalize historical periods and events to emphasize importance."
Invitation to Notice	Hard times had come to America. During the Great Depression of the 1930s, millions of families were struggling to live on incomes so meager that the threat of disaster hung over them day after day. —Russell Freedman, *Children of the Great Depression*
Power Note	*Students may ask why 1930s doesn't have an apostrophe (1930's). Most authoritative style guides suggest the apostrophe isn't needed because the s is lowercase and 1930s is clearly plural. The opener in the second sentence is a prepositional phrase.*
Invitation to Compare and Contrast	Hard times had come to America. During the Great Depression of the 1930s, millions of families were struggling to live on incomes so meager that the threat of disaster hung over them day after day. Big hair and shoulder pads had come to America. During The Eighties, millions of men and women were struggling to find enough hair mousse to make their hair stand up straight.
Power Note	*How would Freedman's sentences have been different if he'd written* The Thirties *rather than the 1930s? Either is correct, but do they have different effects? Why might an author choose one over the other?*
Invitation to Imitate	*Shared Writing*: Together compose a sentence that uses one of the time periods listed in the chart labeled "Capitalize Historical Periods and Events." The invitation to apply will give students the opportunity to try out the pattern with a partner.
Invitation to Apply	Partners choose a historical period and complete a quick Internet search to gather enough information to write a few sentences about the period on an index card. They can use Freedman's example as a guide if they like. Writers make sure the time period is capitalized. (But centuries and the numbers before them are not capitalized.)

Capitalize Historical Periods and Events

Middle Ages	World War II	The Sixties
Machine Age	Cold War	The Seventies
World War I	Vietnam War	The Eighties
Roaring Twenties	Space Age	The Nineties
Great Depression	The Fifties	

Invitation to Celebrate   Share oral presentations of information discoveries. Reports could follow the relative time line in which they occurred, and the index cards can be taped on a piece of butcher paper, creating an actual time line.

Invitation to Edit

What did we learn about writing from Russell Freedman?	
Hard times had come to America. During the Great Depression of the 1930s, millions of families were struggling to live on incomes so meager that the threat of disaster hung over them day after day.	
What changed? What is the effect of the change?	
Hard times had come to america. During the Great Depression of the 1930s, millions of families were struggling to live on incomes so meager that the threat of disaster hung over them day after day.	*America is not capitalized. When the name of a country is not capitalized, we are not honoring it or following the pattern. We capitalize names of places (countries, states, counties, cities, restaurants, and schools).*
Hard times had come to America. During the great Depression of the 1930s, millions of families were struggling to live on incomes so meager that the threat of disaster hung over them day after day.	*Great Depression should be capitalized. When a writer doesn't capitalize a historical time period, it loses its emphasis and may muddle meaning for readers. We capitalize historical time periods.*
Hard times had come to America. During the Great Depression of the 1930's, millions of families were struggling to live on incomes so meager that the threat of disaster hung over them day after day.	*An apostrophe has been inserted in the 1930s. The apostrophe isn't needed for clarity. It could cause readers to think of possessions or contractions.*

What do you notice?

Hard times had come to America. During the Great Depression of the 1930s, millions of families were struggling to live on incomes so meager that the threat of disaster hung over them day after day.

—Russell Freedman, *Children of the Great Depression*

How are they alike and different?

Hard times had come to America. During the Great Depression of the 1930s, millions of families were struggling to live on incomes so meager that the threat of disaster hung over them day after day.

Big hair and shoulder pads had come to America. During The Eighties, millions of men and women were struggling to find enough hair mousse to make their hair stand up straight.

Let's try it out.

Hard times had come to America. During the Great Depression of the 1930s, millions of families were struggling to live on incomes so meager that the threat of disaster hung over them day after day.

Big hair and shoulder pads had come to America. During The Eighties, millions of men and women were struggling to find enough hair mousse to make their hair stand up straight.

Hard times had come to America. During the Great Depression of the 1930s, millions of families were struggling to live on incomes so meager that the threat of disaster hung over them day after day.

What changed? What is the effect of the change?

Hard times had come to america. During the Great Depression of the 1930s, millions of families were struggling to live on incomes so meager that the threat of disaster hung over them day after day.

Hard times had come to America. During the great Depression of the 1930s, millions of families were struggling to live on incomes so meager that the threat of disaster hung over them day after day.

Hard times had come to America. During the Great Depression of the 1930's, millions of families were struggling to live on incomes so meager that the threat of disaster hung over them day after day.

4.7   Honor Everyone's Heritage: Capitalizing Nationalities and Languages

Standard	Capitalize nationalities and languages.
Focus Phrase	"I honor nationalities and language by capitalizing them."
Invitation to Notice	The Golden Lotus is a famous Chinese restaurant, about two hours away from where we live. —Wendy Wan-Long Shang, *The Great Wall of Lucy Wu*
Power Note	*A few teachers are uncomfortable with the comma before the prepositional phrase at the end of the sentence. Our experience is that the kids don't worry about it. If they do talk about the comma, we ask what function it's serving, which is chunking off the last part. In general, we don't need a comma before a prepositional phrase. If this makes you too uncomfortable, you can, of course, cut the prepositional phrase: The Golden Lotus is a Chinese restaurant. But we nudge you to explore the questions. It will work itself out.*
Invitation to Compare and Contrast	The Golden Lotus is a famous Chinese restaurant, about two hours away from where we live. Papuli's is a delicious Greek restaurant, about fifteen minutes from where we live.
Invitation to Imitate	Students imitate Shang's pattern of capitalizing nationalities (or languages) in a sentence about their own experiences.
Invitation to Celebrate	Students share sentences. On second reading, the class stands up and sits down when the nationality or language is mentioned to remember to capitalize them, like standing up for a national anthem.
Invitation to Apply	Divide students into cooperative groups. Groups brainstorm as many nationalities and languages as they can. Create a class collection on chart paper under the focus phrase "I honor nationalities and language by capitalizing them." *Bonus question for students*: Which of the classes you take during the day should be capitalized within a sentence?
Power Note	*We capitalize all subject areas when they're on a schedule, but that's because they're on a schedule following its conventions. If we write a subject area in a sentence, such as math, gym, social studies, or science, it isn't capitalized. However, when the word is derived from a language or nationality, we do: English, Spanish, American history.*

Invitation to Edit

What did we learn about writing from Wendy Shang?	
The Golden Lotus is a famous Chinese restaurant, about two hours away from where we live.	
What changed? What is the effect of the change?	
The Golden Lotus is a famous Chinese Restaurant, about two hours away from where we live.	*The common noun restaurant has been capitalized. Readers could think it is a restaurant named Chinese Restaurant. The word Chinese is capitalized because it is a nationality. It comes from a proper noun or nation of China.*
The Golden Lotus is a famous chinese restaurant, about two hours away from where we live.	*The nationality Chinese (proper adjective technically) needs to be capitalized. When we don't capitalize it, we're not honoring the nationality's importance.*
The Golden Lotus is a famous Chinese restaurant. About two hours away from where we live.	*When the comma is changed to a period, the second half of the sentence becomes a sentence fragment, which can't stand on its own. The period could make readers think these are two separate thoughts.*

Tip: Capitalization Across the Curriculum

As writers continue to notice capitalization and ask why certain words are capitalized, take advantage of these quick opportunities to extend the idea that we capitalize words only for a reason in context. For example, while reading aloud Michael Harris's *What Is the Declaration of Independence?* in social studies, stop and display a sentence that uses capitalization in a new way:

After the Declaration of Independence was finished, it was signed on July 4, 1776.

As we've done previously, ask students what they notice, taking all answers. Name and extend the conversation around the standard of capitalizing historical documents. In our experience these types of patterns, such as historical documents, aren't always ripe for imitation. Instead, we continue to encourage students to highlight these specific historical and geographical capitalization patterns as we encounter them across the curriculum in our reading and writing. Books such as *What Is the Declaration of Independence?* are rich with capitalized historical names and nationalities:

In 1754, Great Britain tried to grab more of North America by invading lands controlled by the French. This led to a war known as the French and Indian War.

In these two sentences, the author demonstrates more purposeful capitalization patterns for proper nouns:

- *Geographical places*: Great Britain and North America
- *Nationalities*: French
- *Historical events*: French and Indian War

What do you notice?

The Golden Lotus is a famous Chinese restaurant, about two hours away from where we live.

—Wendy Shang, *The Great Wall of Lucy Wu*

How are they alike and different?

The Golden Lotus is a famous Chinese restaurant, about two hours away from where we live.

Papuli's is a delicious Greek restaurant, about fifteen minutes from where we live.

Let's try it out.

The Golden Lotus is a famous Chinese restaurant, about two hours away from where we live.

Papuli's is a delicious Greek restaurant, about fifteen minutes from where we live.

The Golden Lotus is a famous Chinese restaurant, about two hours away from where we live.

What changed? What is the effect of the change?

The Golden Lotus is a famous Chinese Restaurant, about two hours away from where we live.

The Golden Lotus is a famous chinese restaurant, about two hours away from where we live.

The Golden Lotus is a famous Chinese restaurant. About two hours away from where we live.

5

What Do Nouns Do?

$\mathcal{N}$ouns are the stuff that things are made of. In fact, the world we live in is made of nouns. Where are you sitting or lying right now? In a *chair*? On a *couch*? In *bed*? All the places where we could be are nouns. Sentences need stuff—or nouns—to be about something. The essential stuff of a basic sentence is referred to as its subject—the *who* or *what* of the sentence. We ask, "*Who* or *what* does or is something?" to identify the subject easily. The subject—or noun—will be the answer. Of course nouns do more than act as subjects of sentences. Writers use nouns all over their sentences to show a clear picture of people, places, and things.

And the more specific our nouns, the more concrete our writing becomes. The word *thing* doesn't give the mind a specific picture. The common noun *bug* does. Choosing a specific bug such as *roach* gives us an even clearer picture. *Steak* and *sand* and *money* all give us an image. Crafting nouns effectively asks writers to find the right one for the job. Each noun is a gift, producing associations for readers, tapping into their backgrounds, and providing them with information that is vital to helping them visualize and understand.

In addition to crafting nouns from broad to specific, authors sharpen images by naming names. When a *boy's* name is *Zack*, he is now not just a *boy*, but one particular boy named *Zack*. To ensure proper nouns get the attention they deserve, writers capitalize them. (See additional example lessons on capitalizing proper nouns in Chapters 1–3.)

Lesson Sets:

What Do Nouns Do?

5.1   Spending Your Allowance: Know Your Nouns

Standard   Use and understand common nouns.

Focus Phrase   "I use nouns to show a picture of people, places, and things."

Invitation to Notice   Jacques saved his allowance, penny by penny, until he had enough to buy a small home-movie camera.
> —Jennifer Berne, *Manfish: A Story of Jacques Cousteau*

Power Note   *The bold words function as* **nouns** *or* **pronouns** *in this particular sentence (pronouns are a type of noun—a noun substitute, in fact):* **Jacques** *saved his* **allowance**, **penny** *by* **penny**, *until* **he** *had* **enough** *to buy a small home-movie* **camera**. *(In this sentence, home-movie is an adjective telling what kind of camera Jacques had.) (See Figure 5.1.)*

Figure 5.1
Jeff invites young writers to notice author Jennifer Berne's craft and convention choices.

Invitation to Compare and Contrast   Jacques saved his allowance, penny by penny, until he had enough to buy a small home-movie camera.
He saved stuff, thing by thing, until he had enough to get something.
Carl saved his treats, bone by bone, until he had enough to open his own PetSmart.

Power Note   *We chose to add a third sentence to this compare-and-contrast invitation: a vague sentence. This vague sentence in the middle demonstrates that nouns aren't always proper nouns. The contrast of common nouns in the second sentence highlights the specific common nouns in sentences one and three.*

Invitation to Imitate   *Imitate Together*: Invite writers to use interactive or shared writing to compose a sentence with you.

Imitate Independently: Students use the model to create their own sentences, using nouns to help our readers see the world they are creating with the stuff of specific nouns.

Invitation to Celebrate

Open a new document on a class computer and write the focus phrase across the top: "I use nouns to show a clear picture of people, places, and things." Throughout the day, students take turns typing in their imitations. Make sure they put their name after an em dash on the line after their sentence like we do in all the lessons:

> *I saved my allowance, dollar by dollar, until I had enough to buy an epic game of Minecraft.*
> —Brice

Power Note

To make the em dash on the keyboard, hit the hyphen key twice. Don't leave a space after the em dash. If the em dash still isn't a solid line, press command + shift + hyphen if you have a PC; on a Mac, it's option + shift + hyphen. The next day, you can edit the sentences as a class. Print the page(s) and distribute them to the class the day after that.

Invitation to Apply

In another content-area class, ask questions as students find an interesting or favorite sentence:

- "Can you tell *who* or *what* it's about?" Students talk it over with a neighbor.
- "Which nouns paint the strongest or weakest pictures?" The class continues the discussion and charts thinking.
- "When you write today, think about how the nouns you use are painting a picture with specific stuff."

Invitation to Edit

What did we learn about writing from Jennifer Berne?	
Jacques saved his allowance, penny by penny, until he had enough to buy a small home-movie camera.	
What changed? What is the effect of the change?	
Jacques save his allowance, penny by penny, until he had enough to buy a small home-movie camera.	*Save is no longer in the past tense, creating a tense-agreement issue with the second verb in the sentence, had. When verbs in the same sentence don't agree, it disturbs the flow of the sentence.*
Jacques saved her allowance, penny by penny, until he had enough to buy a small home-movie camera.	*The pronoun his before allowance was changed to her. Jacques is male, and the pronoun her is female. This change means Jacques is a girl.*
Jacques saved stuff, thing by thing, until he had enough to buy something.	*These unspecific nouns don't create pictures, making the writing unclear.*

What do you notice?

Jacques saved his allowance, penny by penny, until he had enough to buy a small home-movie camera.

—Jennifer Berne, *Manfish: A Story of Jacques Cousteau*

How are they alike and different?

Jacques saved his allowance, penny by penny, until he had enough to buy a small home-movie camera.

He saved stuff, thing by thing, until he had enough to get something.

Carl saved his treats, bone by bone, until he had enough to open his own PetSmart.

Let's try it out.

Jacques saved his allowance, penny by penny, until he had enough to buy a small home-movie camera.

Carl saved his treats, bone by bone, until he had enough to open his own PetSmart.

Jacques saved his allowance, penny by penny, until he had enough to buy a small home-movie camera.

What changed? What is the effect of the change?

Jacques save his allowance, penny by penny, until he had enough to buy a small home-movie camera.

Jacques saved her allowance, penny by penny, until he had enough to buy a small home-movie camera.

Jacques saved stuff, thing by thing, until he had enough to buy something.

5.2   Capital Offense: When to Capitalize, When Not To

Standard	Use and understand proper nouns.
Focus Phrase	"I capitalize proper nouns to show the names of people, places, and things."
Invitation to Notice	That night, Chrysanthemum dreamed that she really *was* a chrysanthemum. —Kevin Henkes, *Chrysanthemum*
Invitation to Compare and Contrast	That night, Chrysanthemum dreamed that she really *was* a chrysanthemum. That morning, Esteban realized he *was* also Stephen.
Invitation to Imitate	*Imitate Together*: Invite writers to use paired writing to compose a sentence. *Imitate Independently*: Students use the model sentence to create their own sentences, using proper nouns for specific names of places, people, and things.
Invitation to Celebrate	*Wall or Door Chart*: At the top of the chart or on butcher paper, write the focus phrase: "I capitalize proper nouns to name people, places, and things." Add sentence strips with sentences students say, write, or find. Highlight capitalization use on teacher and student examples on the chart. (See Figure 5.2.)

Figure 5.2
Proper noun collection

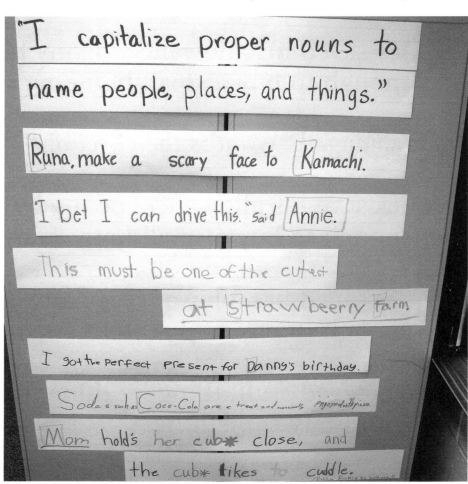

Invitation to Apply Students return to a piece of writing—a writer's notebook entry, a draft, or a completed piece. Using the Rapid Revision technique from Chapter 3, they revise one or two sentences, changing common nouns to proper ones.

Invitation to Edit

What did we learn about writing from Kevin Henkes?	
That night, Chrysanthemum dreamed that she really was a chrysanthemum.	
What changed? What is the effect of the change?	
That night, Chrysanthemum dreamed that she really *was* a Chrysanthemum.	*The second chrysanthemum refers to a type of flower, not a proper noun. When we capitalize it, we are changing the meaning from a flower to a name because "We capitalize names."*
That night, Chrysanthemum dreamed that She really *was* a chrysanthemum.	*The pronoun she has been capitalized. Pronouns like she, he, they, and it are not capitalized. When we capitalize she, it is because it is either the beginning of a new sentence or a name. Either way, we're slowing our reader down.*
That night Chrysanthemum dreamed that she really *was* a chrysanthemum.	*The comma setting off that night as the sentence opener has been deleted. "How does reading the sentence change with no comma?" (There is no pause setting off that night. It might lose emphasis.)*

What do you notice?

That night, Chrysanthemum dreamed that she really *was* a chrysanthemum.

—Kevin Henkes, *Chrysanthemum*

How are they alike and different?

That night, Chrysanthemum dreamed that she really *was* a chrysanthemum.

That morning, Esteban realized he *was* also Stephen.

Let's try it out.

That night, Chrysanthemum dreamed that she really *was* a chrysanthemum.

That morning, Esteban realized he *was* also Stephen.

That night, Chrysanthemum dreamed that she really *was* a chrysanthemum.

What changed? What is the effect of the change?

That night, Chrysanthemum dreamed that she really *was* a Chrysanthemum.

That night, Chrysanthemum dreamed that She really *was* a chrysanthemum.

That night Chrysanthemum dreamed that she really *was* a chrysanthemum.

5.3   One More Mountain to Climb: Proper Nouns

Standard   Use and understand proper nouns.

Focus Phrase   "I capitalize proper nouns to give emphasis to names of people and places."

Invitation to Notice   A 15-year-old named Christopher Harris wanted to become the youngest person to climb Mount Everest.
—Tim O'Shei, *Left for Dead! Lincoln Hall's Story of Survival*

Invitation to Compare and Contrast   A 15-year-old named Christopher Harris wanted to become the youngest person to climb Mount Everest.
An 11-year-old named Tonia Washington wanted to become the youngest person to go to Harvard.

Invitation to Imitate   *Imitate Together*: Invite writers to use paired writing to compose a sentence. (See Figure 5.3.)

Figure 5.3
Third graders talk through their ideas for an imitation through paired writing.

Imitate Independently: Dream Weaver. Students use the model sentence to create their own sentences, using proper nouns to name specific names of places, people, and things to be the best or most at something. (Writers may use *youngest*, but they don't have to.)

Invitation to Celebrate   *If Your Mind Can Conceive It, I Know You Can Achieve It*. At the top of the chart or on butcher paper, write the focus phrase: "I capitalize proper nouns to show specific people, places, and things." Add students' imitation sentences to the chart. (See Figure 5.4.)

Invitation to Apply   Students return to a piece of writing—a writer's notebook entry, a draft, or a completed piece. Using the Rapid Revision technique explained in Chapter 3, they revise one or two sentences, changing common nouns to proper ones.

Figure 5.4
"I Capitalize Proper Nouns" third-grade celebration

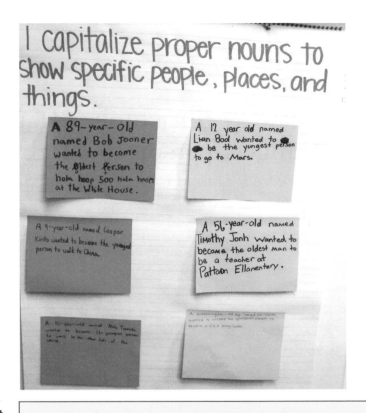

I capitalize proper nouns to show specific people, places, and things.

Invitation to Edit

What did we learn about writing from Tim O'Shei?	
A 15-year-old named Christopher Harris wanted to become the youngest person to climb Mount Everest.	
What changed? What is the effect of the change?	
A 15-year-old named Christopher Harris wanted to become the youngest person to climb mount Everest.	Mount *was changed to lowercase.* Mount Everest *is a proper noun, so* mount *should be capitalized. When it's not, it no longer appears to be the name of a place.* "I capitalize proper nouns to give emphasis to names of people and places."
A 15-year-old named Christopher Harris wanted to become the younger person to climb Mount Everest.	Youngest *was changed to* younger. *This makes the reader ask, "Younger than whom?"* Younger *compares at least two things, whereas* youngest *means "youngest of all." The sentence's meaning is muddled with the change.*
A 15-year-old named Christopher harris wanted to become the youngest person to climb Mount Everest.	Harris *is his last name. "I capitalize proper nouns to give emphasis to names of people and places." When we don't capitalize names, we are communicating that the word is not a name.*

What do you notice?

A 15-year-old named Christopher Harris wanted to become the youngest person to climb Mount Everest.

—Tim O'Shei, *Left for Dead! Lincoln Hall's Story of Survival*

How are they alike and different?

A 15-year-old named Christopher Harris wanted to become the youngest person to climb Mount Everest.

An 11-year-old named Tonia Washington wanted to become the youngest person to go to Harvard.

Let's try it out.

A 15-year-old named Christopher Harris wanted to become the youngest person to climb Mount Everest.

An 11-year-old named Tonia Washington wanted to become the youngest person to go to Harvard.

A 15-year-old named Christopher Harris wanted to become the youngest person to climb Mount Everest.

What changed? What is the effect of the change?

A 15-year-old named Christopher Harris wanted to become the youngest person to climb mount Everest.

A 15-year-old named Christopher Harris wanted to become the younger person to climb Mount Everest.

A 15-year-old named Christopher harris wanted to become the youngest person to climb Mount Everest.

Tip: One or More? Plural Nouns Are More than One

If your noun is one person, one place, or one thing, it's a singular noun. To show that there is more than one noun—two or more—form plural nouns. Most plural nouns are formed by adding an *s* to the end. Words that end in *-s*, *-ss*, *-tch*, *-ch*, or *-sh* need *-es* to become plural. If a word ends in *-y*, you usually change the *y* to *i* and then add *-es*. It's important to remember that not all nouns will follow this pattern. Irregular plural nouns aren't that easy; you just have to know them or look them up. (Also see Lesson 5.6, Add Groups to the Noun Collection: Collective Nouns.)

Irregular Plural Nouns

Singular	Plural
Child	Children
Man	Men
Woman	Women
Foot	Feet
Tooth	Teeth
Leaf	Leaves
Life	Lives
Wife	Wives
Shelf	Shelves

5.4 Give Peas a Chance: Plural Nouns

Standard Use and understand singular and plural nouns.

Focus Phrase "I use plural nouns to show more than one person, place, or thing."

Invitation to Notice It's not the pork chops or the mashed potatoes. It all starts when I'm forced to eat . . . peas!
—George McClements, *Night of the Veggie Monster*

Power Note *You'll notice that to* pluralize *potatoes, writers add -es. The few nouns in English that end in* o *need -es to make them plural (potato/potatoes, tomato/tomatoes).*

Invitation to Compare and Contrast It's not the pork chops or the mashed potatoes. It all starts when I'm forced to eat . . . peas!
It's not the veggie burgers or the kale chips. It all starts when I'm forced to eat . . . smelly broccoli.

Invitation to Imitate *Imitate Together*: Invite writers to use interactive or shared writing to compose a sentence with you.

Imitate Independently: Students use the model to create their own sentences, using plural nouns. (See Figure 5.5.)

Figure 5.5
First graders create pages for a class book with their imitations.

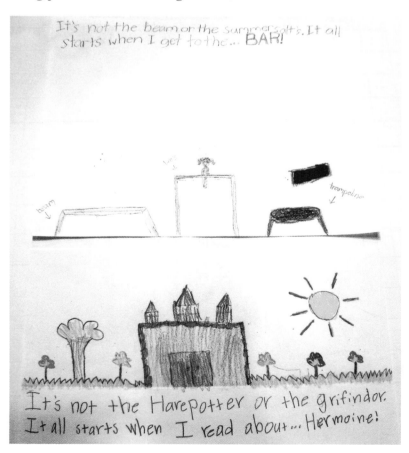

Invitation to Apply   Students write a response to reading with a plural noun. They find a sentence in their reading or writing that uses a plural noun. Then they copy the sentence in their writer's notebook and write a few sentences explaining how they know what the plural noun is and what would change in the sentence if the noun were singular.

Invitation to Edit

What did we learn about writing from George McClements?	
It's not the pork chops or the mashed potatoes. It all starts when I'm forced to eat . . . peas!	
What changed? What is the effect of the change?	
Its not the pork chops or the mashed potatoes. It all starts when I'm forced to eat . . . peas!	*The apostrophe has been deleted from the contraction* it's, *making it a personal possessive pronoun, which changes.* It is = it's, *and* its *always denotes ownership or possession. Possessive personal pronouns don't use apostrophes.*
It's not the pork chops or the mashed potatoes. It all starts when I am forced to eat . . . peas!	*The contraction* I'm *is written out as* I am. *It's still correct, but how is the effect different?*
It's not the pork chops or the mashed potato. It all starts when I'm forced to eat . . . peas!	*The plural noun* potatoes *is changed to a singular noun,* potato. *This version means only one potato was mashed, so it wouldn't be much!*

What do you notice?

It's not the pork chops or the mashed potatoes. It all starts when I'm forced to eat . . . peas!

　　—George McClements, *Night of the Veggie Monster*

How are they alike and different?

It's not the pork chops or the mashed potatoes. It all starts when I'm forced to eat . . . peas!

It's not the veggie burger or the kale chips. It all starts when I'm forced to eat . . . smelly broccoli.

Let's try it out.

It's not the pork chops or the mashed potatoes. It all starts when I'm forced to eat . . . peas!

It's not the veggie burger or the kale chips. It all starts when I'm forced to eat . . . smelly broccoli.

It's not the pork chops or the mashed potatoes. It all starts when I'm forced to eat . . . peas!

What changed? What is the effect of the change?

Its not the pork chops or the mashed potatoes. It all starts when I'm forced to eat . . . peas!

It's not the pork chops or the mashed potatoes. It all starts when I am forced to eat . . . peas!

It's not the pork chops or the mashed potato. It all starts when I'm forced to eat . . . peas!

5.5   Pluralism: More Than One Noun

Standard	Form and use regular and irregular plural nouns.
Focus Phrase	"I use plural nouns to show more than one person, place, or thing."
Invitation to Notice	Everyone was running—men, children, women carrying babies.
	—Linda Sue Park, *A Long Walk to Water*

Power Note   *These plurals are mostly irregular.* Everyone *is an indefinite pronoun, which uses singular noun agreement. Write* men, children, women. *"What are their singular forms? Which plural noun is regular? [Babies] What is its singular form?" A dash can be used to set off information like a comma, as Park has done here.*

Invitation to Compare and Contrast   Everyone was running—men, children, women carrying babies.
People played in the piles of leaves—children, men, and women.

Power Note   *As students talk about how the sentences are alike and different, a few questions may come up with the imitation.* People *is a noncount noun like* men, women, *and* children, *which means it is still treated as a plural, needing a plural verb for agreement. In the past tense, the words are the same—they end in -ed*

Invitation to Imitate   *Imitate Together*: Invite writers to use interactive or shared writing to compose a sentence with you. (See Figure 5.6.)

Figure 5.6
Whitney works with fourth graders to create an imitation through interactive writing.

Imitate Independently: Students use the model to create their own sentences, using plural nouns—regular or irregular.

Invitation to Apply   Students write a response to reading with a plural noun. They find a sentence in their reading or writing that uses a plural noun. Then they copy the sentence in their writer's notebook and write a few sentences explaining how they know what the plural noun is and what would change in the sentence if the noun were singular. (See Figure 5.7.)

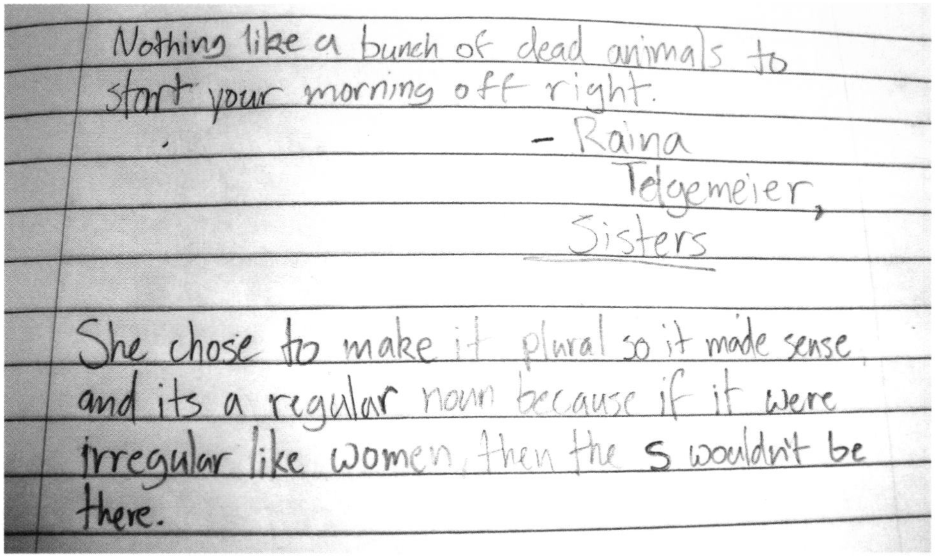

Figure 5.7
Notebook reflection on plural nouns

> Nothing like a bunch of dead animals to start your morning off right.
> — Raina Telgemeier, Sisters
>
> She chose to make it plural so it made sense, and its a regular noun because if it were irregular like women, then the s wouldn't be there.

Invitation to Edit

What did we learn about writing from Linda Sue Park?	
Everyone was running—men, children, women carrying babies.	
What changed? What is the effect of the change?	
Everyone was running—men, children, women carrying babyes.	*The plural noun* babies *is misspelled. The pattern for pluralizing words that end in -y is to change y to i and add -es.*
Everyone was running—men, childrens, women carrying babies.	*An s was added to the end of* children. *Adding an s when none is needed can interrupt your message.* Children *is an irregular plural noun that doesn't end in -s.*
Everyone was running—men, children, woman carrying babies.	*The plural noun* women *has been changed to the singular noun* woman, *which changes how many women there were. When it says* woman, *it means there was only one woman.*

What do you notice?

Everyone was running—men, children, women carrying babies.

—Linda Sue Park, *A Long Walk to Water*

How are they alike and different?

Everyone was running—men, children, women carrying babies.

People played in the piles of leaves—children, men, and women.

Let's try it out.

Everyone was running—men, children, women carrying babies.

People played in the piles of leaves—children, men, and women.

Everyone was running—men, children, women carrying babies.

What changed? What is the effect of the change?

Everyone was running—men, children, women carrying babyes.

Everyone was running—men, childrens, women carrying babies.

Everyone was running—men, children, woman carrying babies.

Tip: Collective Nouns Gather Together Groups

Read aloud Anna Wright's *A Tower of Giraffes: Animals in Groups* and discuss group nouns with the class. (*Class* is a noncount noun in that sentence, by the way.) Start the conversation about a few common collective nouns (see the chart below)

Collective Nouns

People	*Places*	*Things (including* living *things)*
Class of children	Range of mountains	Basket of fruit
Team of players	Library of books	Batch of cookies
Class of students	Forest of trees	Deck of cards
Platoon of soldiers	Suite of rooms	Galaxy of stars
Audience of listeners	Constellation of stars	Wad of bills
Crowd of fans		Swarm of bees or flies
		Bouquet of flowers
		Bunch of grapes
		Fleet of ships or planes
		Set of tools

Note: The articles and verbs that come before and after should be treated as a singular noun—as in one group—for agreement purposes. The *batch* of cookies is burned. Ignore that plural noun *cookies*, because *batch* is the subject and *of cookies* is a prepositional phrase that modifies it. The *bunch* of grapes *falls* on the floor. Collective nouns often give writers trouble because of the prepositional phrase and plural noun that follow them.

"What patterns do you see?" I ask students. They answer or I help them see the following:

- There's an *of* in all of them.
- The word that follows of usually ends in *-s* (plural).
- The first word, the collective noun or group word, is considered one thing.

Close by asking students if they see or hear another word in *collective.* "We are going to *collect* group nouns on this chart." Pointing to the chart, we write the sentence *I have the best* class *in the school.* Explain that just adding an *s* to a word like *teacher* makes it plural, *teachers*, but collective nouns are a whole new way of naming the group as one thing. (If kids say a lot of plural nouns, just start another chart of plural nouns so you can accept answers but see the differences.)

For the rest of the day, we continue to collect collective nouns. The next day I begin the invitational process. For this lesson, young readers will enjoy *An Ambush of Tigers: A Wild Gathering of Collective Nouns* by Betsy R. Rosenthal, from the American Library Association Notable Children's Books List. Third through fifth graders will appreciate the simplicity and beauty of Thomas Bewick's line drawings in Samuel Fanous's *A Barrel of Monkeys: A Compendium of Collective Nouns for Animals.*

5.6   Add Groups to the Noun Collection: Collective Nouns

Standard	Use and understand collective nouns.
Focus Phrase	"I use collective nouns to name groups of people, places, and things as one."
Invitation to Notice	A little crowd bunched up around us, and everyone was really excited.
	—Christopher Paul Curtis, *The Watsons Go to Birmingham—1963*
Power Note	*Bunch can be a collective noun, but here,* bunched *is functioning as a verb to tell what the* crowd *did. The collective nouns are* crowd *and* everyone. *Everyone is also considered an indefinite pronoun.*
Invitation to Compare and Contrast	A little crowd bunched up around us, and everyone was really excited.
	The soccer team surrounded the goal, and the goalie was really excited.
Invitation to Imitate	*Imitate Together*: Invite writers to use interactive, shared, or paired writing to compose a sentence with you. (See Figure 5.8.)
	Imitate Independently: Students use the model to create their own sentences, using a collective noun. Sharing a list of collective nouns will be essential. (See Figure 5.9 and the invitation to celebrate.)

Figure 5.8 (left)
Fifth graders work together to create an imitation through interactive writing.

Figure 5.9 (right)
Collective noun chart

I use collective nouns to name groups of people, places, and things as one.

A little crowd bunched up around us, and everyone was really excited.

The soccer team surrounded the goal, and the goalie was really excited.

I pulled an ace of diamonds from the thick deck, and I was really excited.

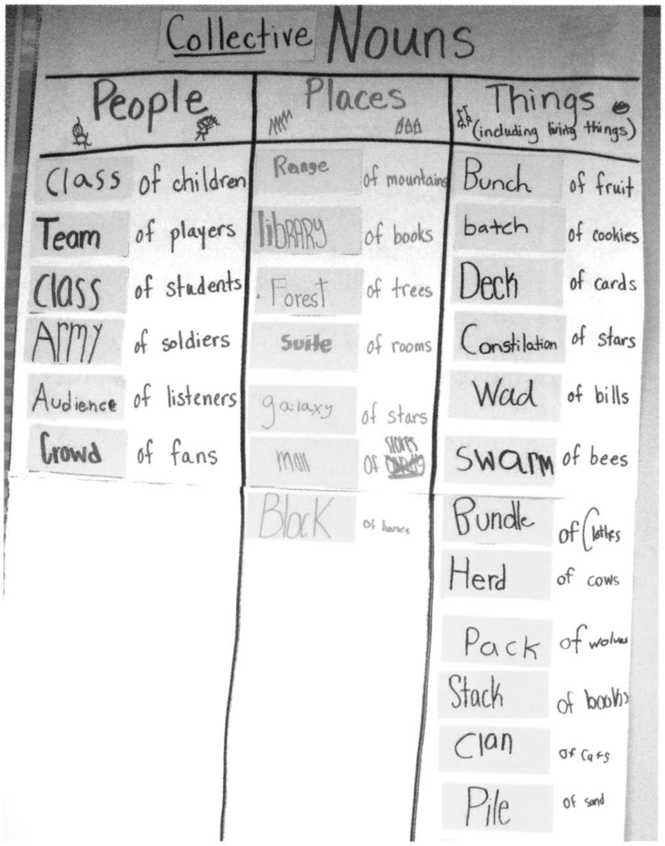

Collective Nouns

People	Places	Things (including living things)
Class of children	Range of mountains	Bunch of fruit
Team of players	library of books	batch of cookies
Class of students	Forest of trees	Deck of cards
Army of soldiers	Suite of rooms	Constilation of stars
Audience of listeners	galaxy of stars	Wad of bills
Crowd of fans	mall of stores	swarm of bees
	Block of horses	Bundle of clothes
		Herd of cows
		Pack of wolves
		Stack of books
		Clan of cats
		Pile of sand

Invitation to Celebrate   We continue adding to our collective noun chart from our reading, writing, and speaking. (See Figure 5.9.)

Invitation to Apply   Collect any collective nouns found in other subject areas. Discuss how the articles and verbs around them treat the collective noun as one entity (singular).

Invitation to Edit

What did we learn about writing from Christopher Paul Curtis?	
A little crowd bunched up around us, and everyone was really excited.	
What changed? What is the effect of the change?	
A little crowd bunches up around us, and everyone is really excited.	The past-tense verbs bunched and was were changed to the present-tense form bunches and is, affecting when the action happened. This version means it's happening now.
A little crowd bunched up around us, and everyone was real excited.	The adverb really was changed to the nonstandard form of real. This has a more casual sound, but in academic settings the pattern is to use really.
An little crowd bunched up around us, and everyone was really excited.	The article a was changed to an. We use the article an in front of singular and collective nouns that start with a vowel sound. When we put an in front of a word that begins with a consonant, we created a break in fluency.

What do you notice?

A little crowd bunched up around us, and everyone was really excited.

—Christopher Paul Curtis, *The Watsons Go to Birmingham—1963*

How are they alike and different?

A little crowd bunched up around us, and everyone was really excited.

The soccer team surrounded the goal, and the goalie was really excited.

Let's try it out.

A little crowd bunched up around us, and everyone was really excited.

The soccer team surrounded the goal, and the goalie was really excited.

A little crowd bunched up around us, and everyone was really excited.

What changed? What is the effect of the change?

A little crowd bunches up around us, and everyone is really excited.

A little crowd bunched up around us, and everyone was real excited.

An little crowd bunched up around us, and everyone was really excited.

6

What Do Verbs Do?

Sentences wouldn't *do* or *be* much without a workhorse verb.
  Tom.
    See? Nothing happens.
Tom cooks.
Add a verb, and now we're cooking—at least Tom is.

Verbs activate sentences, bringing them to life, identifying actions, setting a mood, or telling time. Quite simply, verbs help us *do* and *be*. That's right. In additions to actions, verbs also signal a state of existence, linking nouns or pronouns to a description: *You **are** a magnificent writer.* They even help out other verbs from time to time.

But trouble erupts for many young writers when things get tense. *Tense* comes from the Latin word for time. Sure, when the past tense merely needs *-ed* slapped onto the end to transform to the past, or the present tense needs an *s* attached to its end to be present, or the future tense needs *will* in front of it to catapult a verb into the future, tenses are a cakewalk. Until they're not. Irregular verbs rear their irregular forms, causing young writers overgeneralization problems and confusion. Helping verbs may link us to more problems than solutions. But together, we can face it all with ease—one verb at a time.

Loreen Leedy's *Seeing Symmetry* begins with a great example of verb usage:

Butterfly wings have it.
Triceratops had it.
The word MOM has it.
When you know what to look for, it's easy to start.

Leedy uses the verb *has* in its glorious past- and present-tense irregular forms:

When Leedy writes, *Butterfly wings have it*, we know she used the plural present form of *has* because *butterfly wings* is plural. And to this day, butterfly wings still have symmetry.

Since triceratops are an extinct dinosaur, Leedy writes *Triceratops had it*, using the past form of *has*, which, by the way, is *had* in either plural or singular form. With her verb tense, Leedy acknowledges to the reader that triceratops existed only in the past.

Leedy writes *The word MOM has it*, in the singular present form, because the word *MOM* exists now. Kids often ask why Leedy capitalized all the letters in *MOM*. The kids figure it out, but it takes a good understanding of the concept of symmetry, which by book's end, Leedy gives readers.

Whether past, present, future; linking or helping; progressive or perfect, verbs will always give you the time of day.

Lesson Sets:

What Do Verbs Do?

6.1 Verbs Move: Verbs Mean Action

6.2 Tell It Like It *Is* (*Are, Was, Were, Be, Been,* and *Am*): The Verbs of Being

6.3 Have You Got the Time? Verb Tense

6.4 Highly Irregular: Nonconforming Verbs

6.5 Rain Pummeled the Ground Versus The Ground Was Pummeled by Rain: Finding Your Active Voice

(For more on subject-verb agreement, see Chapter 11, "How Do Nouns and Verbs Agree?")

6.1 Verbs Move: Verbs Mean Action

Standard	Use and understand the function of verbs (action).
Focus Phrase	"I use verbs to show action."
Invitation to Notice	Animals live all around us. They crawl, walk, run, hop, swim, and fly. —Steve Jenkins, *Biggest, Strongest, Fastest*

Power Note *We chose to use two sentences because we thought that for this context it was good to see both, but it has the added benefit of highlighting a period between sentences and how the capitalized they also cues us that a new sentence is beginning. These are important skills to highlight for beginning writers. At some point, the writers will love acting out the list of verbs, which can lead to demonstrating that verbs mean action. We also ask, "What does the word they refer to?" (Pronoun reference and antecedent.)*

Invitation to Compare and Contrast Animals live all around us. They crawl, walk, run, hop, swim, and fly. Puppies live all around us. They bark, jump, and lick.

Power Note *Young writers benefit from a discussion about puppies being a specific animal, baby versus adult. "What does they refer to in the second sentence? How do you know?" (Puppies comes before they and agrees in number because both puppies and they are plural—more than one.)*

Invitation to Imitate *Imitate Together*: Partners choose a subject—a particular animal, person, or living thing. Once they choose it, the pair thinks of actions particular to their subject. While writers work on their imitations, remember that children should always be able to refer to the displayed try-it-out page.

Invitation to Celebrate *Bitten by the Drama Bug*: Pairs present Master-Verb Theater. One of the pair reads their imitation sentence aloud as the other acts out the movements. Readers and actors have the commas to regulate the timing between actions to make adjustments for fluency or phrasing or performance. (See Figure 6.1.)

Figure 6.1
Second-grade partners act out their imitation sentences.

A rose is a rose is a rose. Until it dies. Then it was a rose.
—Constance Hale

Invitation to Apply   *What's Happening?* In guided reading groups, expand on how verbs show what's happening in the text and will be part of any good summary. Invite writers to write a sentence about what is happening. "Did you need verbs to do it? Could you write a sentence about what's happening without verbs? Why or why not?"

Invitation to Edit

What did we learn about writing from Steve Jenkins?	
Animals live all around us. They crawl, walk, run, hop, swim, and fly.	
What changed? What is the effect of the change?	
Animals lived all around us. They crawled, walked, ran, hopped, swam, and flew.	By putting the verbs in the past tense, these two sentences underwent a lot of changes. Putting the action in the past affects the sentences' meaning. We can begin exploring irregular verbs (ran, swam, and flew) and how we form regular verbs by adding -ed to the end. "Which verbs are regular? Which are irregular? How do you know?" This may take a while, but it's worth it.
Animals live all around us They crawl, walk, run, hop, swim, and fly.	The period after the first sentence has been deleted. Periods tell us when a sentence is over. When we don't use periods, our sentences run together (making what we call "run-on" or "fused" sentences). Run-ons may mix up readers.
Animals live all around me. They crawl, walk, run, hop, swim, and fly.	We changed the plural us (more than one) to the singular me. This means that instead of the author including all his readers, he is speaking about just himself. In this version, it sounds like he is sharing his first-person point of view or personal experience rather than including everyone.

Tip: Verbs in Motion: From Simple to Sublime

If your students need a simpler sentence first, try one or more of these from Lola Schaefer's *An Island Grows*:

Stone breaks.
Water quakes.
Magma glows.
Volcano blows.

We also highly recommend Steve Jenkins and Robin Page's *Move!*

A polar bear floats in dark, icy water and slides down a snow-covered hill.

Read aloud *Move!* and *An Island Grows* during your verb study to help build the concept of what verbs do. They mean action. Then use them again with lessons in Chapter 7, "What Do Sentences Do?"

What do you notice?

Animals live all around us. They crawl, walk, run, hop, swim, and fly.

—Steve Jenkins, *Biggest, Strongest, Fastest*

How are they alike and different?

Animals live all around us. They crawl, walk, run, hop, swim, and fly.

Puppies live all around us. They bark, jump, and lick.

Let's try it out.

Animals live all around us. They crawl, walk, run, hop, swim, and fly.

Puppies live all around us. They bark, jump, and lick.

Animals live all around us. They crawl, walk, run, hop, swim, and fly.

What changed? What is the effect of the change?

Animals lived all around us. They crawled, walked, ran, hopped, swam, and flew.

Animals live all around us They crawl, walk, run, hop, swim, and fly.

Animals live all around me. They crawl, walk, run, hop, swim, and fly.

6.2 Tell It Like It *Is* (*Are, Was, Were, Be, Been*, and *Am*): The Verbs of Being

Standard   Use and understand the function of verbs (verbs of being).

Focus Phrase   "I use verbs to tell it like it *is*: *are, was, were, be, been*, and *am*."

Invitation to Notice   Hippos are huge!
—Jonathan London, *Hippos Are Huge!*

Power Note   *Young writers often figure out that verbs are action words, but the verbs of being and helping verbs are often lost on them. Highlight this verb of being (are) by spewing several sentences using are: "My students are smart. We are readers. We are writers." This lesson gives readers an opportunity to explore the verbs of being. To help students understand subject-verb agreement, you may also discuss how is is used for a singular subject (one) and are is used for plural subjects (more than one). Don't forget to ask, "What do exclamation marks do?" (They end the sentence and show yelling or extreme excitement.)*

Invitation to Compare and Contrast   Hippos are huge!
Kittens are sweet.

Power Note   *As students discuss the sentence, underscore that both nouns are plural (more than one) and how we know. Discuss how changing the end punctuation affects how we read a sentence. As a possible extension, change the verbs to singular form. A hippo _____ huge! and A kitten _____ sweet. Can students fill in the verb is without help? (See Figure 6.2.)*

Figure 6.2
First graders compare and contrast the sentences through partner talk.

Invitation to Imitate   *Imitate Together*: Partners choose a subject (perhaps a particular animal, person, or living thing). Once they've chosen it, the pair composes a sentence using *is* or *are*. Coach kids about whether their subject is singular or plural and how that affects the choice of *is* or *are*.

Invitation to Celebrate   *I Am What I Am: First-Person Celebration*. Let's make this personal. Display several titles from Brad Meltzer's Ordinary People Change the World series: *I Am Albert Einstein, I Am Amelia Earhart*, and so on. Make sure you write your name on the board first, showing that *am* is capitalized in Meltzer's books only because verbs are always capitalized in titles. In our sentences, *I* is capitalized, because it always is. Spiral back to an earlier focus phrase, "We capitalize names."

Invitation to Apply   *We Exist!* Jot down the verbs of being (*is, are, was, were, be, been, am*) and display them. Using the verbs of being, students generate their own sentences orally.

Invitation to Edit

What did we learn about writing from Jonathan London?	
Hippos are huge!	
What changed? What is the effect of the change?	
A hippo is huge!	*This subject moved from plural (more than one:* hippos*) to singular (one:* hippo*), which causes the verb to change from* are *to* is *(subject-verb agreement).*
Hippos are Huge!	*The adjective* huge *is capitalized. We don't capitalize adjectives. This slip-up might slow down readers, causing them to think* huge *is a name or part of a title.*
Hippos is huge!	*The subject,* hippos*, doesn't agree with the verb in number. A plural subject takes* are*. Students are great writers. A writer is courageous. When our subjects and verbs don't agree, the flow or syntax sounds off.*

Linking Verbs

All the verbs of being are linking verbs. But they aren't the only ones. **Technically, linking verbs don't show action. They connect the noun to more information about it.** Any sensory verb (think the five senses) could be a linking verb: *smell, look, sound, taste, feel*. There are more (*seem, appear, get*), but in general the distinction is semantic, or at least pedantic. The abstractness of these distinctions crashes against an elementary student's developmental abilities. This is another instance in which we don't feel the need to teach labels. We teach use. And our experience is that young writers naturally use these verbs (helping and linking) without prompting and without needing labels.

Helping Verbs

When the verbs of being come before the main verb of a sentence, they can also be considered helping verbs. But wait—there are more helping verbs: *would, could, should, shall, do, does, did, has, have, had*. As teachers, we have to ask ourselves, *Will kids just use the word can without knowing it's a helping verb?* Our experience is that showing use of these words and discussing them in the context of sentences is more than enough. Children can indeed use *can* without knowing what kind of verb it is. The distinction is of little importance, unless we're trying to create tiny linguists.

(See more about the helping verbs *can, may*, and *might* in "Modal Auxiliaries: Help Wanted" in the tip box at the end of this chapter.)

What do you notice?

Hippos are huge!

—Jonathan London, *Hippos Are Huge!*

How are they alike and different?

Hippos are huge!

Kittens are sweet.

Let's try it out.

Hippos are huge!

Kittens are sweet.

Hippos are huge!

What changed? What is the effect of the change?

A hippo is huge!

Hippos are Huge!

Hippos is huge!

6.3 Have You Got the Time? Verb Tense

Standard Understand and use verb tenses—past, present, and future.

Focus Phrase "I use verbs to show time: past, present, and future."

Invitation to Notice A loud clap of thunder shook the house, rattled the windows, and made me grab her close.
—Patricia Polacco, *Thunder Cake*

A loud clap of thunder shakes the house, rattles the windows, and makes me grab her close.

A loud clap of thunder will shake the house, will rattle the windows, and will make me grab her close.

Power Note *In this invitation to notice, we display three sentences in three tenses to highlight the effect of tense changes. This may seem like jumping ahead, but we find that being flexible with the invitation to notice reaps the benefits of focus and freshness. Discuss with writers how each sentence is alike and different. What are the effects of the differences? Emphasize how verbs tell time—past, present, and future—or when the action* took *place,* takes *place, or* will take *place.*

Invitation to Compare and Contrast A loud clap of thunder shook the house, rattled the windows, and made me grab her close.
The wind howled through the window, rustled the trees, and made me grab Mom's hand.

Power Note *In the imitation sentence,* Mom *is capitalized because it's not preceded by a possessive noun or pronoun. If the tense similarity is not noted, ask, "Are both sentences in the same tense? How do you know?"*

Invitation to Imitate *Imitate Together*: As a class, identify the tense of the original sentence. Together craft a sentence that has serial action in the same tense, making sure each verb agrees. This consistent agreement of tense is part of the craft of parallelism.

Imitate Individually: Students imitate a version of Polacco's sentence, choosing the tense they'd like and used it consistently.

Invitation to Apply *Time Traveling*: Students select a sentence from their independent reading. They identify the sentence's verb tense, and revise and rewrite the sentence into two new versions, using the other two tenses not chosen by the author. Including the original, writers will have three sentences: one each in past, present, and future. Students debrief the decisions made and the effects created by those changes. (See Figure 6.3.)

Figure 6.3
Verb tense sentences

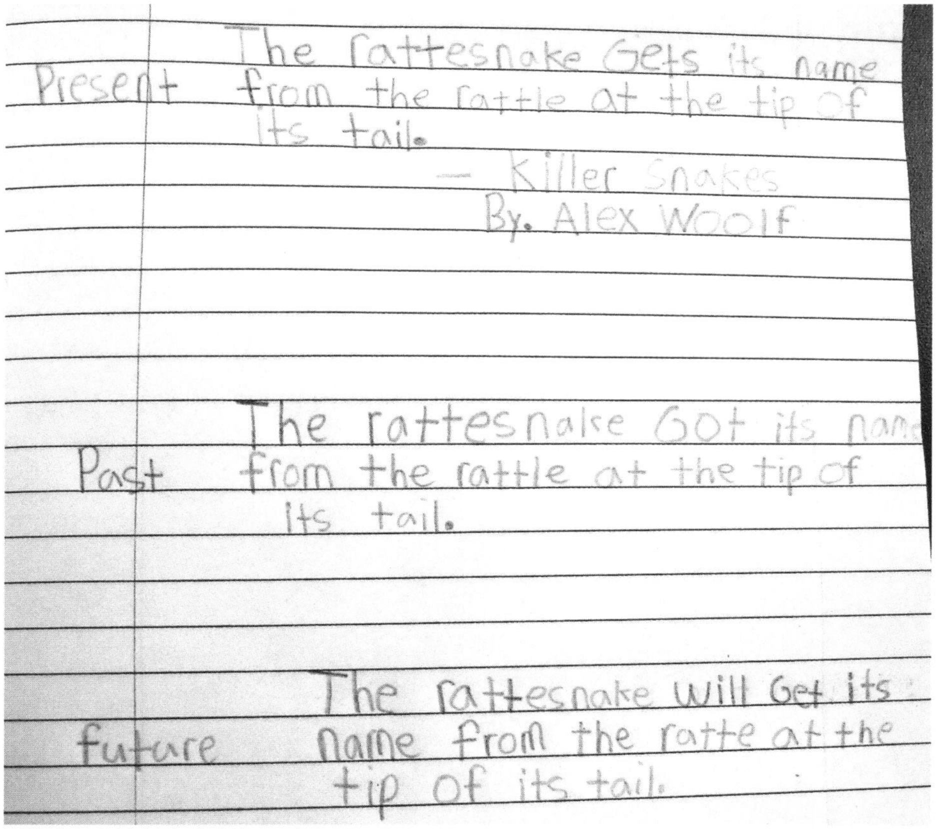

Present The rattesnake Gets its name from the rattle at the tip of its tail.
— Killer snakes By. Alex Woolf

Past The rattesnake Got its name from the rattle at the tip of its tail.

future The rattesnake will Get its name from the ratte at the tip of its tail.

Invitation to Celebrate   Share imitations and applications of time traveling. Play the song "Time Is on My Side," before and after sharing, to add a celebratory tone.

Invitation to Edit

What did we learn about writing from Patricia Polacco?	
A loud clap of thunder shook the house, rattled the windows, and made me grab her close.	
What changed? What is the effect of the change?	
A loud clap of thunder shakes the house, rattled the windows, and made me grab her close.	*The past-tense verb* shook *was changed to* shakes, *which changes the time of the action. For the sentence to work, all three verbs need to be in the same tense. This is one use of parallelism. When verbs in a list are not consistent in tense, the fluency is damaged.*
A loud clap of thunder shook the house, will rattle the windows, and made me grab her close.	*The verb expressing the future,* will, *was inserted in front of* rattle. *Future tense is formed with* will *+ present-tense verb. But all three verbs need to be consistent in tense. When they aren't or are in the wrong combination, it makes for rough reading.*
A loud clap of thunder shook the house, rattled the windows, and makes me grab her close.	*The past-tense form* made *was changed to the present form* makes. *Verbs in a list need to match in tense or they cause readers to trip over words and not focus on the message. Inconsistent tense messes up the time of the sentence as well.*

Tip: Past, Present, and Future

Use of past and present tense is everywhere, so we thought we'd share another sentence that works nicely to show an intentional use of the future tense. Lola Schaefer's *Lifetime: The Amazing Numbers in Animal Lives* is a great read for young writers, especially if you want to see future tense maintained across pages:

> In one lifetime, this rattlesnake will add 40 beads to its rattle.

After a study of Schaefer's sentence and the future tense, rewrite this sentence from Margaret Wild's *Fox* in the future tense to demonstrate what changes when the verb tense changes from present to future.

> Magpie feels the wind streaming through her feathers, and she rejoices.
> —Margaret Wild, *Fox*

What do you notice?

A loud clap of thunder shook the house, rattled the windows, and made me grab her close.

—Patricia Polacco, *Thunder Cake*

A loud clap of thunder shakes the house, rattles the windows, and makes me grab her close.

A loud clap of thunder will shake the house, will rattle the windows, and will make me grab her close.

How are they alike and different?

A loud clap of thunder shook the house, rattled the windows, and made me grab her close.

The wind howled through the window, rustled the trees, and made me grab Mom's hand.

Let's try it out.

A loud clap of thunder shook the house, rattled the windows, and made me grab her close.

The wind howled through the window, rustled the trees, and made me grab Mom's hand.

A loud clap of thunder shook the house, rattled the windows, and made me grab her close.

What changed? What is the effect of the change?

A loud clap of thunder shakes the house, rattled the windows, and made me grab her close.

A loud clap of thunder shook the house, will rattle the windows, and made me grab her close.

A loud clap of thunder shook the house, rattled the windows, and makes me grab her close.

6.4   Highly Irregular: Nonconforming Verbs

Standard   Use and understand irregular verbs.

Focus Phrase   "I check my verbs to make sure they sound right."

Invitation to Notice   My ears rang with crickets, and my eyes stung from staring too long.
—Julie Brinkloe, *Fireflies*

Power Note   *Besides containing two irregular past-tense verbs (*rang* and *stung*), the sentence is compound. For more information on compound sentences, refer to Chapter 18, "Why Do Writers Use Compound Sentences?" When students note the comma or the* and *or both, we can ask, "What's the comma doing when we read it aloud? What's it doing when we read it with just our eyes?" We can repeat these function questions for the coordinating conjunction* and.

Invitation to Compare and Contrast   My ears rang with crickets, and my eyes stung from staring too long.
My ears rang with shouting voices, and my nose drained from the stench of salmon patties.

Power Note   *We chose to put a regular past-tense verb in our imitation to stimulate discussion of how they are alike and how they are different from irregular verbs, deepening awareness. If students don't mention it, ask, "Is* drained *a regular or an irregular verb?" Students can consider: "How do readers know? What are the signals of the regular past tense?"*

Invitation to Imitate   *Imitate Together*: Invite writers to compose a sentence that follows this structure and uses at least one irregular verb. See the 30 Common Irregular Verbs list.

Imitate Independently: Students use the model to create their own sentences, using an irregular verb. Provide a list of common irregular verbs or let them do an Internet search for Top 50 Irregular Verbs.

30 Common Irregular Verbs

		Present	Past		
say	said	think	thought	hear	heard
make	made	tell	told	mean	meant
go	went	become	became	meet	met
take	took	leave	left	run	ran
come	came	feel	felt	pay	paid
see	saw	put	put	sit	sat
know	knew	bring	brought	speak	spoke
get	got	begin	began	grow	grew
give	gave	keep	kept	lose	lost
find	found	hold	held	fall	fell

Invitation to Celebrate

Students share sentences with irregular verbs from their writing and reading. Make a T-chart with "Regular" and "Irregular" on the top and categorize verbs as they're shared. At the end, ask, "As you look at the chart, what patterns do you see?" (Regular past-tense verbs all end in *-ed* to show past tense; often, present-tense regular verbs end in *-s*. Irregular verbs often undergo internal changes, such as vowel changes, to indicate past and present. Sometimes, even we teachers have to look up verb forms when we're unsure.) (See Figure 6.4.)

> The passive voice is always formed by joining an inflected form of *be* with the verb's past participle. Compare *the ox pulls the cart* with *the cart is pulled by the ox.*
> —*The Chicago Manual of Style*

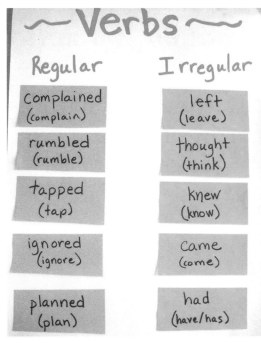

Figure 6.4
T-chart of regular and irregular verbs

Invitation to Apply

Sentence Face-Off: Put students in two lines. One person from each line comes up to the front of the class. The teacher reads from a list of irregular verbs. Whoever uses the verb most creatively and still makes sense wins.

Invitation to Edit

What did we learn about writing from Julie Brinkloe?	
My ears rang with crickets, and my eyes stung from staring too long.	
What changed? What is the effect of the change?	
My ears ringed with crickets, and my eyes stung from staring too long.	The irregular past-tense verb *rang* has been changed to *ringed. This may sound like fingernails on a chalkboard in your readers' heads, causing confusion.*
My ears rang with crickets, and my eyes stung from staring to long.	The homophone *too, which means "very," has been replaced by* to, *which is a preposition. This causes the author's meaning of "very long" to be lost.*
My ears rang with crickets, and my eyes stang from staring too long.	The irregular past tense *stung has been changed to* stang. *The irregular past tense of sting is* stung. *Since stang is not a word, this gets in the way of the author's message.*

What do you notice?

My ears rang with crickets, and my eyes stung from staring too long.

—Julie Brinkloe, *Fireflies*

How are they alike and different?

My ears rang with crickets, and my eyes stung from staring too long.

My ears rang with shouting voices, and my nose drained from the stench of salmon patties.

Let's try it out.

My ears rang with crickets, and my eyes stung from staring too long.

My ears rang with shouting voices, and my nose drained from the stench of salmon patties.

My ears rang with crickets, and my eyes stung from staring too long.

What changed? What is the effect of the change?

My ears ringed with crickets, and my eyes stung from staring too long.

My ears rang with crickets, and my eyes stung from staring to long.

My ears rang with crickets, and my eyes stang from staring too long.

Tip: Why Do Writers Use the Active Voice?

The first thing to know is that kids' primary default is to use the active voice.

Don't lose your cookies over passive versus active voice. This concept is difficult for most writers—and teachers and other adults—to understand. But more than likely, writers will use the active voice most of the time without thinking.

Discussing the active voice requires defining it. Here we will define it, but again, the goal is not to memorize the definition or to identify passive voice. Soak the kids in the active voice that fills the pages of the literature in your classroom and school library. Almost every single sentence we use as a mentor text in this book is in the active voice.

Constance Hale defines it this way in one of our favorite style guides, *Sin and Syntax: How to Craft Wicked Good Prose*: "In the active voice, the subject performs the action. In the passive voice, the subject is acted upon. In classic English sentences in the active voice, the subject starts the show followed by a dynamic verb. The subject is the *agent* or person or thing taking the action: *She reads*. Sometimes there is a direct object: *She reads* The Odyssey. The action flows briskly from the subject through the verb and to the object" (2013, 67).

To be honest, our own definitions have grown through study, trial and error, and oversimplification. We're all for simplification, but identifying passive voice isn't as easy as circling all the verbs of being (*is, are, was, were, be, been, am*) and then taking them all out and replacing them with "active" verbs. Sometimes we need those helpful verbs. (See the tip box on progressive and perfect tense at the end of this chapter.)

All sources will say this about the active voice: in active voice, the subject is doing the action. *Rain filled the gutters*. In passive voice, the subject becomes the object of the action, or the action is being done to the subject. *The gutters were filled by the rain*.

Note that in *the gutters were filled by the rain*, the *be*-verb *were* appears. The action is done to the rain, rather than the rain *doing* the action. The editors of the *Chicago Manual of Style* are quite sure of themselves: "The passive voice is always formed by joining an inflected form of *be* with the verb's past participle" (2010, 235). To understand what they're saying, you may need to brush up on your participles.

Pondering Participles: What's Past Is Past, What's Present Ends in *-Ing*

Many of us know the participle as the *-ing* verb. That's true. Present participles do end in *-ing*: *José is shopping*. But *José was shopping* is still in the active voice, even though there is a participle and a past *be*-verb. As described earlier, *a passive voice construction needs a* be-*verb and a* past *participle. Shopping* is a present participle.

On the other hand, if José receives the action, and there is both a *be*-verb and a *past participle* such as *done*, it becomes passive: *the shopping was done by José*. José is no longer the active doer. In this passive construction, he is receiving the action rather than doing it actively. Often the past participle is the past-tense form of a verb, but it can also end in *-en: written, given, beaten, chosen*. To be sure, you have to look it up.

And sure, *José shops* or *José shopped* is crisper, more active, but it doesn't mean the same thing. We may want to show that José's action is ongoing, thus the participle. (See the section on progressive tenses.)

Still not sure of the difference? Perhaps start by realizing that the standards prefer the active voice, meaning you'll want to model and teach that. The point isn't to identify the passive voice so much as it is to avoid its use and to use active voice, which is our usual default when we're not trying too hard. Perhaps this chart will help.

Playing with Active and Passive Voice		
Tense	*Active Voice*	*Passive Voice*
Simple present	We love books.	The books were loved by us.
Simple past	Yesterday, I loved books.	Yesterday, books were loved by me.
Simple future	We will love books tomorrow.	Books will be loved by us tomorrow.

6.5 Rain Pummeled the Ground Versus The Ground Was Pummeled by Rain: Finding Your Active Voice

Standard Use and understand active voice.

Focus Phrase "I craft active voice to show my subjects acting."

Invitation to Notice Fists of rain pummel the cockpit windshield.
Rivers of quicksilver darkness drown the moon.
  —Robert Burleigh, *Night Flight: Amelia Earhart Crosses the Atlantic*

The cockpit windshield is pummeled by fists of rain.
The moon is drowned by rivers of quicksilver darkness.

Power Note *"What do you notice about the two sets of sentences? Which set of sentences do you prefer? Why?" The second set of sentences change to the passive voice. Analyzing the differences will help students understand the effects of active and passive voice. Though the sets of sentences communicate the same information, the preferred style is to put the actor first and then the action it does next. The passive voice has the action being done to the actor. Sometimes this pattern of power is referred to as SVO (subject-verb-object).*

Invitation to Compare and Contrast Fists of rain pummel the cockpit windshield.
Rivers of quicksilver darkness drown the moon.

Sheets of ice covered the shiny roads.
Layers of snow hid the grass and flowers.

Power Note *When students discuss what they notice, circle back to the fact that nouns come first and action follows. We don't teach passive voice. We soak young writers in the active voice in almost every sentence in Burleigh's book. We're building a pattern by continuously repeating it.*

Invitation to Imitate *Imitate Together*: Invite writers to use interactive or shared writing to compose a sentence with you. As you compose the sentence, repeat the focus phrase, "I craft active voice to show my subjects acting." (See Figure 6.5.)

Figure 6.5
This fifth-grade sentence was created during shared writing.

I use active voice with my verbs to show my subjects acting and being.

sts of rain pummel the cockpit windshield. Rivers of quicksilver rkness drown the moon.

Shared Writing: Write a sentence together showing active voice.

Puddles of ink stained the blank paper.

Figures 6.6, 6.7, and 6.8
Fifth graders work through the process of imitating using active voice.

Imitate Independently: Students use the model to create their own sentences, using active voice. Share successful attempts as you roam around the room coaching. Continue to emphasize that the subject is near the beginning of the sentence and doing or being something. (See Figures 6.6, 6.7, and 6.8.)

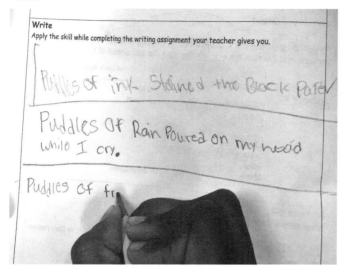

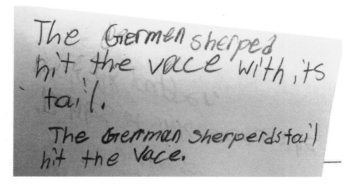

Invitation to Celebrate   Writers make before-and-after versions of sentences in the passive voice and in the shiny active voice.

Invitation to Apply   *I Told You So*: Writers find three active-voice sentences in reading materials found around the classroom. The challenge will be explaining how they know each sentence is in the active voice. Students post them around the classroom or do so electronically, sharing both the active-voice sentences and their explanations about how they can tell they're in the active voice.

Invitation to Edit

What did we learn about writing from Robert Burleigh?	
Fists of rain pummel the cockpit windshield. Rivers of quicksilver darkness drown the moon.	
What changed? What is the effect of the change?	
Fists of rain pummels the cockpit windshield. Rivers of quicksilver darkness drown the moon.	*The verb* pummel *was changed to* pummels. *The subject is tricky: it's* fists. *The prepositional phrase* of rain *can make* pummels *sound right because* rain *is singular, but we have to match the subject* fists, *which is plural. When our verb agreement is off, our fluency falters.*
Fists of rain pummel the cockpit windshield rivers of quicksilver darkness drown the moon.	*There is no period between the two sentences. There is no capital letter at the beginning of the second. As is, this is a fused or run-on sentence, which is difficult for readers to manage.*
Fists of rain pummel the cockpit windshield. The moon is drowned by rivers of quicksilver darkness.	*The second sentence has been changed from active voice to the passive voice. The actor (rivers) comes after the action (drowned). The passive voice is less direct and crisp than the active voice.*

What do you notice?

Fists of rain pummel the cockpit windshield.
Rivers of quicksilver darkness drown the moon.

—Robert Burleigh, *Night Flight: Amelia Earhart Crosses the Atlantic*

The cockpit windshield is pummeled by fists of rain.
The moon is drowned by rivers of quicksilver darkness.

How are they alike and different?

Fists of rain pummel the cockpit windshield.
Rivers of quicksilver darkness drown the moon.

Sheets of ice covered the shiny roads.
Layers of snow hid the grass and flowers.

Let's try it out.

Fists of rain pummel the cockpit windshield.
Rivers of quicksilver darkness drown the moon.

Sheets of ice covered the shiny roads.
Layers of snow hid the grass and flowers.

Fists of rain pummel the cockpit windshield. Rivers of quicksilver darkness drown the moon.

What changed? What is the effect of the change?

Fists of rain pummels the cockpit windshield. Rivers of quicksilver darkness drown the moon.

Fists of rain pummel the cockpit windshield rivers of quicksilver darkness drown the moon.

Fists of rain pummel the cockpit windshield. The moon is drowned by rivers of quicksilver darkness.

Tip: Why Do Writers Use Progressive Tenses?

We know verbs mean action, and we know the tense of our verbs places that action in time. But verbs can also orient actions *in relation to other actions* on a time line. Past, present, and future are the basic tenses, and they stick around even when we twist and bend deeper into tense, crafting time in more precise ways. In some cases, writers need to show a little more information about when something happens, especially in relation to something else that happens in the same sentence but at a different time. For example, we might want to show that an action is *ongoing* and *keeps going*: the progressive tense.

Progressive Tenses		
Writers use progressive tenses to show ongoing actions that continue.		
(A verb of being + a present participle)		
Past Progressive	*was/were* + present participle (*-ing* verb)	His mind filled with thoughts of all the amazing things that **were keeping** his friend from imagining him. —Dan Santat, *The Adventures of Beekle: The Unimaginary Friend*
Present Progressive	*is/are/am* + present participle (*-ing*)	This **is taking** forever. —Dan Santat, *Are We There Yet?*
Future Progressive	*will be* + present participle (*-ing*)	"Zack has done some careful research and **will be leading** this meeting." —Jeff Anderson, *Zack Delacruz: Me and My Big Mouth*

Or we may want to show that an action was ongoing for a time but has come to an end: the perfect tense.

Perfect Tense		
Writers use the perfect tense to show an **ongoing action that has come to an end**, usually in relationship to *another event (verb)* in the same sentence.		
(A *have*-verb form + past participle)		
Past Perfect (sometimes called pluperfect)	*had* + past participle	Mom *says* by then they **had told** her all about me. —R. J. Palacio, *Wonder*
Present Perfect	*has/have* + past participle	Mom *says* they **have told** her all about me.
Future Perfect (*will have*)	*will have* + past participle	Mom *says* by then they **will have told** her all about me.

When would I want to use either of these tenses? you may be thinking. There is a purpose to these additional tenses. They show multiple events at multiple times in the same sentence. The good news is that they are still talking in past-present-future language, but with a new "ongoing" twist. Study the two sentences from Christina Soontornvat's *The Changelings*:

> By midday, the changelings **were dragging** from the heat. They **hadn't seen** or **heard** any sign of the Unglers during their whole trip, so Seldom eased up on the grueling pace and agreed they could take turns dipping in the creek.

In the first sentence from the excerpt, *were dragging* is the past progressive, showing an ongoing action that continues. Soontornvat wants us to know the changelings have been dragging and are still dragging, seemingly

(continued)

without end. On the other hand, in the second sentence, *hadn't seen* or *heard* means that they've been listening and looking in an ongoing way, but up to this moment they haven't seen or heard. This is called the past perfect.

To show this information yet another way, we'll take a sentence from William Alexander's *Goblin Secrets* and put it in every tense, from simple to progressive to perfect:

Tense	Simple	Progressive	Perfect
Past	Lights **burned** through the fog-filled dark. —William Alexander, *Goblin Secrets*	Lights **were burning** through the fog-filled dark.	Lights **had burned** through the fog-filled dark.
Present	Lights **burn** through the fog-filled dark.	Lights **are burning** through the fog-filled dark.	Lights **have burned** through the fog-filled dark.
Future	Lights **will burn** through the fog-filled dark.	Lights **will be burning** through the fog-filled dark.	Lights **will have burned** through the fog-filled dark.

Modal Auxiliaries: Help Wanted!

Modal auxiliaries? Seriously? Sometimes standards ask things of nine-year-olds that most adults would have trouble understanding. But we're not about identification, so it's doable. We're putting use into usage. Labels don't give power. The patterns do. That said, let's dump the term *auxiliary* and just go with *helping verbs*. Helping verbs allow other verbs to do more, such as

- adjust time (*will, is, did*);
- indicate necessity (*must, should*);
- show ability (*can*); and
- show a condition like permission or possibility (*may* and *might*).

To illustrate, when Rebecca Stead uses the word *might* in this sentence from *When You Reach Me*, she is using it to show the possibility that something may happen:

I quickly turned my back on him, worried that he **might** recognize me and come over.

In fact, in addition to permission, *may* is often used to convey possibility, as seen here in this installment of Kathleen Krull's Giants of Science series, *Isaac Newton*:

Sunlight **may** *appear* white. But Newton proved that white light is made up of colors mixed together: violet, indigo, blue, green, yellow, orange, and red.

The helping verb *can* **might** also show possibility, but is often used to expresses capacity and ability. Can you use the word *can* without knowing it's a modal auxiliary? Sure. In the past tense, *can* becomes *could*, and in the infinitive, *can* becomes *able to*. Ugh! And if this is bugging you as an adult, then why not give up making kids ask, "May I go to the restroom?" *Can I go to the restroom?* is perfectly acceptable. If you don't agree, check a current authoritative guide to word usage. For more about helping verbs, also see Lesson 6.2.

7

What Do Sentences Do?

Short sentences can be quite powerful. They are the source from which all sentences emanate—the seed, the foundation, the beginning. Think of the craft that goes into writing short sentences. If we write a sentence with only two words, we carefully choose the noun and verb. And if we've just written four long sentences and then suddenly punch our reader with a short one, that succinct sentence will be accentuated. Short sentences are the beginning of crafting all other sentences. Everything starts there.

Simple sentences are our first attempts to string words together; we join a noun with a verb to get a need met. Jeff's mother says that when he was four years old, one of his first sentence attempts came at 4:00 a.m., poking her awake from sleep. "Want egg, Mama."

From this utterance, his mother understood, Jeff meant *I want an egg*. But as he grew, his demands became more specific: "I want scrambled eggs, Mama." Most of us, like young Jeff, naturally developed an ability to make our sentences clearer and more meaningful—whether to demand things we wanted or to tattle on that irritating kid who was kicking our desk.

First graders say, "He's kicking my desk" without knowing that they chose to use *kicking*, the present participle (or present progressive) to connote an ongoing action. They are merely saying what they've observed. The first graders are communicating, sending a message. One more time, it's not about the labels.

That said, to operate in complete sentences, young writers need to understand at least two basic tools: subjects and verbs. Later, adding to these two basic tools will help writers develop more complex constructions—compound and complex sentences—and even avoid run-ons and fragments. But for now, just subjects and verbs. We're not asking students to label all the parts of speech—ever. We're not asking students to gnash their teeth over whether their predicate is a complete one or not. We'll make sentences with subjects and verbs, intuitively and intentionally stringing words together and making sense.

Lesson Sets:

What Do Sentences Do?

7.1 Subject-Verb Chomp: The Teeth of a Sentence
7.2 Subject and Verb Plus One: Adding to the Basic Noun and Verb
7.3 More Than Anything: Just Being Simple Sentences

7.1   Subject-Verb Chomp: The Teeth of a Sentence

Standard Use and understand simple sentences.

Focus Phrase "I use a noun and a verb in my sentences."

Invitation to Notice Dragonflies swoop.
    —Lola M. Schaefer, *Swamp Chomp*

Power Note *If students don't notice that the sentence contains only two words, ask the group, "Is this a sentence?" Nudge them to back up their answers with evidence from the model. "How do you know it's a sentence?" Lead them to the conclusion that it is a sentence because it answers two important questions:*

- *Who or what does or is something? (dragonflies—the subject)*
- *What are they or what do they do? (swoop—the verb)*

Sadly for most elementary students, groups of words that start with a capital letter and end with a period aren't necessarily sentences. For them, fragments are. Run-ons are. But it's all about the noun and the verb.
    Uncover the second excerpt from Swamp Chomp:

    Mosquitoes flit. Sit.

Power Note *Continue the invitation to notice after you uncover "Mosquitoes flit. Sit."*
    "How many sentences do you see here?"
    "Is Sit *a sentence?" (There's no subject. There's only action. We wouldn't get into it unless it's asked, but to be clear,* Sit *is not meant as a command here.)*
    "How could we make Sit *into a sentence?" Record the class's answers on a chart or whiteboard. Here are some possibilities:*

- *Mosquitoes flit and sit.*
- *Mosquitoes flit, and mosquitoes sit.*
- *Mosquitos flit. Mosquitos sit.*

Students may not be able to label a compound predicate in the first example (one subject with two verbs) or a compound sentence in the second example, but those options are stored in their syntactic language pools in their heads, which they tap into to speak. It's never about the label. It's about making sense. Too many abstract labels confuse rather than clarify things for young writers. Our focus is on nouns and verbs—for now. We can change the term noun *to* subject, *but we'd argue to continue using the term* verb *rather than* predicate *because of the difficult sound of the word. Just say* predicate *to a room full of adults and I bet you'll hear groans.*

Invitation to Compare and Contrast Dragonflies swoop.
Toddlers wobble.

Invitation to Imitate

Imitate Together: Invite writers to use interactive or shared writing to compose a sentence with you.

Students laugh.

Imitate Independently: Students use the model sentences to compose their own sentences, imitating the two-word pattern with a strong subject (noun) and verb. There will be issues, so roam around and support, asking the questions "Who or what does or is something?" and "What are they and what do they do?" If a child tries to use a sentence with a helping verb, the sentence will most often need to become three words, unless it can be recast. *Delphine is smart*. We do have another option to delete the helping verb but still retain the young author's meaning: *Delphine reads* or *Delphine studies*.

Invitation to Celebrate

Make a skinny wall chart with the "sentence test" questions: "Who or what does or is something?" and "What are they or what do they do?" Students add the two-word sentences they wrote during the invitation to imitate. (See Figure 7.1.)

Figure 7.1
Sentence test chart

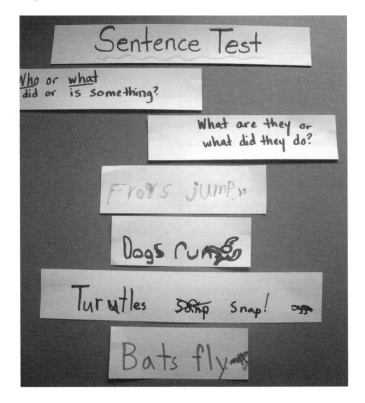

Invitation to Apply

Stop and Talk! Throughout the day encourage students to stop and pause when they come to sentences they like. The teacher or student may write the sentence on a chart. During invitation time the next day or next several days, use the sentence test to find the subject(s) and verb(s) in the collected sentences. These can be added to the chart started in the invitation to celebrate.

Invitation to Edit

What did we learn about writing from Lola Schaefer?	
Dragonflies swoop.	
What changed? What is the effect of the change?	
Dragonfly swoop.	The plural subject dragonflies— the who or what—has been changed to the singular dragonfly. If we were to leave dragonfly, we'd have to change our verb to the singular form to match: Dragonfly swoops. Subjects and verbs have to agree in number. If they don't, readers are thrown off our message. (For more information, see Chapter 11, "How Do Verbs and Nouns Agree?")
Dragonflies Swoop.	The verb swoop is capitalized. We capitalize the first word of sentences or names of people, places, and things, but not verbs or other words after the first one. When we do, our reader may think this is a person named Dragonfly Swoop or the title of a book.
Dragonflys swoop.	An -s is added to the end of the subject, dragonfly. This causes stops and starts for the reader. The plural pattern for words ending in -y hasn't been followed. Change the -y to -i and add -es. When we don't follow patterns, it calls attention away from the message.

Power Note   All the information we'll learn about sentence patterns, even sentence fragments, will come back to this simple lesson of pairing a subject and verb to
create a sentence. If you want more practice for your students similar to that
in Lesson 7.1, try April Pulley Sayre's Squirrels Leap, Squirrels Sleep (or you
might save it for when you and your students add prepositional phrases to
simple sentences). Everything else students will learn in Patterns of Power is
about addition, adding to the subject and the verb. "The Power of Detail" and
"The Power of Combining" will continue this process of addition. For a simple
view into adding to the two-word sentence, we've provided another lesson.

What do you notice?

Dragonflies swoop.

—Lola M. Schaefer, *Swamp Chomp*

Mosquitoes flit. Sit.

How are they alike and different?

Dragonflies swoop.

Toddlers wobble.

Let's try it out.

Dragonflies swoop.

Toddlers wobble.

Dragonflies swoop.

What changed? What is the effect of the change?

Dragonfly swoop.

Dragonflies Swoop.

Dragonflys swoop.

7.2   Subject and Verb Plus One: Adding to the Basic Noun and Verb

Standard	Use and understand simple sentences.
Focus Phrase	"I use a noun and a verb in my sentences."
Invitation to Notice	Her skin prickles.

        —Laurel Snyder, *Swan: The Life and Dance of Anna Pavlova*

Power Note   *After the process of listening and responding to student noticing, if it hasn't been discussed, ask, "Is this is a sentence?" Nudge writers to back up their answers. "How do you know?" Lead them to the conclusion that it is a sentence because it answers two important questions:*

- *Who or what did or is something? (skin—the subject)*
- *What are they or what did they do? (prickles—the verb)*

"What do we need to take away to make it so that it isn't a sentence?" If they suggest taking away her, *show them how* skin prickles *still passes the sentence test. The word* her *just tells us whose skin prickles, a personal possessive functioning as an adjective.*

Invitation to Compare and Contrast	Her skin prickles. His ears throb.
Invitation to Imitate	*Imitate Together*: Invite writers to compose a sentence using paired writing. *Imitate Independently*: Students use the model sentences to compose their own sentences, imitating the three-word pattern with a strong subject (noun) and verb and another word of their choice. The third word will very likely be a possessive, but I don't think we need to demand that here. There will be issues, so roam around and support the students, asking, "Who or what does or is something?" and "What are they and what do they do?" Remember, if a child tries to use a sentence with a helping verb, technically it has three words: *Carl is rambunctious.*
Invitation to Celebrate	Students add three-word sentences to the skinny wall chart with the "sentence test" questions: "Who or what does or is something?" and "What are they or what do they do?" (See Figure 7.2.)
Invitation to Apply	Continue encouraging writers to stop, pause, and look closely at the sentences they admire. We may write the sentences they discover on a chart. The next day or for the next several days, during invitation time, use the sentence test to find the subject(s) and verb(s) in the collected sentences. They can be added to the chart started in the invitation to celebrate. This may take a few extra days, but this pattern is foundational and needs a lot of exposure to develop in young writers.

Figure 7.2
Sentence test extended wall chart

Invitation to Edit

What did we learn about writing from Laurel Snyder?	
Her skin prickles.	
What changed? What is the effect of the change?	
Her prickles.	The subject skin, *which is the thing that prickles, is missing. Her can't be the subject. (It's the objective case. See Chapter 10, "What Do Pronouns Do?") She can be a subject in this case, but the possessive pronoun (*her*) can't. This version of the sentence doesn't make sense.*
Her skin prickle.	Prickles *has been changed to* prickle. *Sometimes when our subjects and verbs don't agree, it sounds like baby talk. The subject* skin *is singular, and singular verbs often take an s at the end. This is the pattern with* prickles.
Her skin.	The verb *prickles is gone. This is no longer a sentence. Without the verb, the subject,* skin, *isn't doing anything. The verb isn't there to answer the second question of the sentence test, "What are you or what do you do?" Therefore, this is not a sentence. This version doesn't do anything.*

What do you notice?

Her skin prickles.
—Laurel Snyder, *Swan: The Life and Dance of Anna Pavlova*

How are they alike and different?

Her skin prickles.

His ears throb.

Let's try it out.

Her skin prickles.

His ears throb.

Her skin prickles.

What changed? What is the effect of the change?

Her prickles.

Her skin prickle.

Her skin.

7.3   More Than Anything: Just Being Simple Sentences

Standard   Use and understand simple sentences.

Focus Phrase   "I use a noun and a verb in my sentences."

Invitation to Notice   More than anything, Audrey wanted to be a ballerina.
—Margaret Cardillo, *Just Being Audrey*

Power Note   *After the process of listening and responding to student noticing, continue asking, "Is this a sentence?"*

Nudge writers to back up their answers. "How do you know?" Lead them to the conclusion that it is a sentence because it answers two important questions:

- *Who or what does or is something? (Audrey—the subject)*
- *What are they or what did they do? (wanted—the verb)*

Invitation to Compare and Contrast   More than anything, Audrey wanted to be a ballerina.
More than anything, Jonathan wanted to be a gaming designer.

Power Note   *Some of you may think these aren't simple sentences. The label doesn't matter, but just between us, it is a simple sentence. A complex sentence needs at least two clauses. The opener "more than anything" is a phrase, not a clause, so even though we set off the phrase with a comma, it's still a simple sentence, and it's easy to find the subject and verb. (More than anything is an adverbial phrase showing the intensity of how important her wanting to be a ballerina was to Audrey.) See more about the difference between clauses and phrases in Chapter 20, "Why Do Writers Use Complex Sentences?"*

Invitation to Imitate   *Imitate Together*: Invite writers to use interactive or shared writing to compose a sentence with you.

More than anything, we want a couch for the reading area.

Imitate Independently: Students use the model sentence to create their own sentences, imitating the pattern of a simple sentence about something they want more than anything.

Invitation to Celebrate   Create a dream board where everyone posts their dreams in the form of this imitation. For fun, they can use the first person or third person to write the sentence about their dream. (See Figure 7.3.)

Invitation to Apply   Continue encouraging writers to stop, pause, and look closely at the sentences they admire, even longer ones. Students use the sentence test to find the subject(s) and verb(s) in their collected sentences.

Figure 7.8
Dream board celebration

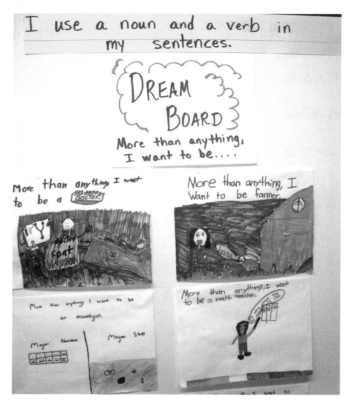

Invitation to Edit

What did we learn about writing from Margaret Cardillo?	
More than anything, Audrey wanted to be a ballerina.	
What changed? What is the effect of the change?	
More than anything Audrey wanted to be a ballerina.	*There is no comma setting off the opener. The reader needs the pause for emphasis and the comma to chunk the sentence. When it's not there, the words run together.*
More than anything, audrey wanted to be a ballerina.	*Audrey's name isn't capitalized. When we don't capitalize names, we confuse our reader. This version communicates that Audrey isn't a name.*
More then anything, Audrey wanted to be a ballerina.	*The* than, *which compares, has been changed to* then, *which shows time. (Some people remember this common pattern by thinking* then *has to do with time because both* then *and* time *have an e in them. Compare and* than *both have an a. When authors mean to compare, they confuse their readers when they use a time word such as* then.

What do you notice?

More than anything, Audrey wanted to be a ballerina.

—Margaret Cardillo, *Just Being Audrey*

How are they alike and different?

More than anything, Audrey wanted to be a ballerina.

More than anything, Jonathan wanted to be a gaming designer.

Let's try it out.

More than anything, Audrey wanted to be a ballerina.

More than anything, Jonathan wanted to be a gaming designer.

More than anything, Audrey wanted to be a ballerina.

What changed? What is the effect of the change?

More than anything Audrey wanted to be a ballerina.

More than anything, audrey wanted to be a ballerina.

More then anything, Audrey wanted to be a ballerina.

8

What Do End Marks Do?

A ll good things must come to an end—even sentences.

Sentences aren't sentences until they're finished off with a period, a question mark, or an exclamation point. With the stroke of the pen or the tap of a key on our keyboard, writers direct how sentences are read. Do you want your sentence to make some noise or show some excitement? Use an exclamation point. If you'd like a sentence to ask a question, with the reader's voice going up at the end, conclude with a question mark. And if you're merely stating something without any fanfare, just the facts, conclude with a period. Just three end marks total to learn, with only three jobs to do.

When writers take care with their end marks, they not only enhance sentence boundaries, but also tell you if a sentence is a statement, question, or exclamation. They orchestrate how we read the sentences that unfurl before us, one after the other.

> In writing, punctuation plays the role of body language. It helps readers hear you the way you want to be heard.
> –Russell Baker

Lesson Sets:

What Do End Marks Do?

8.1 Choral Read Our Way to the End: Punctuation Voices

8.2 Never Fear: End Marks Are Here!

8.3 You Finish My Sentences: Readers Need Periods

8.4 Messy Room: Question Marks and Exclamation Points

8.5 Advanced End Mark Exploration

Tip: Give Me Some Space, Man! How Many Spaces After an End Mark?

Not spaces. Space. According to the *Chicago Manual of Style*, when keyboarding, "one space, not two, should be used between two sentences—whether the first ends in a period, a question mark, an exclamation point, or a closing quotation mark" (2010, 308). Welcome to the twenty-first century.

8.1 Choral Read Our Way to the End: Punctuation Voices

Power Note When studying end punctuation, students need to experience how punctuation adds voice and rhythm to writing. Choral reading can build this understanding. Begin by displaying the excerpt from Eric Litwin's Pete the Cat: Rocking in My School Shoes.

- *Read the excerpt together with the teacher's voice guiding the reading.*
- *Read it again with an emphasis on what the punctuation tells us to do with our voices. Discuss what each mark tells us.*
- *Choose two or three lines to highlight and read them again with the focus on the punctuation guiding the change in voice.*
- *Read the entire excerpt again.*

Students may read only the bold sentences. And we like to do a stage whisper for the last three lines about reading in his school shoes.

Pete is sitting at his desk when his teacher says, "Come on, Pete, down that hall to a room with books on every wall."
Where is Pete going?
The library!
Pete has never been to the library before!
Does Pete worry?
Goodness, no!
He finds his favorite book and sings his song: "I'm **reading in my school shoes, I'm reading in my school shoes, I'm reading in my school shoes."**

—Eric Litwin, *Pete the Cat: Rocking in My School Shoes*

8.2   Never Fear: End Marks Are Here!

Standard   Use punctuation marks at the end of sentences.
Use interrogative and exclamatory sentences.

Focus Phrase   "I use end marks to help the reader."

Invitation to Notice   Does Pete worry?
Goodness, no!

Invitation to Compare and Contrast   Does Pete worry?
Goodness, no!

Does your voice go up at the end of question?
Yes, it does!

Invitation to Imitate   *Imitate Together*: Invite writers to compose a sentence with you, using interactive or shared writing.

Invitation to Celebrate   *Punctuation Theater*: Students perform their sentences in pairs, exaggerating their question and exclamation voices!

Invitation to Apply   While they're reading and writing, invite students to note which end marks are used most often. Collect a few examples and discuss which end marks the students use the most in their own writing. Discuss why that is. (See Figure 8.1.)

You may also explore questions and exclamations in a deeper way at this point. "When you look at several questions, do you see anything else they have in common?" "When you look at several exclamatory sentences, do you see anything in common among them?" Perhaps students see that exclamations are often short or that sentences that end in question marks have question words at the beginning. You might start a wall chart of question words or refer to them and highlight them in some way in the sentences from your earlier celebrations. You might also display several books from Scholastic's Who Would Win? series by Jerry Palotta and any other books formatted in question-and-answer style you can get your hands on.

For a continued study of the exclamation point, question mark, and period, consider reading aloud *Oh, No!* by Candace Fleming.

Figure 8.1
A first-grade student notices the punctuation used in the class book created by his class.

What do you notice?

Does Pete worry?
Goodness, no!

—Eric Litwin, *Pete the Cat: Rocking in My School Shoes*

How are they alike and different?

Does Pete worry?
Goodness, no!

Does your voice go up at the end of question?
Yes, it does!

Let's try it out.

Does Pete worry?
Goodness, no!

Does your voice go up at the end of question?
Yes, it does!

8.3   You Finish My Sentences: Readers Need Periods

Standard   Use punctuation marks at the end of sentences.

Focus Phrase   "I use end marks to move my reader from sentence to sentence."

Invitation to Notice

Power Note   *Print and distribute the excerpt without end marks from Dan Gutman's* Million Dollar Shot. *The periods are missing. If a word started a sentence and wouldn't be capitalized on its own, it's lowercase here. If the word that started a sentence would be capitalized no matter what—such as the pronoun I—it was left capitalized. As editors, young writers insert periods with a caret (^) and draw three lines under any first word of a sentence that needs to be capitalized. We model, using the first paragraph and saying, "I'll show you how." We read aloud the first paragraph, running it together as written without periods (let's get one thing straight from the start I can shoot). "Are there any places where an end mark would help the reader?" Students will easily accept the period after shoot, but some may not understand why we need a period between the words start and I. Read it aloud both ways, with the period and without, and talk about why having the period separate it is better.*

Also remind editors that if the pronoun I wasn't already capitalized, we'd need to indicate the first word of the sentence by capitalizing it. We do that by putting three lines under it. Student writers in pairs or groups of three punctuate and capitalize the first word of the new sentence when needed for the rest of Gutman's passage. (All the end marks in this passage are periods. You can decide whether to tell the students that.)

After the periods and capital letters at beginnings of sentences have been inserted, the class shares their choices and their thinking behind them. The next day we will compare and contrast them with Gutman.

What do you notice?

let's get one thing straight from the start I can *shoot*

I can shoot the daylights out of a basketball I've always had a special talent for throwing stuff at targets I can toss a soda can into the recycling bucket from across the room no problem I can fire a snowball at a tree across the street and hit it nine times out of ten

it's like a sixth sense sometimes I set up a bunch of toy soldiers on a table and pick them off with a rubber band one by one other kids are amazed I can shoot a bow and arrow like a laser beam I'm always winning stuff at carnivals

of course, being a great shooter isn't good enough in a real game you've got to be able to dribble the ball you've got to be able to pass you've got to be able to handle pressure

I was never good at those things I get rattled when I'm playing the game the other kids are always shouting, sticking their hands in my face everybody's running around it's all a blur too much pressure

but give me a basketball and put me on the foul line with nobody guarding me I can sink it like I said, I can *shoot*

Invitation to Compare and Contrast   *How are they alike and different?*

Power Note   *Groups compare and contrast the places where they inserted periods with the spots in which Dan Gutman placed them. Have them talk through choices that Gutman made versus theirs.*

Tip: Are Commands Imperative?

Some standards ask students to use imperative sentences. And they will. They already do. Have you ever heard these words uttered in your classroom? "Stop it!" "Don't." But can't we just call them commands? The first definition of *imperative* in the *Oxford English Dictionary* is "expressing a command" or "request" (2009).

Read these three sentences aloud.

Sit.
Sit?
Sit!

With just a period, the word *sit* seems more like a kind request. This is a simple command. The word *sit* with a question mark isn't a command at all. It's a question, and you knew how to read it, didn't you? End marks do more than terminate a sentence.

Now let's change the punctuation: *Sit!* How did your voice change? What is the purpose of the exclamation point? It's a command in this sentence through and through, isn't it? We find that kids figure out commands on their own without an abstract conversation about the imperative mood and the understood *you*—the two things that allow a command to be a type of sentence, even though it's often a lonesome verb hanging out alone with an end mark. Confused yet? If you were eight, you would be.

So, standards call them imperatives. We call them commands because that's what they do. And we call them that without explaining that grammarians have decided that these are labeled sentences in the imperative mood and contain a subject that isn't even there: the *you* is understood to be there, according to grammarians, so it's a sentence. Kids are less confused when we call it a command, not a sentence. Leave it at that. Less is actually clearer in this instance. We're preparing writers, not linguists.

When the curiosity or interest intersects with a developmentally appropriate example, dive in headfirst if you like and discuss commands. But until then, don't add another abstraction, which will most likely lead to more confusion than clarity.

How are they alike and different?

Let's get one thing straight from the start. I can *shoot*.

I can shoot the daylights out of a basketball. I've always had a special talent for throwing stuff at targets. I can toss a soda can into the recycling bucket from across the room. No problem. I can fire a snowball at a tree across the street and hit it nine times out of ten.

It's like a sixth sense. Sometimes I set up a bunch of toy soldiers on a table and pick them off with a rubber band one by one. Other kids are amazed. I can shoot a bow and arrow like a laser beam. I'm always winning stuff at carnivals.

Of course, being a great shooter isn't good enough in a real game. You've got to be able to dribble the ball. You've got to be able to pass. You've got to be able to handle pressure.

I was never good at those things. I get rattled when I'm playing the game. The other kids are always shouting, sticking their hands in my face. Everybody's running around. It's all a blur. Too much pressure.

But give me a basketball and put me on the foul line with nobody guarding me. I can sink it. Like I said, I can *shoot*.

—Dan Gutman, *The Million Dollar Shot*

8.4   Messy Room: Question Marks and Exclamation Points

Standard	Use question marks for interrogatives (questions). Use exclamation points for exclamatory sentences.
Focus Phrase	"I use question marks to end questions." "I use exclamation points to show shouting or strong feeling."
Invitation to Notice	Do you see this? This is Melvin's sneaker! I found it under his bed in a cracker box!

        —Nick Bruel, *Who Is Melvin Bubble?*

Power Note   *Read aloud* Who Is Melvin Bubble? *by Nick Bruel. Afterward, students look again at a few sentences from* Who Is Melvin Bubble?

Invitation to Compare and Contrast

Do you see this? This is Melvin's sneaker! I found it under his bed in a cracker box!

Do you see this room? Clothes cover every inch of the floor!

Power Note   *It's valid to notice three sentences versus two, that both are about messy rooms, and that both have question marks and exclamation points. Talk through the effects and deeper similarities as well. (Both questions start with the question word* do. *In both cases the writer is talking directly to the reader by using the second person. There are more specifics in the original.)*

Invitation to Imitate

Imitate Together: Invite writers to use paired writing to compose a sentence. They may use the topic of a messy room or choose some other way to use a question mark and an exclamation point in two or so sentences.

Imitate Independently: Students use the model sentence to create their own questions and exclamations.

Invitation to Celebrate

Exaggeration Nation: We can't always yell in school for many reasons, but for special occasions, we can exaggerate how we read aloud sentences that end in exclamation points. Have fun! Won't you? Students read aloud their sentence, exaggerating their voices to match what the punctuation directs them to do.

Invitation to Apply

In one class period—or some other set period of time—students track how many sentences they come across that end in periods, question marks, and exclamation points. Some kids like keeping track on three sticky notes and then come to the chart and make hash marks. (See Figure 8.2.) They'll discover that we use a lot more periods than anything else. Or do we? Explore the books in your class and find out.

Figure 8.2
End mark tally chart

What Mark Will You Leave Behind?

 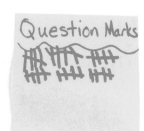 

Invitation to Edit

What did we learn about writing from Nick Bruel?	
Do you see this? This is Melvin's sneaker! I found it under his bed in a cracker box!	
What changed? What is the effect of the change?	
Do you see this. This is Melvin's sneaker! I found it under his bed in a cracker box!	*In the first sentence, the question mark has been changed to a period. This could slow readers and impede their understanding.*
Do you see this? This is Melvin's sneaker. I found it under his bed in a cracker box!	*In the second sentence, the first exclamation point is changed to a period. It's still correct, but it's no longer yelling. And Nick Bruel wanted to show that Melvin's mother was having some strong feelings.*
Do you see this? This is Melvins sneaker! I found it under his bed in a cracker box!	*In the second sentence, the possessive apostrophe has been deleted. This changes the meaning to more than one Melvin, which doesn't make sense.*

What do you notice?

Do you see this? This is Melvin's sneaker! I found it under his bed in a cracker box!

—Nick Bruel, *Who Is Melvin Bubble?*

How are they alike and different?

Do you see this? This is Melvin's sneaker! I found it under his bed in a cracker box!

Do you see this room? Clothes cover every inch of the floor!

Let's try it out.

Do you see this? This is Melvin's sneaker! I found it under his bed in a cracker box!

Do you see this room? Clothes cover every inch of the floor!

Do you see this? This is Melvin's sneaker! I found it under his bed in a cracker box!

What changed? What is the effect of the change?

Do you see this. This is Melvin's sneaker! I found it under his bed in a cracker box!

Do you see this? This is Melvin's sneaker. I found it under his bed in a cracker box!

Do you see this? This is Melvins sneaker! I found it under his bed in a cracker box!

8.5 Advanced End Mark Exploration

We know punctuation has a purpose, that each mark has a particular meaning and causes the words before it to be read in certain ways. As you talk about these ending marks with young writers, you might add to the discussion by exploring these excerpts from literature. What do they tell us about end punctuation?

Write? Write. Write!

After discussion of the excerpts above, invite students to collaborate to develop their own creative reference to one of the end marks. It can be a paragraph with dialogue, a comparison, a metaphor, a poem, or a song. It's their creation. This writing activity gives them a further opportunity to get creative and explore common things through an uncommon lens. Allow them to choose their genre, such as poetry, narrative, or essay. (See Figure 8.3.)

Figure 8.3
A fifth grader plays with words as he reflects on the question mark.

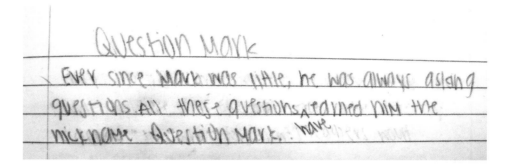

Exclamation Point

Mom looked at me, furious. I thought she would slap me for the first time in my life. She didn't. She stomped away. I stood there, wishing she had slapped me. You're supposed to put an exclamation point at the end of strong feelings. A slap would have felt like that. But instead, her heels clicked out her punctuation, dot dot dot. . . .

—Esme Raji Codell, *Sahara Special*

"I baked you an applesauce cake!"

"Please don't use exclamation points in front of our children," said Mrs. Dullard.

—Sara Pennypacker, *Meet the Dullards*

Period

Isabelle kept staring at her. Raymie stared back. She made her soul smaller and smaller. She imagined it becoming as tiny as the period at the end of a sentence. No one would ever find it.

—Kate DiCamillo, *Raymie Nightingale*

Question Mark

This excerpt is from a classroom celebrating National Punctuation Day.

"Can I yell something out, Miss?" Chewy asked, squinting.
"Well, you're at the question mark station: can you?"
"Mrs. Harrington, can I go to the restroom?!" he shouted, then broke down giggling and wiping his runny nose. "Can I say anything that's not a question?"
"Will you?" jumped in Mrs. Harrington. When she moved her hands, I noticed her fingernails were painted red. It was like she wanted to date punctuation.

—Jeff Anderson, *Zack Delacruz: Me and My Big Mouth*

The Power of Pairs

Two heads are better than one. People who are married live longer. Stories and essays begin and end, with bookends holding the writing together. Readers love pairs and the beauty of balance, the magnificence of a perfect match, two halves making a whole.

For instance, writers need apostrophes to combine a pair of words into one contraction. We love shortening things even more than we love pairs. In *The Day the Crayons Quit*, a contraction helps the gray crayon's complaint sound conversational, squeezing together the subject–helping verb pair *you* and *are*: "You're killing me!"

Pronouns pair themselves with noun antecedents. And as noun substitutes, pronouns must match their nouns. Whereas the list of nouns is forever growing, pronouns stay a finite set bound with another noun—male or female, plural or singular.

Careful pairing crafts a perfect match for reader ease. If our verbs are in singular form but our noun is plural, *they is off*. Disagreements between subject-verb pairs clunk, and jostle the flow of writing. A noun-verb pair that doesn't agree grates on the nerves and takes the reader out of meaning and into confusion.

Nouns and verbs aren't the only pairs. Certain punctuation comes only in pairs as well: quotation marks, parentheses, and brackets. Readers appreciate it when writers sprinkle dialogue into their narrative prose. But if writers open a quote to show that a character's mouth is beginning to move, and they don't close the quotes when the character's jaw stops flapping, then readers are left puzzled. Same thing goes for parentheses and brackets—they have to be together, enclosing.

Writers need pairs, and young writers need to know how to craft them with balance, grace, and effectiveness.

It ain't whatcha write, it's the way atcha write it.
—Jack Kerouac

What Do Apostrophes Do?

Everybody likes a shortcut. Apostrophes give readers and writers the gift of brevity, helping them crisply communicate ownership and competently combine pronouns with shortened verbs. *That's* nice. See, *that's* a contraction of *that is*. The apostrophe shows where we squeezed the letter *i* out. That's a contraction.

But wait; there's more. Who doesn't love owning things? Often people are quite concerned with what's theirs and what's someone else's. Apostrophes help us spread the wealth of ownership in our prose in a compact way. An apostrophe-*s* can do that: *We tripped on Carl's bone*. I don't have to use any additional words to explain that the bone belongs to Carl. By writing his name and adding an apostrophe-*s* after it, the reader knows whose bone it is.

As a matter of craft, using contractions indicates a casual and conversational tone. If writers want to make their writing less formal, to sound more like talking, they use contractions. *That's informal*. If writers want to sound more formal, they choose to write the words out. *That is formal*. Ooh-la-la! Even though they mean the same thing, each choice affects the reader differently.

The best writing is often economical, with every word doing work. Using apostrophe-*s* after a noun and before another noun acts like a nice, compact adjective, telling whose noun it is.

Lesson Sets:

What Do Apostrophes Do?

9.1 Let's Eat: Apostrophes of Restaurant Ownership

Standard Recognize and use possessive apostrophes.

Focus Phrase "I add an apostrophe-*s* to show ownership."

Invitation to Notice They passed Fadil's Falafel, Tony's Pizza, and Dot's Deli.
  —Yangsook Choi, *The Name Jar*

Power Note *Students often note that the restaurants are owned. Ask, "How do you know?" You may have to explain what* falafel *is—a Middle Eastern food, specifically a spicy mixture of ground chickpeas or fava beans shaped into a ball or patty and fried.* Deli *is short for delicatessen; delis usually serve foods such as sandwiches, cold cuts, salads, and pickles.*

Invitation to Compare and Contrast They passed Fadil's Falafel, Tony's Pizza, and Dot's Deli.
I saw Jennifer's shoes, Delia's iPad, and the dog's toys on the living room rug.

Power Note *Students see from the imitations that restaurants are not the only thing we own, and we use an apostrophe-*s *after all singular nouns to indicate what is owned or possessed.*

Invitation to Imitate *Imitate Together*: Invite writers to use interactive or shared writing to compose a sentence with you.

  I tripped over John's backpack.

Imitate Independently: Students use the model sentences to compose their own sentences, using apostrophes to show ownership. If students try to show plural ownership, help them out and discuss the difference with the class when you think they are ready.

Invitation to Celebrate Students share their imitations. The teacher writes the name of the student who's sharing on the board and asks, each time, "What do I need to add to the name to show ownership?" (An apostrophe-*s*.)

  Terry's sentence

Invitation to Apply Wall charts give us a way to organize our thinking and group like concepts with like concepts. This chart was originally used in Jeff's book *Mechanically Inclined* (2005), and we have found its organization helpful in understanding the concept of apostrophes. This is only the first half of the chart, where we begin with the idea that apostrophes do two things: show possession or show where letters have been removed from a verb. (See Figures 9.1 and 9.2.)

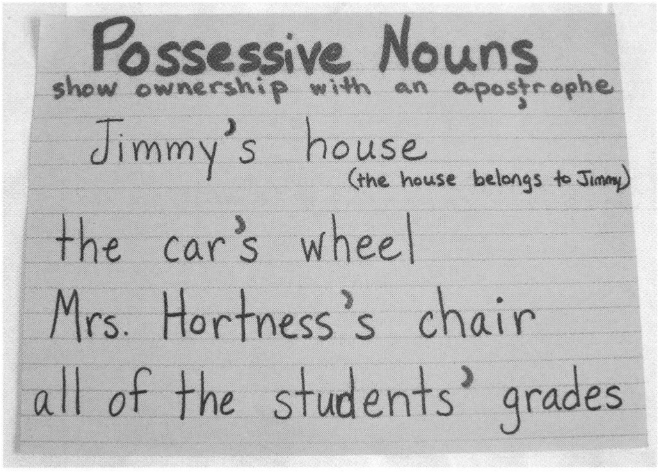

Figure 9.1 (left)
Apostrophe chart, possessive nouns

Figure 9.2 (below)
Apostrophe chart, with possessive nouns and contractions

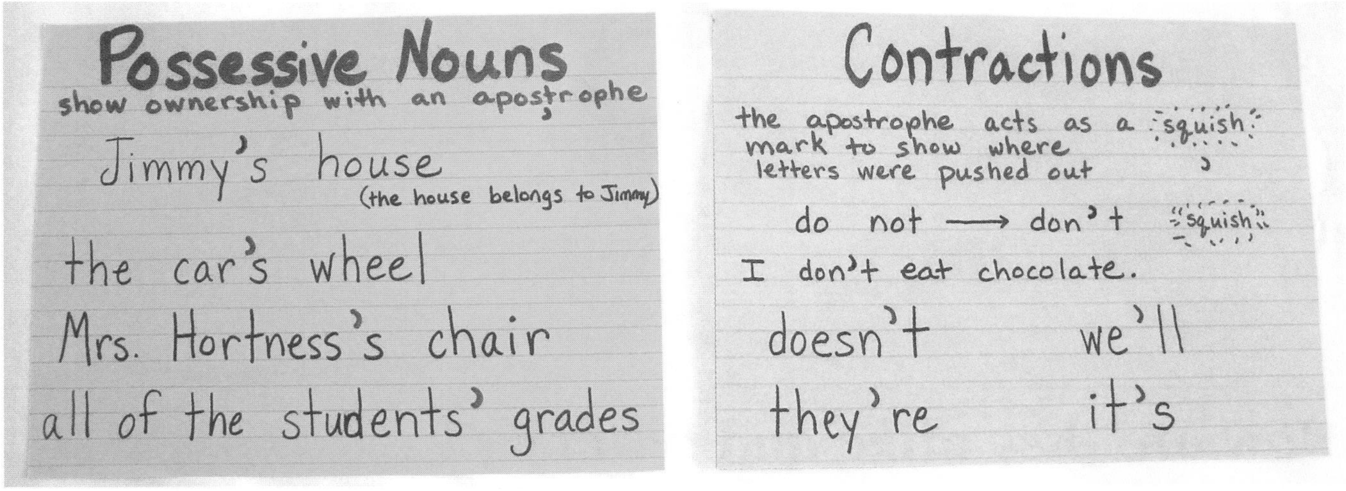

Invitation to Edit

What did we learn about writing from Yangsook Choi?	
They passed Fadil's Falafel, Tony's Pizza, and Dot's Deli.	
What changed? What is the effect of the change?	
They passed Fadil's Falafel, Tonys Pizza, and Dot's Deli.	*The apostrophe has been deleted from* Tony's, *making it no longer possessive. It would actually mean more than one Tony, but it wouldn't show whose pizza place it is.*
They passed Fadil's falafel, Tony's Pizza, and Dot's Deli.	*The first letter of falafel is changed from a capital to lowercase. Since* falafel *is part of the name of the restaurant, it must be capitalized too.*
They passed Fadil's Falafel Tony's Pizza, and Dot's Deli.	*The comma between* Fadil's Falafel *and* Tony's Pizza *has been deleted, making the two restaurant names run together. The comma provides the separation readers need.*

What do you notice?

They passed Fadil's Falafel, Tony's Pizza, and Dot's Deli.
—Yangsook Choi, *The Name Jar*

How are they alike and different?

They passed Fadil's Falafel, Tony's Pizza, and Dot's Deli.

I saw Jennifer's shoes, Delia's iPad, and the dog's toys on the living room rug.

Let's try it out.

They passed Fadil's Falafel, Tony's Pizza, and Dot's Deli.

I saw Jennifer's shoes, Delia's iPad, and the dog's toys on the living room rug.

They passed Fadil's Falafel, Tony's Pizza, and Dot's Deli.

What changed? What is the effect of the change?

They passed Fadil's Falafel, Tonys Pizza, and Dot's Deli.

They passed Fadil's falafel, Tony's Pizza, and Dot's Deli.

They passed Fadil's Falafel Tony's Pizza, and Dot's Deli.

9.2 Apostrophe Family Reunion: Contractions and Possessives

Standard	Use an apostrophe to form contractions and possessives.
Focus phrase	"I use apostrophes to show either ownership or contraction."
Invitation to Notice	Today is my family reunion. I can't wait for my grandmother's cheese chowder! —Mike Curato, *Little Elliot, Big Family*
Power Note	*We chose to use two sentences for this activity to give it a context and make it easier to imitate later. It gives us a chance to see who knows what a reunion is and, if appropriate, talk about the prefix re-, meaning "again."*
Invitation to Compare and Contrast	Today is my family reunion. I can't wait for my grandmother's cheese chowder! Tonight is my family's party. I can't wait for my abuelo's tamales.
Power Note	*We chose to use an extra possessive apostrophe (family's) in our imitation to highlight differences about when we use apostrophes and when we don't. It also might open up the possibility of students using more than one in their imitations. Note how painlessly we're teaching them to use adverbs such as today and tonight as time-markers. Don't be concerned if they're not labeled. It's about use.*
Invitation to Imitate	*Imitate Together*: Invite writers to use interactive or shared writing to compose a sentence with you.
	Next month is my aunt's wedding. I can't wait to eat Aunt Sheila's wedding cake.
	Imitate Independently: Students use the two models to compose their own sentences, using apostrophes to show ownership and at least one contraction. We wouldn't suggest pushing them to include things like this when they're writing an essay, but when they're writing only one or two sentences, this is a way to nudge them to apply the skill to their meaning-making process.
Invitation to Celebrate	*Dueling Recorders*: Two students. Two markers. Students share sentences while two recorders alternate writing whose sentence we're listening to. (See Figure 9.3.)

Figure 9.3
Dueling recorders

Invitation to Edit

What did we learn about writing from Mike Curato?	
Today is my family reunion. I can't wait for my grandmother's cheese chowder!	
What changed? What is the effect of the change?	
Today is my family reunion. I can't wait for my Grandmother's cheese chowder!	Grandmother *is capitalized. We capitalize* Grandma *or* Grandpa, *or* Mom *and* Dad, *only when there is no possessive pronoun in front of it or it's substituting for their name.*
Today is my family reunion. I can't wait for my grandmothers cheese chowder!	*The possessive apostrophe on* grandmothers *has been deleted. The apostrophe shows whose cheese chowder it is. This version may cause a reader to think there is more than one grandmother.*
Today is my family reunion. I cannot wait for my grandmother's cheese chowder!	*The contraction* can't *has been changed to* cannot. *Both are correct, but the contraction is less formal.*

Tip: *Whose* or *Who's*: Who Knows *Who Owns* or *Who Is*?

Sometimes students are flummoxed by choosing between writing *whose* or *who's*. If you mean to say *who is*, use the contraction *who's*. *Who's* is a contraction. Always.

> "Who's lost?"
> —Kate DiCamillo, *Flora and Ulysses*

If you mean to communicate ownership, like in the sentence below, use the possessive pronoun *whose*. Personal pronouns never use apostrophes for ownership or possession. When there's an apostrophe with a pronoun, it's a contraction.

> Despereaux looked at his father and saw an old mouse whose fur was shot through with gray.
> —Kate DiCamillo, *The Tale of Despereaux*

What do you notice?

Today is my family reunion. I can't wait for my grandmother's cheese chowder!

—Mike Curato, *Little Elliot, Big Family*

How are they alike and different?

Today is my family reunion. I can't wait for my grandmother's cheese chowder!

Tonight is my family's party. I can't wait for my abuelo's tamales.

Let's try it out.

Today is my family reunion. I can't wait for my grandmother's cheese chowder!

Tonight is my family's party. I can't wait for my abuelo's tamales.

Today is my family reunion. I can't wait for my grandmother's cheese chowder!

What changed? What is the effect of the change?

Today is my family reunion. I can't wait for my Grandmother's cheese chowder!

Today is my family reunion. I can't wait for my grandmothers cheese chowder!

Today is my family reunion. I cannot wait for my grandmother's cheese chowder!

9.3   Apostrophes Look Like Fingernails: Contractions

Standard   Use apostrophes to form contractions.

Focus Phrase   "I use an apostrophe to show where I squeezed letters out (contraction action!)."

Invitation to Notice

Power Note   *Students read each passage with a partner and talk about what they notice.*

> "Teddy, it's the third day of school. Can you please save daydreaming until day four?"
> "Strange but true, Ms. Raffeli, I'm not daydreaming. I'm thinking about fingernails and you'll be happy to know it's related to the math unit we're working on."
> —Molly B. Burnham, *Teddy Mars: Almost a World Record Breaker*

Power Note   *We chose to use a larger chunk of text so we could see apostrophes used in different ways over time in a text. Of course, this same text could be used to teach dialogue, but we are still seeing and studying dialogue without it being our focus.*

Invitation to Compare and Contrast

> "Teddy, it's the third day of school. Can you please save daydreaming until day four?"
> "Strange but true, Ms. Raffeli, I'm not daydreaming. I'm thinking about fingernails and you'll be happy to know it's related to the math unit we're working on."

> "Sophia, it's the second day of school. Can you please save lip glossing for day four?"
> "Strange but true, Mrs. Harrington. I'm not lip glossing. I'm lip moisturizing, which will help me when it's time to turn and talk, because my lips will move better."

Power Note   *Many patterns emerge in the discussion: quotation marks, humor, tone (sarcasm—saying something like you mean it when you don't), and revealing character. Go with what the students notice, honoring and naming and extending it, but at some point bring it back to the focus phrase: "I use an apostrophe to show where I squeezed letters out (contraction action!)."*

Invitation to Imitate   *Imitate Together*: Invite students to use paired writing to compose a sentence. Writers try to incorporate some "contraction action," squeezing letters out and leaving behind the squish mark, which is actually called an apostrophe.

Imitate Independently: Students use the models to compose their own paragraphs using several contractions. "Why might you choose to use dialogue?"

(Because people use contractions in speech.) Encourage them to use the model if they have questions about the quotation marks. "Writing can teach us when we look closely at it, rereading and noting."

Invitation to Celebrate

Two Listeners; Contraction Action! Students share sentences. On the whiteboard or chart paper, two listeners record any contractions they hear or read during our celebratory sharing. Squish! (See Figure 9.4.)

Figure 9.4 Contraction action!

Invitation to Apply

With a partner, students write a sentence or two about our science or math work, using at least one contraction. After students share, the class can cheer, "Contraction action! SQUISH!"

Invitation to Edit

What did we learn about writing from Molly B. Burnham?	
"Strange but true, Ms. Raffeli, I'm not daydreaming. I'm thinking about fingernails and you'll be happy to know it's related to the math unit we're working on."	
What changed? What is the effect of the change?	
"Strange but true, Ms. Raffeli, I am not daydreaming. I'm thinking about fingernails and you'll be happy to know it's related to the math unit we're working on."	The contraction I'm *was changed to* I am, *which signals more formality and is less conversational. Contractions are used in dialogue because that's often how we talk.*
"Strange but true, Ms. Raffeli, I'm not daydreaming. I'm thinking about fingernails and you will be happy to know it's related to the math unit we're working on."	The contraction you'll, *meaning* "you will," *was changed to* you will. *Both constructions have the same meaning, but the effect of each is slightly different. The contraction is more casual and generally used when talking.*
"Strange but true, Ms. Raffeli, I'm not daydreaming. I'm thinking about fingernails and you'll be happy to know its related to the math unit we're working on."	The apostrophe from it's *was deleted, turning the meaning of* its *to ownership.* It's = it is. Its = ownership.

What do you notice?

"Teddy, it's the third day of school. Can you please save daydreaming until day four?"

"Strange but true, Ms. Raffeli, I'm not daydreaming. I'm thinking about fingernails and you'll be happy to know it's related to the math unit we're working on."

—Molly B. Burnham, *Teddy Mars: Almost a World Record Breaker*

How are they alike and different?

"Teddy, it's the third day of school. Can you please save daydreaming until day four?"

"Strange but true, Ms. Raffeli, I'm not daydreaming. I'm thinking about fingernails and you'll be happy to know it's related to the math unit we're working on."

"Sophia, it's the second day of school. Can you please save lip glossing for day four?"

"Strange but true, Mrs. Harrington. I'm not lip glossing. I'm lip moisturizing, which will help me when it's time to turn and talk, because my lips will move better."

Let's try it out.

"Teddy, it's the third day of school. Can you please save daydreaming until day four?"

"Strange but true, Ms. Raffeli, I'm not daydreaming. I'm thinking about fingernails and you'll be happy to know it's related to the math unit we're working on."

"Sophia, it's the second day of school. Can you please save lip glossing for day four?"

"Strange but true, Mrs. Harrington. I'm not lip glossing. I'm lip moisturizing, which will help me when it's time to turn and talk, because my lips will move better."

"Strange but true, Ms. Raffeli, I'm not daydreaming. I'm thinking about fingernails and you'll be happy to know it's related to the math unit we're working on."

What changed? What is the effect of the change?

"Strange but true, Ms. Raffeli, I am not daydreaming. I'm thinking about fingernails and you'll be happy to know it's related to the math unit we're working on."

"Strange but true, Ms. Raffeli, I'm not daydreaming. I'm thinking about fingernails and you will be happy to know it's related to the math unit we're working on."

"Strange but true, Ms. Raffeli, I'm not daydreaming. I'm thinking about fingernails and you'll be happy to know its related to the math unit we're working on."

Tip: **Pairing Plurals with Possessives: A Special Note for Those Whose First or Last Names End in -s, -ch, or -z and Those Who Love Them**

Nothing about apostrophes stirs a group of people up like possessive apostrophes with names or words that end in -s, -ch, or -z. First, there are two issues often conflated with plurals and possessives. Most adults are incredibly irritated when writers incorrectly use an apostrophe-s to communicate pluralization. For the first example, we'll use a noun that doesn't end in s. *Banana's* is not the plural form of *bananas*. *Bananas* is. There could be an occasion to use the apostrophe-s with a singular *banana* like this: *the banana's skin is speckled.* But if we were talking about more than one banana, we'd write *The bananas' skins are speckled.* Because the s at the end of the word is a plural s, writers need only add an apostrophe to it. These issues do intersect in certain circumstances, however, as the chart in this tip box shows. It's time we give people whose names end in -s, -ch, and -z a break.

Conventions are agreements. But even something as common as this is not a settled matter according to every source. The Associated Press doesn't follow the same pattern, so always check which style guide you're expected to use.

And even if you don't like a convention, it's still the convention. Here's what the *Chicago Manual of Style,* the *Publication Manual of the American Psychological Association*, and the Modern Language Association's *MLA Handbook* recommend:

Names That End in -s, -z, and -ch
Singular and Plural Versus Singular and Plural Possessive

Singular	Plural
Mrs. Ross	The Rosses A plural form of Mrs. Ross, Mr. Ross, and their kids Ron and Rona.
Mr. Gonzalez	The Gonzalezes Everyone in the Gonzales family—plural is more than one.
Chris	Chrises Uncommon, but you could say, "I have three Chrises in my class." We pluralize names that end in -s, -ch, or -z by adding -es to the end, like all nouns that end in these letters.

Versus

Singular Possessive	Plural Possessive
Mrs. Ross's yard	The Rosses' yard looks nice.
Mr. Gonzalez's pool	The Gonzalezes' pool shimmers.
Chris's phone	(Though it might be incredibly rare, it is possible to say, "**The Chrises's** behaviors are similar.")
Like all **singular** nouns, **singular names** that end in -s, -ch, or -z require an **apostrophe-s** to show possession or ownership.	Like all **plural nouns**, **plural names** that end in -s (only because they're pluralized) require an apostrophe only. This shows that the name is both plural and possessing something.

What Do Pronouns Do?

Pronouns are the substitutes, plain and simple. They link to nouns that came before them. These nouns are called the pronouns' antecedents. An antecedent noun defines the pronoun as singular or plural and as first, second, or third person, and sometimes tells us its gender, male or female.

The *Oxford English Dictionary* defines *antecedent* as "a thing or circumstance which goes before or precedes in time or order." In other words, what came before this pronoun?

For example, when you write a story about Marsha, pronouns give you a way to say something other than *Marsha, Marsha, Marsha*! We don't have to repeat Marsha's name in an endless loop. Instead, we can call in a sub. Since *Marsha* is female, the substitute is *she* for *Marsha* or *hers* for *Marsha's*. In fact, pronouns' main function is to give writers a way to clearly and concisely refer to characters or people without using their names over and over and over. Look at pronouns at work in Carl Hiaasen's *Scat* in Figure 10.1.

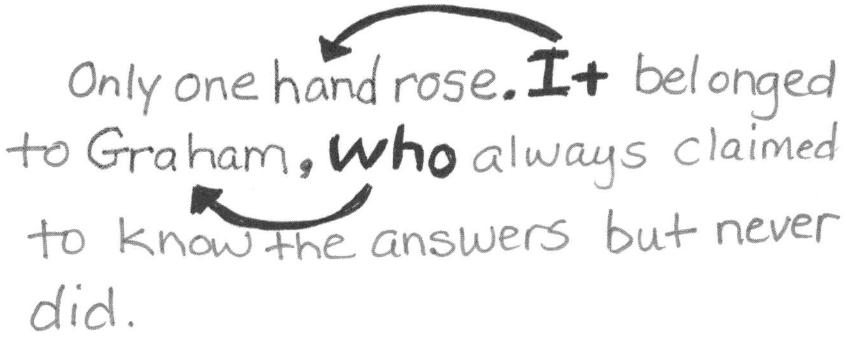

Figure 10.1
The pronoun *it* refers to *hand*, and *who* links to the antecedent *Graham*. We suggest students imagine these little arrows pointing to a noun antecedent, tracing with their finger. In revision, using a bright pen to draw arrows to noun antecedents in a draft can ensure clear pronoun-antecedent linkage, with agreement in number and person.

> Only one hand rose. **It** belonged to Graham, **who** always claimed to know the answers but never did.

As an author's craft move, pronouns also identify a character or writer's point of view. The point of view determines what information is shared in the writing. Each voice or point of view (POV) has a different purpose:

Pronouns Reveal Point of View

- **The first person, or *I* voice:** First person is close to the content and can be a more revealing or personal filter, but first-person POV can't see inside other characters' heads, only what he or she can observe.

- **The second person, or *you* voice:** Second person is rarely used on an entire piece; it usually just pops in to involve the reader or ask a question.

- **The third person, or *he-she-it* voice:** Third person is the most removed from the content, an observer who is outside the situation. This can be a more objective, reporting POV, but that all depends on the tone the author uses—that is, attitude and word choice. (Third person can flex to omniscient status, where it can see all things, even inside others' heads, but that's a bit heavy for now.)

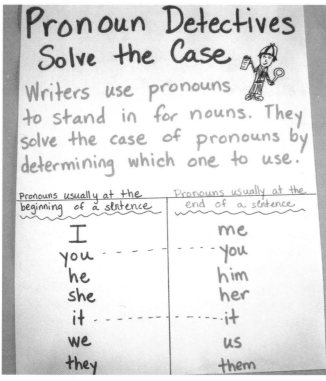

Figure 10.2 Whitney's pronoun case chart

Distance in point of view can matter. As we often repeat, every choice a writer makes affects readers, including point of view.

Besides linking back to nouns, another elementary pronoun standard is pronoun case. There are three pronoun cases: subjective, objective, and possessive. In this chapter, we'll focus on two cases—subjective and objective. See the word *subject* and *object* within these terms? These two words give us our best hint at the usage pattern. Some pronouns act as subjects in the subjective case. The pronoun *I* is in the subjective case because it's the first-person pronoun used as a subject. If we want to write in the first person and show the narrator receiving something, it's the pronoun *me*—the objective case. But don't worry! We don't even have to get that deep into the weeds with pronoun case, because students do much of it with automaticity. When they don't, it's better to address the common pronouns with a chart, like Whitney did with a first-grade class as shown in Figure 10.2.

Pronouns are all about the references, so let's get off their case.

Lesson Sets:

What Do Pronouns Do?

10.1 Standing In for a Crayon: Pronouns and Antecedents

10.2 *Magic Tree House* Pronouns: Possession

10.3 Indefinitely *Save Me a Seat*: *Everybody* Loves Indefinite Pronouns

---

Tip: Avoid the "He or She" Said/"S/he" Said Trap: *They* and *Their* Aren't Singular Pronouns

Consider the word *writer*. It's not yet clear whether this particular writer is *he* or *she*. We could reference the word *writer* with both pronouns (*he or she*), but many readers find that awkward. A trick of the trade is to change the singular *writer* to the plural *writers*. Then you can use *they* and *their* to refer to the *writers* and still agree in number and person. Plus you won't have to worry about the gender. It can distract your reader if you use *their* or *they* to refer to singular antecedents.

10.1   Standing In for a Crayon: Pronouns and Antecedents

Standard	Ensure subject-verb and pronoun-antecedent agreement.
Focus Phrase	"I use pronouns to substitute for nouns."

Invitation to Notice

> Hey Duncan,
> It's me, Red Crayon. We need to talk. You make me work harder than any of the other crayons.
> —Drew Daywalt, *The Day the Crayons Quit*

Power Note   *After kids notice things about the sentence, ask them who each pronoun is referring to and how they know. To make it easier to follow, ask about the pronouns in the order in which they appear in the sentence:*

- *Who is me? How do you know?*
- *Who is we? How can you tell?*
- *Who is you? What clues are you given?*
- *Who is the second me? How are you sure?*

Invitation to Compare and Contrast

> Hey Duncan,
>
> It's me, Red Crayon. We need to talk. You make me work harder than any of the other crayons.
>
> Hey Mom,
>
> It's me, Tiara. We need to talk. You make me do the dishes and you don't make Darron do anything.
>
> Sincerely yours,
> Tiara

Power Note   *We chose to put a closing in our imitation, so students will sign their own notes in later applications. After you review the pronoun-antecedent connections, you may want to review patterns we use with personal letters. For a lesson focused on the conventions of letter openings and closings, see Chapter 4, Lesson 4.5: "A Crayon Has Reasons: Capitalization in Letter Openings and Closings."*

Invitation to Imitate   *Imitate Together*: As a shared writing activity, lead students in writing a letter from something they use in school to the principal or an audience of their choice, modeling pronoun case and antecedent reference.

> Dear Mrs. Miller,
>
> As yellow pencils we are feeling ignored. Everyone wants a bright-colored mechanical pencil. They don't need to be sharpened like us. Well, la-di-da is all we have to say to that. We think that as our school's principal, you need to make sure all pencils are valued equally.
>
> Sincerely,
> No. 2

Imitate Independently: Students use the models to create their own letters or notes as an item from a list of school supplies to another student in the room. Students make sure pronouns are linked to noun antecedents in number and person.

Invitation to Celebrate

Students deliver letters to the name they chose. Recipients receive and read letters, and perhaps reply. To extend the celebration with a splash of color, students may use a highlighter or crayon to draw lines from pronouns to their noun antecedents.

Invitation to Apply

From a subject other than language arts, share a list of three or more sentences with pronouns in them. Have kids link the pronouns to their antecedents with an arrow on the Smartboard or document camera. (See Figure 10.3.)

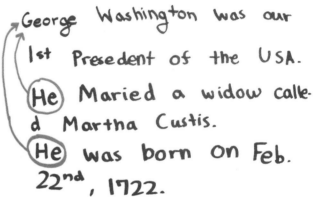

Figure 10.3 Student Work in Social Studies

Fun Fact: #ICYMI: In CASE You Missed It

In terms of case (subject or object), indefinite pronouns are one of the few pronouns that can always be used in either subjective or objective case.

Everybody loves somebody, but nobody loves everybody.

Bonus points if you know the other pronoun that can be used in both cases. I'm not going to tell you.

Invitation to Edit

What did we learn about writing from Drew Daywalt?	
Hey Duncan, It's me, Red Crayon. We need to talk. You make me work harder than any of the other crayons.	
What changed? What was the effect of the change?	
Hey Duncan It's me, Red Crayon. We need to talk. You make me work harder than any of the other crayons.	*The comma after the letter opening has been deleted. Letter openings or greetings are followed by a comma (or colon if you want to get into block form).*
Hey Duncan, It's me, Red Crayon. We need to talk. You make her work harder than any of the other crayons.	*The first-person pronoun* me *is changed to the third-person* her. *We don't know the gender of the crayon, but we don't need to. It's in the first person, and the Red Crayon is talking about him- or herself.*
Hey Duncan, Its me, Red Crayon. We need to talk. You make me work harder than any of the other crayons.	*The apostrophe from* it's *has been deleted. Now it no longer says,* "It is me." It's = It is Its = ownership *This changes the meaning to ownership of me, which is confusing to readers.*

What do you notice?

Hey Duncan,
It's me, Red Crayon. We need to talk. You make me work harder than any of the other crayons.

—Drew Daywalt, *The Day the Crayons Quit*

How are they alike and different?

Hey Duncan,
It's me, Red Crayon. We need to talk. You make me work harder than any of the other crayons.

Hey Mom,

It's me, Tiara. We need to talk. You make me do the dishes and you don't make Darron do anything.

Sincerely yours,
Tiara

Let's try it out.

Hey Duncan,
It's me, Red Crayon. We need to talk. You make me work harder than any of the other crayons.

Hey Mom,

It's me, Tiara. We need to talk. You make me do the dishes and you don't make Darron do anything.

Sincerely yours,
Tiara

Hey Duncan,
It's me, Red Crayon. We need to talk. You make me work harder than any of the other crayons.

What changed? What is the effect of the change?

Hey Duncan
It's me, Red Crayon. We need to talk. You make me work harder than any of the other crayons.

Hey Duncan,
It's me, Red Crayon. We need to talk. You make her work harder than any of the other crayons.

Hey Duncan,
Its me, Red Crayon. We need to talk. You make me work harder than any of the other crayons.

10.2 *Magic Tree House* Pronouns: Possession

Standard	Use and understand possessive pronouns. (Possessive pronouns agree in number and person.)
Focus Phrase	"I match my pronouns by number, person, and ownership."
Invitation to Notice	Jack pulled his scarf tighter.

Annie lifted up her long dress and ran to a tree close to the river. Jack held on to his hat and ran after her.

Jack and Annie were wearing their nice, dry clothes again.
—Mary Pope Osborne, *Magic Tree House: Revolutionary War on Wednesday*

Power Note *We thought it would be valuable to look at a few more sentences with pairs and males and females, so this invitation has four sentences. Students explore Mary Pope Osborne's sentences. After noticings, ask kids what pronouns refer to and how they know, including possessive pronouns. Discuss number (plural and singular), person (gender), and possession (ownership). Ask, "How does the antecedent define them?"*

Invitation to Compare and Contrast Jack pulled his scarf tighter.
Emma pulled her belt tighter to keep her jeans from sagging.

Power Note *For ease, we chose one of Osborne's sentences to take us through the rest of the process, but feel free to give students the other options if you like. When students say one sentence is about a girl and one is about a boy, ask them, "Why is that important for what we're learning?" (Pronouns need to match in number and person.) When they point out a pronoun, ask, "What is that pronoun doing?" (A pronoun stands in or substitutes for a noun antecedent.) "I match my pronouns by number, person, and ownership."*

Invitation to Imitate *Imitate Together*: Invite writers to use interactive or shared writing to compose a sentence with you. "I match my pronouns by number, person, and ownership."

Juan took off his hat because it was making his head sweat.

Imitate in Pairs: Student pairs use the models to compose their own sentence, using pronouns with clear noun antecedents about any subject they choose.

Invitation to Celebrate Students share their sentences aloud, reading them twice. We applaud writers for the hard work of making pronouns agree in number, person, and possession with their noun antecedents.

Invitation to Apply *Lights, Clothes, Action*: Students write about getting dressed, naming the clothes and then later referring to them with pronouns.

Invitation to Edit

What did we learn about writing from Mary Pope Osborne?	
Jack pulled his scarf tighter.	
What changed? What is the effect of the change?	
Jack pulled her scarf tighter.	The possessive pronoun her refers to a female. Jack is male, so to agree or match, the pronoun needs to be his. When pronouns don't agree in gender, it can confuse readers.
Jack pulled their scarf tighter.	The possessive pronoun their refers to a plural noun (more than one). Jack is a singular noun, so to agree or match, the pronoun needs to be his. When pronouns don't match in number, they scuttle meaning.
Jack pull his scarf tighter.	The -ed has been deleted from the verb pulled. This dropped ending makes the action no longer in the past. To be in the present pattern, an s would need to be added to the end: Jack pulls. When verb tense is off, it feels jarring to readers.

Tip: Reflexive Pronouns: The Selfie of Pronouns (or Is It *Selvies*?)

Myself, yourself, himself, herself, itself, ourselves, yourself, yourselves, themselves. The first thing to know about reflexive pronouns is don't use them unless you need to. Don't think you'll sound smarter if you use one. Usually they make you sound inelegant and aren't needed. (For example, never say, "I, myself . . .") You need a reflexive pronoun only when the subject of the sentence is also the object, like the example in Figure 10.4 from Christina Soontornvat's *The Changelings*.

See the same thing modeled here in William Alexander's *Goblin Secrets* with a plural subject. A plural subject needs a plural object, of course:

Sometimes *they* made up names for *themselves*.

And like all pronouns, the reflexive ones agree in number and person:

He clenched his hands and strained forward, but *he* couldn't force *himself* to move.

Figure 10.4 The reflexive changelings

We find that addressing reflexive pronouns as writers need them in their writing or when we come across a successful example in our reading is the best way in. Point to a reflexive pronoun. "Explain how we know the writers used the right word here." For example, you might ask, "How did William Alexander know to use *themselves* in the first sentence and *himself* in the second?" Doing an effective job of teaching pronoun-antecedent agreement is three-quarters of the battle on this persnickety pronoun.

What do you notice?

Jack pulled his scarf tighter.

Annie lifted up her long dress and ran to a tree close to the river. Jack held on to his hat and ran after her.

Jack and Annie were wearing their nice, dry clothes again.

> —Mary Pope Osborne, *Magic Tree House: Revolutionary War on Wednesday*

How are they alike and different?

Jack pulled his scarf tighter.

Emma pulled her belt tighter to keep her jeans from sagging.

Let's try it out.

Jack pulled his scarf tighter.

Emma pulled her belt tighter to keep her jeans from sagging.

Jack pulled his scarf tighter.

What changed? What is the effect of the change?

Jack pulled her scarf tighter.

Jack pulled their scarf tighter.

Jack pull his scarf tighter.

10.3 Indefinitely *Save Me a Seat*: *Everybody* Loves Indefinite Pronouns

Standard	Use indefinite pronouns.
Focus Phrase	"*Indefinite* pronouns are indefinite and don't need antecedents."
Invitation to Notice	

Save Me a Seat: Indefinite Pronouns	
All	We don't have a cook anymore, so Amma has to prepare all the meals herself.
Nobody	There's a long table against the back wall. Nobody ever sits there because it's near the trash cans.
Anything	My stomach grumbles. I haven't eaten anything since lunch.
Everything	My mom and dad are both pretty smart people, but the truth is, they don't know everything.

All sentences are from *Save Me a Seat* by Sarah Weeks and Gita Varadarajan

Power Note *Indefinite pronouns are the sneaky snakes of pronouns. No antecedent needed. Nothing at all. See what we did there? Nothing is indefinite—indefinable. You know you're complaining if you use a lot of indefinite pronouns: He does it all the time. Everybody hates me. Nobody ever listens. I didn't understand anything (all words that end in -one, -thing, or -body).*

Indefinite pronouns flit around sentences, dripping with indefiniteness and independent as all get-out because they aren't tied to any antecedent. In fact, they're so indefinite about number and person, they can make subject-verb agreement tougher than a two-dollar steak.

Invitation to Compare and Contrast My mom and dad are both pretty smart people, but the truth is, they don't know everything.

My dogs Carl and Paisley are both pretty good dogs, but the truth is, they aren't good dogs all the time.

Power Note *Highlight that everything and all are indefinable and don't require an antecedent. "Indefinite pronouns are indefinite and don't need antecedents."*

Invitation to Imitate *Imitate Together*: Invite writers to compose a sentence with a partner that uses an indefinite pronoun. A chart of indefinite pronouns—words that end in -*one*, -*thing*, or -*body*—might help kids. (They are all treated as singular nouns for agreement purposes, as is another indefinite pronoun: *each*.) The indefinite pronouns *several, few, many,* and *all* are always treated as plural.

Imitate Independently: Students use the models to compose their own sentences, using pronouns with clear noun antecedents about any subject they choose.

Patterns of POWER

206 *Patterns of* **POWER**

Invitation to Celebrate Students share their sentences aloud, reading them twice. We clap for writers working hard on using indefinite pronouns.

Invitation to Apply As a group, students write a list of complaints that use indefinite pronouns. They may use resources to build their choices of indefinite pronouns.

Invitation to Edit

What did we learn about writing from Sarah Weeks and Gita Varadarajan?	
My mom and dad are both pretty smart people, but the truth is, they don't know everything.	
What changed? What is the effect of the change?	
My mom and dad are both pretty smart people, but the truth is, they don't know anything.	*The indefinite pronoun* everything *has been changed to* anything. *Though both are indefinite pronouns, they have different meanings, so the sentence's message is changed in regard to how much her parents know.*
My Mom and dad are both pretty smart people, but the truth is, they don't know everything.	*The first m in* mom *is capitalized. When words for family members such as* parent *or* grandparent *are preceded by a possessive noun or pronoun, they aren't capitalized (*my mom/Mom, your dad/Dad, her grandma/Grandma, his grandpa/Grandpa*).*
My mom and dad are both pretty smart people, but the truth is, they don't know nothing.	*The indefinite pronoun* everything *has been changed to* nothing. *The meaning is changed, and now we have a double negative.*

Tip: Indefinite Agreement: Making It Definite

An indefinite pronoun is usually singular. For a moment of Zen, check out this quote from Lama Surya Das:

Everything passes. Nothing remains.

This treating of indefinite pronouns as singular subjects remains true with all the words that end in *-thing*, *-body*, and *-one*, as well as *any, some, one, other (another)*, and *none*. However, Das was on to something. This singular rule doesn't remain true for these indefinites. If you think about it, it makes sense that these words are treated as plural when it comes to agreement: *all, both, many, few*. They aren't singular in any way. The conventions are about meaning and making sense.

Tip: Who or Whom: What's Up with Them?

For whom am I writing this? For someone who wants an oversimplified, accurate-most-of-the-time trick to help select the right word for the job. When you can't decide whether to use *who* or *whom*, ask yourself this: is there a preposition in front of it? If there is, choose *whom*. When the word does not follow a preposition, use *who*. That'll get you by. Authors Alexander and DiCamillo illustrate who or whom in the following sentences:

"This is not safe," said a man who stood next to Rownie.
—William Alexander, *Goblin Secrets*

"The whiskers of whom?"
—Kate DiCamillo, *The Tale of Despereaux*

What patterns do you notice with these indefinite pronouns?

Save Me a Seat: Indefinite Pronouns	
All	We don't have a cook anymore, so Amma has to prepare all the meals herself.
Nobody	There's a long table against the back wall. Nobody ever sits there because it's near the trash cans.
Anything	My stomach grumbles. I haven't eaten anything since lunch.
Everything	My mom and dad are both pretty smart people, but the truth is, they don't know everything.
All sentences are from *Save Me a Seat* by Sarah Weeks and Gita Varadarajan	

How are they alike and different?

My mom and dad are both pretty smart people, but the truth is, they don't know everything.

My dogs Carl and Paisley are both pretty good dogs, but the truth is, they aren't good dogs all the time.

Let's try it out.

My mom and dad are both pretty smart people, but the truth is, they don't know everything.

My dogs Carl and Paisley are both pretty good dogs, but the truth is, they aren't good dogs all the time.

My mom and dad are both pretty smart people, but the truth is, they don't know everything.

What changed? What is the effect of the change?

My mom and dad are both pretty smart people, but the truth is, they don't know anything.

My Mom and dad are both pretty smart people, but the truth is, they don't know everything.

My mom and dad are both pretty smart people, but the truth is, they don't know nothing.

How Do Verbs and Nouns Agree?

an't subjects and verbs just get along? Be ye singular or plural, ye nouns shall bind together in number. Past-tense verbs almost always end in *-ed*, but watch out, present tense: your verbs change with the person.

When verbs are plural in the present tense, they don't need an *s* because the *s* is in the plural nouns. (Think more than one.)

On the other hand, when verbs are matched with a singular noun, the verb needs the *s* (remember, singular nouns need an *s* on the verb in the present tense). If we recast Spires's sentences with the singular *she* and *he*, we need to add an *s* to the verb.

> They race. They eat. They explore. They relax.
> —Ashley Spires, *The Most Magnificent Thing*

She races. He eats. She explores. He relaxes.

Verbs standing in agreement make reading clear and easy to follow. When nouns and verbs are not in agreement, it can make our prose sputter or clang, and make our reader look for something less disagreeable to read.

Lesson Sets:

How Do Nouns and Verbs Agree?

11.1 They All Saw a Verb: Verbs Make Friends with Nouns

11.2 Everyday Agreement: Nouns and Verbs

11.3 Clothes Cloze: Finding Verbs That Agree in Number and Person

11.1   They All Saw a Verb: Verbs Make Friends with Nouns

Standard   Use verbs that agree with singular and plural nouns.

Focus Phrase   "I make sure my nouns and verbs are friends."

Invitation to Notice

Power Note   *Read aloud Brendan Wenzel's Caldecott Medal–winning* They All Saw a Cat *to the class at some point before this lesson. You may even read it multiple times and have them repeat what will become our invitation-to-notice sentence: "Yes, they all saw a cat!"*

Yes, they all saw a cat.
   —Brendan Wenzel, *They All Saw a Cat*

Power Note   *"Is this sentence happening now, in the present, or did it happen in the past? How do you know?" Students may say some version of this: "It had to have happened in the past because it's already in a book, and if it were happening now, we'd be seeing it or writing it." If this comes up, we explain, "We can write in any tense we want, whether it's the past, present, or the future. We just have to make sure our verbs match."*

Invitation to Compare and Contrast   Yes, they all saw a cat.
No, we did not see a dog.

Power Note   *These sentences provide the perfect opportunity to address the use of a comma after yes or no at the beginning of sentences. This is a comma rule that elementary-aged children are expected to know. Kids may also contrast the pronouns in the two sentences. The pronoun they is third person plural, while the pronoun we is first person plural.*

Invitation to Imitate   *Imitate Together*: Invite writers to use interactive, or shared writing to compose a sentence with you.

Imitate in Pairs: Pairs of students use the model sentences to compose a sentence in which nouns and verbs agree. Say, "Make sure you and your partner can explain how or why your nouns and verbs agree in your sentence."

Invitation to Celebrate   *A Round of How Do You Know?* Students share their sentences aloud or on the document camera, explaining how they know the noun and verb agree.

Invitation to Apply   Writers return to their own recent writing and check for subject-verb agreement with a partner. After they help each other, debrief by asking, "What did you notice? What do you still wonder? What's something you need to pay extra attention to as a writer or reader?" (See Figure 11.1.)

Figure 11.1
A fourth grader uses subject-verb agreement while writing poetry.

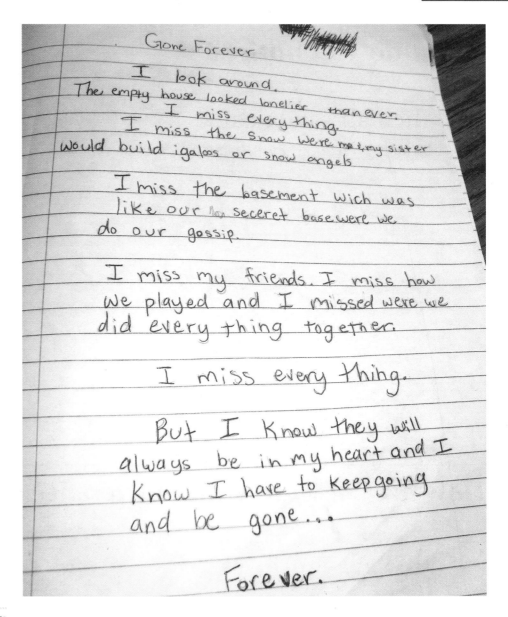

Gone Forever

I look around.
The empty house looked lonelier than ever.
I miss every thing.
I miss the snow were me & my sister
would build igaloos or snow angels

I miss the basement wich was
like our seceret base were we
do our gossip.

I miss my friends. I miss how
we played and I missed were we
did every thing together.

I miss every thing.

But I know they will
always be in my heart and I
know I have to keep going
and be gone...

Forever.

Invitation to Edit

What did we learn about writing from Brendan Wenzel?	
Yes, they all saw a cat.	
What changed? What is the effect of the change?	
Yes, they all seen a cat.	The verb saw *has been changed to* seen. *It doesn't sound right because the verb* seen *always needs another verb to help it out (*have seen, has seen, will have seen, had seen, is seen, was seen, will be seen*).*
Yes they all saw a cat.	*The comma after* yes *has been deleted, which causes less separation after the answer* yes. *When sentences begin with* yes *or* no, *they're usually set off with a comma.*
Yes, they all see a cat.	Saw *has been changed to the present-tense form of the verb* see. *That affects the meaning because it puts the sentence in the present tense, causing it to say that they all see the cat right now.*

What do you notice?

Yes, they all saw a cat.

—Brendan Wenzel, *They All Saw a Cat*

How are they alike and different?

Yes, they all saw a cat.

No, we did not see a dog.

Let's try it out.

Yes, they all saw a cat.

No, we did not see a dog.

Yes, they all saw a cat.

What changed? What is the effect of the change?

Yes, they all seen a cat.

Yes they all saw a cat.

Yes, they all see a cat.

11.2   Everyday Agreement: Nouns and Verbs

Standard   Use singular and plural nouns with matching words in sentences.

Focus Phrase   "I make sure my verbs match my nouns."

Invitation to Notice   Every Saturday after lunch, Mr. Watson goes outside.
Mercy follows him.
They stand in the driveway. Together, they admire Mr. Watson's convertible.
      —Kate DiCamillo, *Mercy Watson Goes for a Ride*

Power Note   *Don't be discouraged if students still begin the conversation with "It starts with a capital letter" or repeat a focus phrase such as "We capitalize names." That's important for a time. Simply decrease the amount of time you spend emphasizing and restating as students' understandings progress. Say, "Yes, and what else?" If no one uses the words* plural *and* singular, *it might be a good time to review. That's academic language students need to discuss noun-and-verb agreement.*

Invitation to Compare and Contrast   Every Saturday after lunch, Mr. Watson goes outside.
Mercy follows him.
They stand in the driveway. Together, they admire Mr. Watson's convertible.

Every Sunday after dinner, my dad goes into the garage and sits in his recliner. I follow him, but he doesn't like it. Together, he and my mom tell me to go play in my room.

Power Note   *Of course our focus is on nouns and verbs agreeing, but in addition, we chose to make our imitation one paragraph rather than three. Students will notice, but may not be able to fully articulate it. We can start or continue our conversation about choice in paragraphing. "Which do you prefer as a reader? Which do you prefer as a writer?" Don't be shy about throwing in terminology about paragraphs if students are interested (for example,* indent, paragraph, tab key*).*

Invitation to Imitate   *Imitate Together*: Invite writers to use interactive, or shared writing to compose a sentence with you.

> Every day after the bell rings, Mr. Anderson takes the roll. We say we're here. Together, we make sure the paperwork is done so we can get to our real work.

Imitate in Pairs: Pairs of students use the model sentences to compose a sentence in which nouns and verbs agree. Say, "Make sure you and your partner can explain how or why your nouns and verbs agree in your sentence."

Invitation to Celebrate   *A Round of How Do You Know?* Student pairs share their sentences aloud or on the document camera if one is available. The authors of the sentence ask for volunteers to explain how the nouns and verbs in their sentences agree or disagree. The sentence writers agree or disagree, and the discussion about how nouns and verbs agree continues.

Invitation to Apply   Writers return to their own recent writing and check for subject-verb agreement with a partner. After they help each other, debrief by asking, "What did you notice? What do you still wonder? What's something you need to pay extra attention to as a writer or reader?"

Invitation to Edit

What did we learn about writing from Kate DiCamillo?	
Every Saturday after lunch, Mr. Watson goes outside. Mercy follows him. They stand in the driveway. Together, they admire Mr. Watson's convertible.	
What changed? What is the effect of the change?	
Every Saturday after lunch, Mr. Watson goes outside. 　Mercy follows him. 　They stands in the driveway. Together, they admire Mr. Watson's convertible.	*The plural verb* stand *has been changed to* stands, *which puts the noun and the verb out of agreement.* They stand *is the pattern. When our subjects and verbs don't match in number, they confuse the reader.*
Every Saturday after lunch, Mr. Watson goes outside. 　Mercy follow him. 　They stand in the driveway. Together, they admire Mr. Watson's convertible.	Mercy *is a singular noun. In the present tense, we add* –s *to regular verbs, so the pattern of singular present tense is* Mercy follows. *When we don't follow the pattern, our readers may be confused.*

What do you notice?

Every Saturday after lunch, Mr. Watson goes outside.
Mercy follows him.
They stand in the driveway. Together, they admire Mr.
Watson's convertible.

—Kate DiCamillo, *Mercy Watson Goes for a Ride*

How are they alike and different?

Every Saturday after lunch, Mr. Watson goes outside.
Mercy follows him.
They stand in the driveway. Together, they admire Mr.
Watson's convertible.

Every Sunday after dinner, my dad goes in the garage
and sits in his recliner. I follow him, but he doesn't
like it. Together, he and my mom tell me to go play in
my room.

Let's try it out.

Every Saturday after lunch, Mr. Watson goes outside.
Mercy follows him.
They stand in the driveway. Together, they admire Mr. Watson's convertible.

Every Sunday after dinner, my dad goes in the garage and sits in his recliner. I follow him, but he doesn't like it. Together, he and my mom tell me to go play in my room.

Every Saturday after lunch, Mr. Watson goes outside.
Mercy follows him.
They stand in the driveway. Together, they admire Mr. Watson's convertible.

What changed? What is the effect of the change?

Every Saturday after lunch, Mr. Watson goes outside.
Mercy follows him.
They stands in the driveway. Together, they admire Mr. Watson's convertible.

Every Saturday after lunch, Mr. Watson goes outside.
Mercy follow him.
They stand in the driveway.
Together, they admire Mr. Watson's convertible.

11.3   Clothes Cloze: Finding Verbs That Agree in Number and Person

Standard   Recognize and correct inappropriate shifts in verb tense.

Focus Phrase   "My verbs agree in number and tense."

Invitation to Notice

Power Note   *We are going to switch things up a bit in this lesson. We want consistency of tense. We want students to sustain tense across a work. We found that using a cloze activity in which we have taken out several verbs works on many fronts.*

First give students this handout and have them fill in the verbs. Ask, "What will we have to think about?" (It has to make sense, and the verbs have to match the nouns. We also have to pay attention to tense—past, present, and future. We usually stay in one tense.) Then repeat the focus phrase: "My verb tenses agree."

Distribute Lesson 11.3 Handout A.

Invitation to Compare and Contrast

Power Note   *Show students the original text the cloze activity was taken from and think about why the author made the choices she did.*

Invitation to Imitate   Students brainstorm places where they like to shop or go. They choose one place and use Handout C to imitate Ami Polonsky's paragraphs from *Threads*.

Invitation to Celebrate   *Read-Around!* Students read their paragraphs to their table partners, listening to each other for noun and verb agreement and consistency of tense.

Lesson 11.3 Handout A

Directions: With your group read the two passages and insert a verb that makes sense in each blank. What do you need to consider?

She spots a display of silky scarves and _____ over to them. "These are awesome!" she _____ over her shoulder. I _____ her and _____ again as I _____ through the scarves.

They _____ thin and soft, and touching them _____ me _____ of spring. I _____ up one with green and turquoise splotches, _____ it around my neck, and _____ in a nearby mirror.

Lesson 11.3 Handout B

Teacher Directions: Before the lesson, photocopy a set of this list of words for each group that will participate in the cloze activity. Cut the list into little rectangles the size of the words. (Don't leave a lot of extra white space around the words. Think magnetic poetry.) Put each cut-up list in its own envelope.

calls	sighed
sift	picked
follow	made
're	spotted
walks	think
think	walked
pick	called
spots	were
makes	looked
tie	followed
look	tied
sigh	sifted

Next, distribute envelopes with precut word lists, one per group. Students need to follow these steps:

- Place all words faceup.
- Sort them into at least two groups.
- Discuss how they sorted the words into categories.
- After discussion, sort by tense (past and present).
- Choose a tense and place the words in the corresponding spaces.
- Discuss why they chose the words they did.

Lesson 11.3 Handout C

She spots a display of silky scarves and walks over to them. "These are awesome!" she calls over her shoulder. I follow her and sigh again as I sift through the scarves.

They're thin and soft, and touching them makes me think of spring. I pick up one with green and turquoise splotches, tie it around my neck, and look in a nearby mirror.

—Ami Polonsky, *Threads*

_____

_____

_____

_____

_____

_____

_____

_____

12

Which Punctuation Comes in Pairs?

One flip-flop won't do you much good if you want to walk on the beach. You need a pair. Like flip-flops, some punctuation marks—quotation marks and parentheses—work only when they come in pairs. These marks appear in pairs to enclose speech or added information, bookending them as they open and close. Put simply, quotation marks and parentheses are like potato chips. You can't have just one.

And quotation marks are the most often used of these indubitable duos. They always come with a buddy, and if they don't, you've left your reader in the dark about where your quotation begins or ends. Most often it's the closing marks that are forgotten, running speech and exposition together. If you open a quote, you must close the quote. Period. These two curly marks ("") show where words are spoken aloud or where an exact quote is extracted from a written work. They show where dialogue or quotations begin (") *and* end (").

Dialogue may literally begin and end with quotation marks, but our lessons will explore the craft of adding dialogue tags as well as looking at how effective dialogue reveals character and moves the narrative along. Watch the power of punctuation pairs drawn from Jeff's middle grade fiction book *Zack Delacruz: Just My Luck* (2016):

> "I don't think I've ever seen so many empty buildings in one place." I gulped. Graffiti covered almost every surface.
>
> "No, sir." Marquis shook his head. I wondered if his stomach twisted like mine.
>
> Janie pointed. "See that green building over there that looks like a slice of key lime pie?"
>
> We nodded. The building—totally lime green from top to bottom—set at a disturbing angle, a giant wedge of danger.
>
> "The one with the windows all bricked in?" Marquis fidgeted with the zipper on his warm-up jacket.
>
> "Yep," Janie said. "We're finally here."

Through the dialogue, we know that Marquis and the narrator Zack are afraid. We also see how dialogue isn't only about the enclosing marks or the words said. Dialogue is surrounded by who's saying what and little shards of setting and action detail, so the dialogue doesn't come off like talking heads.

And who could pass up a sweet pair of parentheses? It's never "paren-thesi." That's not a thing, by the way. (It takes two, baby.) Although quotation marks and parentheses' cousins square brackets ([/]) and curvy braces ({/}) always pair up, we focus only on quotation marks and parentheses since they appear more often in prose. We leave brackets to technical information and braces to computer coding. Even though craft-wise, the three pairs of symbols all contain clarifying information (added detail), the *Chicago Manual of Style* warns that braces and brackets are not interchangeable with parentheses.

Pairs of parentheses are not used as often in fiction as in nonfiction, but they always give the author a way to efficiently add clarifying information (definitions, examples, asides). See what we did there? Here's an aside from Zack, the narrator of the Zack Delacruz series:

> Now my pants only covered the front of my legs and bottom half of the back of my legs—just below my biscuit. (That's what Dad calls butts. Don't ask.)

Lesson Sets:

Which Punctuation Comes in Pairs?

12.1 Nerdy Talk: Quotation Marks

12.2 Judy Moody Ring: Dialogue

12.3 Are They In or Out? Dialogue and End Marks

12.4 Insects (Gross!): Parentheses (Provide Extra Information)

12.1   Nerdy Talk: Quotation Marks

Standard   Identify that quotation marks indicate dialogue.

Focus Phrase   "I use quotation marks to show people talking."

Invitation to Notice   "Trying to be cool is exhausting," said the new bird.
—Aaron Reynolds, *Nerdy Birdy*

Power Note   *Our main focus is that the quotation marks show talking. Everything else is gravy for our youngest writers. Remember to honor, name, and extend responses. "Yes, after the quotation mark, writers identify who's talking. We call that a dialogue tag. We use dialogue tags to identify who's speaking."*

Invitation to Compare and Contrast   "Trying to be cool is exhausting," said the new bird.
"Trying to remember everyone's name is exhausting," said the new student.

Power Note   *Exhausting may be a big word, but young writers with a flair for the dramatic love using it. Remember to repeat the focus phrase, "I use quotation marks to show people talking."*

Invitation to Imitate   Students use interactive writing to compose an imitation of something said aloud and tagged with a speaker.

Invitation to Apply and Celebrate   TEXTploring: Students explore at least three texts around the room and see if dialogue is included. After thumbing through each text, they put a sticky note on it with either *Yes* or *No*. (See Figure 12.1.)

Figure 12.1
A first grader determines where quotation marks are used in this Big Book from shared reading.

Invitation to Edit

What did we learn about writing from Aaron Reynolds?	
"Trying to be cool is exhausting," said the new bird.	
What changed? What is the effect of the change?	
"Trying to be cool is exhausting, said the new bird.	*The end quotation mark is gone. This doesn't help readers see when the talking ends.*
"Trying to be cool is exhausting," the new bird said.	*Said has been moved from the front of the dialogue tag or identifier to the end. It doesn't change the meaning. Sometimes writers put the identifier before said and sometimes they put it after.*
Trying to be cool is exhausting," said the new bird.	*The opening quotation mark is missing, so readers won't know which words are being spoken aloud.*

What do you notice?

"Trying to be cool is exhausting," said the new bird.
—Aaron Reynolds, *Nerdy Birdy*

How are they alike and different?

"Trying to be cool is exhausting," said the new bird.

"Trying to remember everyone's name is exhausting," said the new student.

Let's try it out.

"Trying to be cool is exhausting," said the new bird.

"Trying to remember everyone's name is exhausting," said the new student.

"Trying to be cool is exhausting," said the new bird.

What changed? What is the effect of the change?

"Trying to be cool is exhausting, said the new bird.

"Trying to be cool is exhausting," the new bird said.

Trying to be cool is exhausting," said the new bird.

12.2 Judy Moody Ring: Dialogue

Standard Use commas and quotation marks in dialogue.

Focus Phrase "I open and close words spoken aloud with quotation marks."

Invitation to Notice All morning, Judy raised her mood-ring hand, even when she didn't know the answer.

Even Mr. Todd noticed the ring. "What's that you've got there?" he asked Judy.

"A mood ring," Judy said. "It predicts stuff. Like what mood you're in."

"Very nice," said Mr. Todd. "Let's hope everybody's in the mood for the math test."

—Megan McDonald, *Judy Moody Predicts the Future*

Power Note *Students will note a lot of dialogue conventions; begin a list on chart paper. However, give the most time to the opening and closing quotation marks, repeating the focus phrase, "I open and close words spoken aloud with quotation marks."*

Invitation to Compare and Contrast All morning, Judy raised her mood-ring hand, even when she didn't know the answer.

Even Mr. Todd noticed the ring. "What's that you've got there?" he asked Judy.

"A mood ring," Judy said. "It predicts stuff. Like what mood you're in."

"Very nice," said Mr. Todd. "Let's hope everybody's in the mood for the math test."

Power Note *The next day, display the excerpt from* Judy Moody Predicts the Future *again. Compare and contrast sentences that use dialogue with those that don't. Also discuss how dialogue is tagged. List students' noticings about dialogue, creating a list of dialogue patterns. With your guidance as the recorder of responses, students generate a list like the one shown in Figure 12.2.*

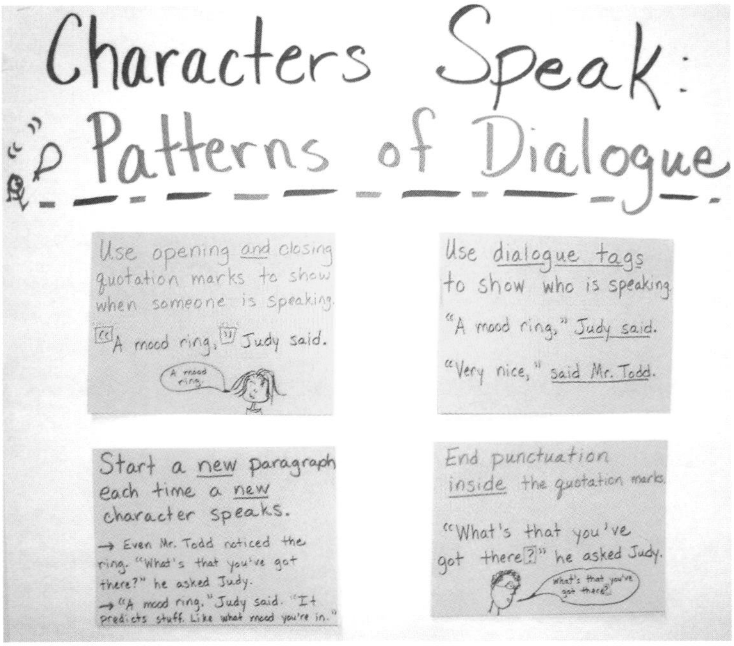

Characters Speak: Patterns of Dialogue

- Use opening and closing quotation marks to show when someone is speaking aloud (Figure 12.2, top left).
- Use dialogue tags to show who is speaking (Figure 12.2, top right).
- Start a new paragraph each time a new character speaks (Figure 12.2, bottom left).
- End punctuation goes inside the quotation marks (Figure 12.2, bottom right).

Figure 12.2 Characters speak chart, part 1

Invitation to Imitate   *Imitate Together*: Invite writers to compose a few sentences of dialogue, focusing on opening and closing quotes around words spoken aloud. Writers may use a class-generated list to refine their dialogue.

Imitate in Pairs: Students work in pairs the next day or use the model to create their own sentence.

Invitation to Celebrate   *Dialogue Drama*: Pairs rehearse and perform dialogue.

Invitation to Apply   Writers dig out an old narrative from their writing folder or writer's notebook. Did they use dialogue? Do they need to make any changes? What do they know now that they didn't know then?

Invitation to Edit

What did we learn about writing from Megan McDonald?	
Even Mr. Todd noticed the ring. "What's that you've got there?" he asked Judy. "A mood ring," Judy said. "It predicts stuff. Like what mood you're in."	
What changed? What is the effect of the change?	
Even Mr. Todd noticed the ring. "What's that you've got there? he asked Judy. "A mood ring," Judy said. "It predicts stuff. Like what mood you're in."	*In the first paragraph, when Mr. Todd is talking, the opening quotation mark is there, but the closing one isn't. We need the closing quotation mark to know when Mr. Todd stops talking aloud.*
Even Mr. Todd noticed the ring. "What's that you've got there?" he asked Judy. "A mood ring," Judy said. It predicts stuff. Like what mood you're in."	*In the second paragraph, after the dialogue tag* Judy said, *Judy starts speaking again, but the opening quotation mark that starts her continued dialogue has been deleted. Quotation marks come in pairs, and one of the pair is missing.*

What do you notice?

All morning, Judy raised her mood-ring hand, even when she didn't know the answer.

Even Mr. Todd noticed the ring. "What's that you've got there?" he asked Judy.

"A mood ring," Judy said. "It predicts stuff. Like what mood you're in."

"Very nice," said Mr. Todd. "Let's hope everybody's in the mood for the math test."

—Megan McDonald, *Judy Moody Predicts the Future*

How are they alike and different?

Look at the sentences that use dialogue and the sentences that don't use dialogue.

All morning, Judy raised her mood-ring hand, even when she didn't know the answer.

Even Mr. Todd noticed the ring. "What's that you've got there?" he asked Judy.

"A mood ring," Judy said. "It predicts stuff. Like what mood you're in."

"Very nice," said Mr. Todd. "Let's hope everybody's in the mood for the math test."

Let's try it out.

All morning, Judy raised her mood-ring hand, even when she didn't know the answer.

Even Mr. Todd noticed the ring. "What's that you've got there?" he asked Judy.

"A mood ring," Judy said. "It predicts stuff. Like what mood you're in."

"Very nice," said Mr. Todd. "Let's hope everybody's in the mood for the math test."

Even Mr. Todd noticed the ring. "What's that you've got there?" he asked Judy.

"A mood ring," Judy said. "It predicts stuff. Like what mood you're in."

What changed? What is the effect of the change?

Even Mr. Todd noticed the ring. "What's that you've got there? he asked Judy.

"A mood ring," Judy said. "It predicts stuff. Like what mood you're in."

Even Mr. Todd noticed the ring. "What's that you've got there?" he asked Judy.

"A mood ring," Judy said. It predicts stuff. Like what mood you're in."

12.3 Are They In or Out? Dialogue and End Marks

Standard	Use punctuation to show dialogue (quotation marks, commas, and end marks).
Focus Phrases	"I open and close words spoken aloud with quotation marks." "I set off dialogue tags with punctuation." "I place end punctuation inside quotation marks."
Invitation to Notice	At this point, there was a long silence. The three of them stared out at Lake Clara. The water glittered and sighed.

    "There's a lady who drowned in this lake," said Raymie. "Her name was Clara Wingtip."

    "So?" said Beverly.

    "She haunts it," said Raymie. "In my father's office, there's a photo of the lake from the air, and you can see Clara Wingtip's shadow under the water."

    Beverly snorted. "I don't believe in fairy tales."

    "You can hear her weeping sometimes," said Raymie. "That's what they say."

    "Really?" said Louisiana. She arranged her barrettes and put her hair behind one ear and leaned in toward the lake. "Oh," she said. "I hear it. I hear the weeping."

    Beverly snorted.

    Raymie listened.

    She heard weeping, too.

    —Kate DiCamillo, *Raymie Nightingale*

Power Note *Read aloud the entire passage and have students respond orally with thoughts or connections to it. After they respond to the text, have students freewrite about something that sticks with them: a disagreement with a friend, a haunted place or superstition, or being at a lake or body of water with friends.*

Invitation to Compare and Contrast

Power Note *The next day, display the entire excerpt from* Raymie Nightingale *again. For a compare-and-contrast discussion and extension of the question "What do you notice?" have students compare and contrast sentences that use dialogue with those that don't, including how dialogue is tagged and broken up, and so on. Create a list of dialogue patterns from anything the students note about dialogue.*

With your guidance as the recorder of responses, students will generate a list like this. (Figure 12.3)

Figure 12.3
This chart began in Lesson 12.2 and we added to it in this lesson. However, the same chart can be created from the beginning with this lesson.

- Use opening and closing quotation marks to show when someone is speaking aloud (Figure 12.3, top row, left column).
- Use dialogue tags to show who is speaking (Figure 12.3, top row, right column).
- Start a new paragraph each time a new character speaks (Figure 12.3, second row, left column).
- End punctuation goes inside quotation marks (Figure 12.3, second row, right column).
- If a dialogue tag appears after the dialogue, separate the dialogue from the tag with a comma if what's being said is a statement. Always use a question mark if it's a question and an exclamation mark to indicate strong feeling or shouting (Figure 12.3, third row).
- Dialogue can be split by inserting a dialogue tag in the middle. (Figure 12.3, bottom, middle):

"You can hear her weeping sometimes," said Raymie. "That's what they say."

"Really?" said Louisiana. She arranged her barrettes and put her hair behind one ear and leaned in toward the lake. "Oh," she said. "I hear it. I hear the weeping."

Invitation to Imitate	*Imitate Independently*: Students use the model and the class-generated list to edit and revise their freewrite responses.
Invitation to Celebrate	Writers read the dialogue they created to a small group.
Invitation to Apply	*Recording Session*: Students reread their dialogue several times, rehearsing it, and then perform it using voices. If you have a way for students to record their voices, this can add a layer of audience awareness and excitement to make "the script" just right.

Invitation to Edit

What did we learn about writing from Kate DiCamillo?	
"You can hear her weeping sometimes," said Raymie. "That's what they say."	
What changed? What is the effect of the change?	
"You can hear her weeping sometimes" said Raymie. "That's what they say."	*The comma after the first line of dialogue has been deleted. When the comma or end punctuation doesn't end the talking, it makes it harder to read.*
"You can hear her weeping sometimes," Raymie said. "That's what they say."	*The* said *comes after the speaker's name instead of before it, which doesn't change the meaning. "Is there a different effect when* said *is in a different place?" Some prefer the noun to come first.*
"You can hear her weeping sometimes," said Raymie. "That's what they say.	*The closing quotation mark is missing from the end of the second line of dialogue. It's as important as the period. It shows where the talking aloud stops.*

What do you notice?

At this point, there was a long silence. The three of them stared out at Lake Clara. The water glittered and sighed.

"There's a lady who drowned in this lake," said Raymie. "Her name was Clara Wingtip."

"So?" said Beverly.

"She haunts it," said Raymie. "In my father's office, there's a photo of the lake from the air, and you can see Clara Wingtip's shadow under the water."

Beverly snorted. "I don't believe in fairy tales."

"You can hear her weeping sometimes," said Raymie. "That's what they say."

"Really?" said Louisiana. She arranged her barrettes and put her hair behind one ear and leaned in toward the lake. "Oh," she said. "I hear it. I hear the weeping."

Beverly snorted.

Raymie listened.

She heard weeping, too.

—Kate DiCamillo, *Raymie Nightingale*

How are they alike and different?

Let's try it out.

At this point, there was a long silence. The three of them stared out at Lake Clara. The water glittered and sighed.

"There's a lady who drowned in this lake," said Raymie. "Her name was Clara Wingtip."

"So?" said Beverly.

"She haunts it," said Raymie. "In my father's office, there's a photo of the lake from the air, and you can see Clara Wingtip's shadow under the water."

Beverly snorted. "I don't believe in fairy tales."

"You can hear her weeping sometimes," said Raymie. "That's what they say."

"Really?" said Louisiana. She arranged her barrettes and put her hair behind one ear and leaned in toward the lake. "Oh," she said. "I hear it. I hear the weeping."

Beverly snorted.

Raymie listened.

She heard weeping, too.

—Kate DiCamillo, *Raymie Nightingale*

"You can hear her weeping sometimes," said Raymie. "That's what they say."

What changed? What is the effect of the change?

"You can hear her weeping sometimes" said Raymie. "That's what they say."

"You can hear her weeping sometimes," Raymie said. "That's what they say."

"You can hear her weeping sometimes," said Raymie. "That's what they say.

When elementary students think about quotations, they think dialogue. But there is a bit more. When writing research text, for example, writers need a way to show when they are quoting directly from a written work, such as a book or article. Sometimes we want the primary source's exact words. To do this we need to enclose the exact words we're extracting from the written work in quotation marks. Note how Robert Byrd encloses a quote from another work in his book *Electric Ben* (2012):

> Benjamin Franklin, Thomas Jefferson, John Adams, Roger Sherman, and Robert Livingston met to draft the Declaration of Independence. "I wish I had written it myself," Franklin noted. Jefferson had written, "We hold these truths to be sacred and undeniable," in his draft. Franklin changed the wording to, "We hold these truths to be self-evident," deeming this more logical.

When students are ready, start collecting works like this and studying how quotes are embedded in essay and explanatory texts they write.

Some punctuation marks—like commas and dashes—that often stand on their own can come in pairs when something needs to be enclosed in the middle of a sentence. For example, commas, which often appear by themselves, can pair up, too, especially when a writer inserts a thought or idea into the middle of his or her sentence.

> Later, in math class, Janie passed a note.
> —Jeff Anderson, *Zack Delacruz: Just My Luck*

> Here, he believed, anything could be accomplished.
> —Robert Byrd, *Electric Ben*

Same goes for dashes when they—like the comma—are enclosing a clause or phrase. In *Just Being Audrey*, author Margaret Cardillo interrupts her sentence with the definition of a French term:

> Audrey struggled with e*n pointe*—dancing on her toes—but she loved a challenge.

And in Robert Byrd's *Electric Ben*, the author clarifies what he means by *the oldest* in the situation about which he writes:

> Benjamin Franklin—then seventy—was the oldest.

We tell students to think of using enclosing marks this way: if the words enclosed could be lifted out by their handles—two dashes or two commas—the remaining words still make up a sentence, and the meaning of the sentence wouldn't change, you set the words off with both marks. For example, removing the words enclosed by dashes in Byrd's sentence, above, still leaves us with a complete sentence and doesn't change its meaning: *Benjamin Franklin was the oldest.* Sometimes, as Strunk and White explain in the *Elements of Style* (2000), the information is so necessary for the sentence, we don't need to enclose the information with commas or dashes. (*People **who live in glass houses** shouldn't throw stones.*)

12.4   Insects (Gross!): Parentheses (Provide Extra Information)

Standard	Use parentheses to enclose clarifying information.
Focus Phrase	"Parentheses help me add information efficiently."
Invitation to Notice	At some point in its life cycle, an insect has three parts to its body (head, thorax, abdomen) and six jointed legs. —Sarah Albee, *Bugged: How Insects Changed History*
Power Note	*When students mention the possessive pronoun its, it's worth it to write on the board its = ownership and it's = it is. When students mention parentheses, remember to ask, "What are the parentheses doing when you read the text aloud and when you read it with just your eyes?" Discuss the relationship between what's in the parentheses and what's in the sentence. "Why do you think a writer might use them?" At conversation's end, ask, "Who can predict the mistake most often made with parentheses?" (As with quotation marks, writers forget to close them once they're opened.)*
Invitation to Compare and Contrast	At some point in its life cycle, an insect has three parts to its body (head, thorax, abdomen) and six jointed legs. At some point in their lives, kids go through at least three stages of school (elementary, middle, and high school).
Power Note	*When students notice something with a function, like a comma or a pair of parentheses, don't forget to ask, "What's that set of parentheses doing when I read the text out loud? What's that set of parentheses doing when I read it with just my eyes?" Function is key.*
Invitation to Imitate	*Imitate Independently*: Students use the model sentences to create their own sentences, using parentheses to add information for clarification (such as definitions or examples).
Power Note	*If students ask to deviate from the model, say, "Why don't you try your idea and see what happens?"*
Invitation to Celebrate	Students share their sentences aloud, reading them twice.
Invitation to Apply	*Nonfiction Parentheses Hunt and List*: Put students in groups of three. Have them investigate an animal and write one to three sentences about what they learn, using at least one list. (See Figure 12.4.)

Gorillas eat mainly plants (leaves, vines, stems) and fruit. Mountain gorillas also eat worms and snails. (yuck!)

Figure 12.4
An example of nonfiction writing using parentheses

Invitation to Edit

What did we learn about writing from Sarah Albee?	
At some point in its life cycle, an insect has three parts to its body (head, thorax, abdomen) and six jointed legs.	
What changed? What is the effect of the change?	
At some point in its life cycle, an insect has three parts to its body and six jointed legs.	*The parentheses and the added information are gone, leaving the reader without the clarity of an insect's three parts.*
At some point in its life cycle, an insect has three parts to its body (head, thorax, abdomen and six jointed legs.	*The closing parenthesis (second one) is gone. This affects the meaning, because in this structure, it never ends. The closing parenthesis has the effect of containing or stopping the clarification.*
At some point in its life cycle, an insect has three parts to its body (head thorax, abdomen) and six jointed legs.	*The comma between* head *and* thorax *has been deleted. Without the comma's separation, it seems like there is such a thing as a "head thorax."*

What do you notice?

At some point in its life cycle, an insect has three parts to its body (head, thorax, abdomen) and six jointed legs.

—Sarah Albee, *Bugged: How Insects Changed History*

How are they alike and different?

At some point in its life cycle, an insect has three parts to its body (head, thorax, abdomen) and six jointed legs.

At some point in their lives, kids go through at least three stages of school (elementary, middle, and high school).

Let's try it out.

At some point in its life cycle, an insect has three parts to its body (head, thorax, abdomen) and six jointed legs.

At some point in their lives, kids go through at least three stages of school (elementary, middle, and high school).

At some point in its life cycle, an insect has three parts to its body (head, thorax, abdomen) and six jointed legs.

What changed? What is the effect of the change?

At some point in its life cycle, an insect has three parts to its body and six jointed legs.

At some point in its life cycle, an insect has three parts to its body (head, thorax, abdomen and six jointed legs.

At some point in its life cycle, an insect has three parts to its body (head thorax, abdomen) and six jointed legs.

The Power of Details

Life is so rich, if you can write down the real details of the way things were and are, you hardly need anything else.
—Natalie Goldberg

The most effective and efficient way to add detail to our writing is to carefully choose our nouns and verbs. A concrete noun and a just-right verb can communicate most everything a writer needs to say. But often readers need more. Readers crave detail to answer their questions, to fill in the missing pieces.

A multitude of conventional structures beyond nouns and verbs have the power to describe in deeper detail. What are the structures of detail that writers need at their fingertips?

- Adjectives
- Adverbs
- Prepositions

These structures give us ways to stylistically spice up our writing with details, to sweeten our prose with the plumpness of size, location, color, and degree.

You ask, "How many people are coming to dinner?" so you know how much to prepare. Are *four* people coming or are *eight* people coming? Those nifty numbers in the previous sentence are adjectives, telling how many *people*. Technically the adjectives modify the noun *people*, clarifying the exact number. *People*, a frequently used collective noun, sometimes needs an adjective to explain **what kind of people** (nice ones, of course) or **how many people**. Adjectives fit that bill because they modify nouns by explaining what kind and how many.

Instead of modifying nouns, adverbs can modify verbs, adjectives, and other adverbs. Most often adverbs answer the question How? For example, in Rebecca Stead's Newbery Medal winner, *When You Reach Me*, she uses the word quickly to show how—the intensity or degree with which she turned:

I *quickly* **turned** my back on him, worried that he might recognize me and come over.

Why isn't *quickly* considered time? We like to think it's more about *how* the action occurred, but it doesn't matter: adverbs can both modify verbs and convey time. It isn't about the label, is it? Like *quickly*, many adverbs end in *-ly*, but some don't. *Sometimes*, we need more information in our sentence than even a noun, verb, or adjective can provide. In the previous sentence, the adverb *sometimes* tells *when* (in a how-ish or frequency way) we need more information.

Not all the time.

Sometimes.

Now you know how it works: *sometimes* you need *-ly* and *often* you don't. *Soon*, or perhaps *someday*, it will make sense. (If you didn't catch it, all the words in italics are *adverbs*.)

In the "The Power of Details" section, we'll explore the following structures:

- What Do Adjectives Do?
- What Do Comparatives and Superlatives Do?
- What Do Adverbs Do?
- What Do Prepositions Do?

"Oh my Lord! I don't have time to explain every little detail."
—Gertie, from Kate Beasley's *Gertie's Leap to Greatness*

13

What Do Adjectives Do?

To begin the study of adjectives with young writers, we define them by the three basic questions they answer:

- *What kind?*
- *How many?*
- *Which one?*

In short, writers use adjectives to narrow the field from everything to something particular. For example, if someone said, "Please go get the drinks out of my car," and you'd never seen her car, you'd ask, "Which car?" Or you might ask, "What kind of drinks?" or "How many drinks do you want?" Once these questions are answered, the field has been narrowed. Her car no longer looks like all the other cars in the parking lot, and there is no question how many or which drinks to bring. That's how adjectives work for people, who just happen to be writers and readers, too: adjectives narrow or limit.

It's easy to spew abstract terms when explaining grammar. But telling primary or intermediate writers to add adjectives to *narrow* or *limit* a noun would only confuse them. Even saying, "Adjectives *describe*" is abstract. It may be true that adjectives describe, but how does that nugget of information delineate adjectives from any other part of speech? Doesn't all language describe? Don't specific nouns and verbs give pictures to our readers as well? Though adjectives do describe, we begin with the basics, what's easiest for young writers to grasp:

Adjectives tell what kind and how many. (See Figure 13.1.)

To communicate the precise function of a part of speech in a way that makes sense, we show young writers what adjectives do in writing and reading.

How many?
three   several
a   an

What kind?
peaceful   weird
green   honest
funny   bright

Adjectives
tell more about nouns

Which one?
the
this
that

Figure 13.1 Adjectives anchor chart

245

And the best way to show adjectives at work is to read a text which uses them, so we lift a few sentences with adjectives for students to study. If children don't see adjectives, we rewrite the sentences without them, like on the far-right column in this chart of excerpts from Jen Bryant's *Six Dots*. Looking at both versions, we ask students, "What changed?" Students compare and contrast the original version containing adjectives with the revised version without them.

Adjectives at Work in Jen Bryant's *Six Dots: A Story of Young Louis Braille*		
Adjectives Answer Questions	**Now You See It!**	**Now You Don't**
How many?	*Six Dots*	*Dots*
What kind?	My hard bed was in a damp, crowded room.	My bed was in a room.
What kind?	In Papa's hands, the rough leather strips became smooth and useful.	In hands, the strips became.

Power Note   *In Bryant's third sentence, the word* Papa's *is possessive, but it's functioning as an adjective.*

The now-you-see-it-now-you-don't method comes in handy when teaching any author move that readers aren't noticing. Take out the move, and compare and contrast the sentences with and without it. This helps students see what adjectives or any move will do.

Lesson Sets:

What Do Adjectives Do?

13.1   What Kind of Chimpanzee? Adjectives Answer Questions
13.2   Good Enough: Adjectives Before Nouns
13.3   Ink a Link: Using Adjectives After the Verb
13.4   Photographic Memory: Crafting Adjectives
13.5   The Describing Verb: Showing an Action or Use with *-ing* Adjectives

Adjectives are consorts, never attending a party alone, preferring to hook themselves on the arm of a sturdy noun. Adjectives embellish their companions, defining the qualities of the person, place, or thing they're escorting, and sharing relevant details whenever possible.
  –Constance Hale, *Sin and Syntax*

13.1　　What Kind of Chimpanzee? Adjectives Answer Questions

Standard	Use and understand adjectives, including descriptive adjectives and articles.
Focus Phrase	"I use adjectives to tell what kind and how many."
Invitation to Notice	Jane had a stuffed toy chimpanzee named Jubilee. 　　　—Patrick McDonnell, *Me . . . Jane*

Power Note　*Students may notice the past tense of the irregular verb had and the capital Js, but they may not mention the adjectives. If that happens, apply the now-you-see-it, now-you-don't approach to conventions. Show them McDonnell's original sentence with adjectives, and then delete both adjectives in a revised version: Jane had a chimpanzee named Jubilee. (See Figure 13.2.) Ask students, "How does this change the meaning of the sentence?" Revise the sentence with only one adjective: Jane had a stuffed chimpanzee named Jubilee. Then ask students, "How is this different?" The students compare and contrast the sentences side by side. Eventually they'll say something about how it tells/doesn't tell what kind of chimpanzee Jubilee is, or how this version reads as if Jubilee were a taxidermic chimpanzee hanging above the fireplace. Then rewrite the sentence using only the other adjective—Jane had a toy chimpanzee named Jubilee—and continue the conversation until you say the focus phrase, "I use adjectives to tell what kind and how many." (And yes, the article tells us how many.)(See Figure 13.2.)*

Figure 13.2
Now you see it.

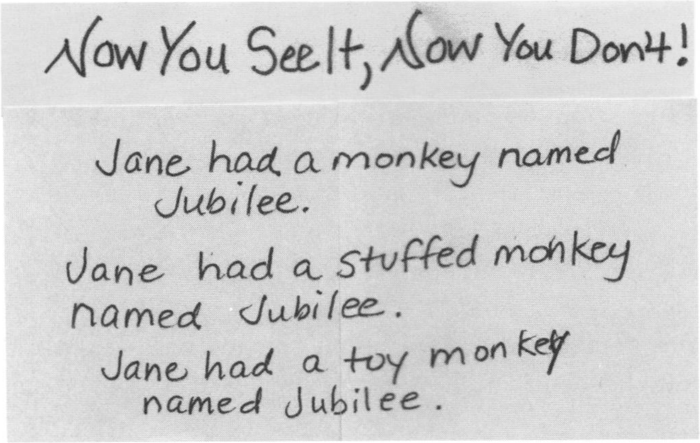

Invitation to Compare and Contrast　Jane had a stuffed toy chimpanzee named Jubilee.
I have a German shepherd named Paisley.

Power Note　*Usually a student asks, "Why isn't shepherd capitalized when German is?" Students may want to know that we don't capitalize dog breeds in prose. German is capitalized only because its root is the proper noun Germany. If there were an Australian shepherd, Australian would be capitalized, but shepherd wouldn't because it doesn't come from a proper noun. The same is true for Mexican pottery, Spanish oak, and Italian food. Technically, these capitalized words are called proper adjectives because they're adjectives telling what kind and their origins are proper nouns. In this case, the proper nouns are a country or nationality. (See Chapter 4's capitalization Lesson 4.7, "Honor Everyone's Heritage: Capitalizing Nationalities and Languages" for more information.)*

Invitation to Imitate　*Imitate Together*: Invite writers to use interactive or shared writing to compose a sentence with you.

Our class has a hamster named Mr. Burrito.

Imitate Independently: Writers compose their own sentences about something they *have* or *had*, using adjectives to tell what kind and how many.

Invitation to Celebrate

Figure 13.3
Also add adjectives found in the wild—from books they're reading or in texts found in other subject areas.

Fun Fact: The articles *an* and *a* originate from the Old English Anglian dialect meaning "*one.*"

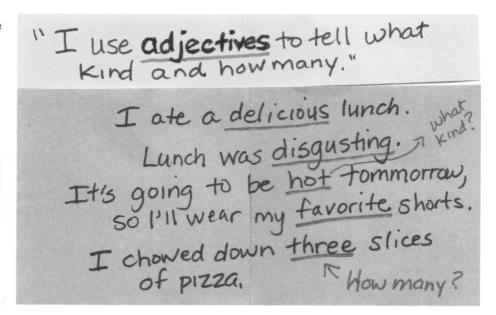

"I use **adjectives** to tell what kind and how many."

I ate a *delicious* lunch.
Lunch was *disgusting*. ↗ what kind?
It's going to be *hot* tommorrow, so I'll wear my *favorite* shorts.
I chowed down *three* slices of pizza.   ↖ How many?

Power Note   *Of course, students reading aloud their imitations is always a celebration, but sometimes we'll want to extend the celebration and the learning by capturing the convention on a wall chart. The focus phrase can be written across the top, and examples of the convention in action will keep the concept alive and ripe for clarification.*

Invitation to Apply   Have student pairs write a sentence or two about science or math work, using an adjective to tell what kind and how many.

Invitation to Edit

What did we learn about writing from Patrick McDonnell?	
Jane had a stuffed toy chimpanzee named Jubilee.	
What changed? What is the effect of the change?	
Jane has a stuffed toy chimpanzee named Jubilee.	*The past-tense verb* had *was changed to* has, *meaning that Jane still has Jubilee in the present rather than that she had Jubilee in the past. The sentence is no longer true.*
Jane had a toy chimpanzee named Jubilee.	*The adjective* stuffed *was deleted, affecting the picture in the reader's mind. Now the reader could be picturing Jubilee as small and plastic.*
Jane had a stuffed chimpanzee named Jubilee.	*The word* toy *has been deleted, which may cause some confusion about what kind of stuffed chimpanzee Jane had. Many students picture a taxidermic chimpanzee with this lone adjective.*

Tip: #AdjectiveProblems: An Overabundance of Adjectives

After your first adjectives lesson (or any convention lesson, really), expect young writers to overuse them. Allow this at first, because it is part of gaining mastery and fluency. But be careful of overcelebrating the overuse of adjectives. We don't want to encourage adjective strings (lists of adjectives). Nouns rarely need more than one adjective. As a long-term goal, we will help students see that adjective strings do not make our writing stronger—especially when a more specific noun or verb could do the job better. Our goal is not this:

> The long, green, pretty, excellent snake scared the frightened, horrified, and screaming children.

But rather:

> The slippery green snake startled the children.

See? Just the right verb, *startled*, can do the work of three adjectives. Furthermore, not every noun needs an adjective, especially if we choose a specific one (*collie* versus *dog*, *toddler* versus *kid*, *minivan* versus *car*). Writers choose the right adjectives for the job. In most cases, fewer adjectives can be stronger than a list of adjectives.

When students are ready to pare down their use of adjectives, compare their adjective strings to how authors use adjectives in the books in your classroom. Do they use lots of strings? If they don't, maybe we should consider that fact. That's the pattern of adjective use. This comes over time. Trust the process by allowing overuse without encouraging it.

Tip: Articles as Adjectives: *A*, *An*, and *The*

Note how Patrick McDonnell uses the article *a* to tell how many chimpanzees in the sentence from *Me . . . Jane*. It's not that we want writers to memorize the term *articles* as much as we want them to see how the articles *a* and *an* may help answer the question of how many.

When the article *the* precedes a particular noun, plural or singular, one or many, it defines which one(s). (See the chart for more information.) Adding the article *the* into the mix allows us to add one more phrase to our adjective focus phrase:

> "I use adjectives to tell what kind, how many, and which one(s)."

Sometimes articles are called limiting adjectives. (Remember, adjectives limit or narrow by telling what kind and how many.) Articles are also included under the term *determiners* as well. They determine which one or how many. Does all this abstract terminology make your head spin? It's easy to imagine how dropping abstract terms like this would scare eight-year-olds. They need to use *a, an,* and *the*, not memorize the terminology surrounding them. Teach the information in the chart for use in the context of writing and reading, and move forward.

We Are One: Articles as Adjectives
A, *An*, and *The*

Article	Mentor Text	Extensions
A	I wish I could be smart like a fox. —Eric Carle, *The Mixed-Up Chameleon*	Compare and contrast the use of *a* and *an* in Carle's and Breen's sentences. Ask students, "How are *a* and *an* alike and different?"
An	"I'm building an airplane," she told them. —Steve Breen, *Violet the Pilot*	*A* and *an* work the same way, telling how many. In English we use *an* when the word following it starts with a vowel sound and *a* when the word that follows it begins with a consonant sound.
The	At home, Wemberly worried about the tree in the front yard. —Kevin Henkes, *Wemberly Worried* Jimmy McClean walked among the buffalo berry thickets along the Smoking Earth River. —Joseph Marshall III, *In the Footsteps of Crazy Horse*	Use the article *the* to identify a particular noun (person, place, thing, or idea), singular or plural, one or many. The two pronunciations of *the* throw some readers for a loop. Say "thee" if the next word starts with a vowel sound. Say "thuh" if the next word starts with a consonant sound.

What do you notice?

Jane had a stuffed toy chimpanzee named Jubilee.
—Patrick McDonnell, *Me . . . Jane*

How are they alike and different?

Jane had a stuffed toy chimpanzee named Jubilee.

I have a German shepherd named Paisley.

Let's try it out.

Jane had a stuffed toy chimpanzee named Jubilee.

I have a German shepherd named Paisley.

Jane had a stuffed toy chimpanzee named Jubilee.

What changed? What is the effect of the change?

Jane has a stuffed toy chimpanzee named Jubilee.

Jane had a toy chimpanzee named Jubilee.

Jane had a stuffed chimpanzee named Jubilee.

13.2   Good Enough: Adjectives Before Nouns

Standard   Use and understand descriptive adjectives.

Focus Phrase   "I usually place adjectives before nouns to tell what kind or how many."

Invitation to Notice   Because I am a dog with a good nose and fine ears, I can hear that he is not breathing easily.
   —Patricia MacLachlan, *The Poet's Dog*

Power Note   *Some teachers react to this sentence from Newbery Medal–winning author Patricia MacLachlan with something like, "I don't let my kids use plain adjectives like* good *and* fine.*" If you're thinking something along those lines, consider two things:*

- *Be careful about taking words away from young writers. This can make drafting more difficult and sets a tone of right and wrong, acceptable versus unacceptable.*
- *This lesson's intention is to help students see where adjectives are usually placed and what they do. These words won't distract learners from function, but will set them up to use their own adjectives. Award-winning writers for children and adults use plain adjectives. Why would we ask something of our young writers that we don't ask from professional writers?*

Invitation to Compare and Contrast   Because I am a dog with a good nose and fine ears, I can hear that he is not breathing easily.
Because I am a kid with an old baseball and worn glove, I can see her hitting a home run easily.

Power Note   *This time our imitation deviates from the original in the second part of the sentence. We did this to emphasize our goal of making sense. We try to follow the author's original pattern, but if making sense dictates something different, making sense wins.*

Invitation to Imitate   *Imitate Together*: Invite writers to use paired writing to compose a sentence, using adjectives before nouns. (See Figure 13.4.)

Figure 13.4
Fourth graders work in pairs to create an imitation of the sentence.

Imitate Independently: Students use the model to create their own sentence, using adjectives before nouns.

Invitation to Celebrate

Adjectives Before Nouns: Create a class book either in print or digitally that demonstrates how adjectives work to clarify nouns. In addition to becoming part of the class library, this *Adjectives Before Nouns* book can be shared with others outside the classroom. Students might take it home and read it to someone, or the class might share it with a younger classroom, the principal, the librarian, a volunteer, or a literacy coach. Allow students to be creative. As a class, pick a theme, topic, or genre.

Invitation to Apply

How Many Times? In math word problems, students highlight all the number adjectives that tell "how many" with a crayon, map pencil, or highlighter. Throughout the day, have them continue to highlight the use of number adjectives, emphasizing them whenever they're spoken aloud: "Everybody does it at least *one* time." "I've told you *two* times to shout only the number adjective. How *many* times do I have to repeat myself? *Three* times? *Four* times?"

Invitation to Edit

What did we learn about writing from Patricia MacLachlan?	
Because I am a dog with a good nose and fine ears, I can hear that he is not breathing easily.	
What changed? What is the effect of the change?	
Because I am a dog with a good nose and fine ears, i can hear that he is not breathing easily.	The pronoun I is not capitalized. When we don't capitalize the pronoun I, it gets lost on the page. "I always capitalize the pronoun I."
Because I am a dog with a good nose and ears, I can hear that he is not breathing easily.	One of the adjectives (fine) is deleted. Although the sentence still makes sense, a bit of the detail is no longer there, creating a less vivid image.
Because I am a dog with a good nose and fine ears I can hear that he is not breathing easily.	The comma is deleted, causing the sentence parts to run together. A comma separates a dependent clause from the rest of the sentence, which makes it easier for the reader to chunk and know what goes together.

What do you notice?

Because I am a dog with a good nose and fine ears, I can hear that he is not breathing easily.

—Patricia MacLachlan, *The Poet's Dog*

How are they alike and different?

Because I am a dog with a good nose and fine ears, I can hear that he is not breathing easily.

Because I am a kid with an old baseball and worn glove, I can see her hitting a home run easily.

Let's try it out.

Because I am a dog with a good nose and fine ears, I can hear that he is not breathing easily.

Because I am a kid with an old baseball and worn glove, I can see her hitting a home run easily.

Because I am a dog with a good nose and fine ears, I can hear that he is not breathing easily.

What changed? What is the effect of the change?

Because I am a dog with a good nose and fine ears, i can hear that he is not breathing easily.

Because I am a dog with a good nose and ears, I can hear that he is not breathing easily.

Because I am a dog with a good nose and fine ears I can hear that he is not breathing easily.

13.3   Ink a Link: Using Adjectives After the Verb

Standard Use and understand descriptive adjectives.

Focus Phrase "I can link adjectives with the verbs of being."

Invitation to Notice Shadows, he thought, are like ink. They are shady and shifty and mysterious.
—Brianne Farley, *Ike's Incredible Ink*

Power Note *It's important for students to see that adjectives don't always come before the noun. Now they have another option when adjectives fall after a be-verb, linking the noun to an adjective. Students may wonder why, in the second sentence, Farley chose to use* ands *instead of* commas *to join this list of three adjectives. "Can you do that?" Writers can, in fact. We rewrite the sentence with commas and compare and contrast it with the one with* ands: They are shady, shifty, and mysterious. *"How do the two sentences differ in their effect? Which do you like better? Why might an author choose to use the two* ands?"

Invitation to Compare and Contrast Shadows, he thought, are like ink. They are shady and shifty and mysterious. Lies, he thought, are like slime. They are messy and sticky and troublesome.

Power Note *If students don't note the pronoun reference or connection between the pair of plural nouns* lies *and* shadows *and the pronoun* they, *ask, "How do we know what the word* they *at the beginning of the second sentence refers to?" (The pronoun* they *refers to the words* shadows *and* lies.) *"How do we know* shadows *and* lies *are plural?" Try asking instead of explaining. "How do we know* they *is plural?" This engages students in thinking about the purpose and craft behind an author's choices.*

Invitation to Imitate *Imitate Together*: Invite writers to use interactive or shared writing to compose a sentence with you. (See Figure 13.5.)

Imitate Independently: Students use the models to create their own sentences, using adjectives after a verb. Posting some linking verbs will help show writers the menu of options available.

Invitation to Celebrate As students read their sentences aloud, the listeners stand up each time an adjective is used. When the next adjective is used, they sit down . . . and when the next adjective is used, they stand up again . . . and so on. Add sentences to the adjective wall chart.

Invitation to Apply Use adjectives as a tool to respond personally to a read-aloud or independent reading. Students use stems to respond to reading, remembering, "We use adjectives to tell what kind, how many, and which one." Writers may choose from the examples of possible patterns shown in Figure 13.6.

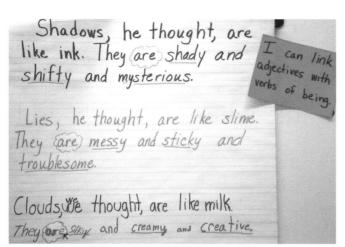

Figure 13.5 This third-grade sentence was created during shared writing imitation.

Figure 13.6 Adjectives in personal responses

Invitation to Edit

What did we learn about writing from Brianne Farley?	
Shadows, he thought, are like ink. They are shady and shifty and mysterious.	
What changed? What is the effect of the change?	
Shadows, he thought, are like ink. They is shady and shifty and mysterious.	Is *comes after* They. *The sentence does not sound right because the verb* is *does not agree with the pronoun* they. *When our pronouns do not agree with our verbs, the sentence does not sound right, which causes reader confusion.*
Shadows, he thought, are like ink. They are shady, shifty, and mysterious.	*The conjunction* and *is replaced with a comma. This is another way to list adjectives. Although it may change the emphasis or sentence fluency, it doesn't change the meaning.*
Shadows, he thought, are like ink. They are shady shifty and mysterious.	*The conjunction* and *is deleted. Because there is no comma or conjunction, the adjectives run together. When listing these adjectives, we need to separate them with commas or conjunctions.*

Fun Fact: Using a conjunction repeatedly instead of commas in a list is a literary device called *polysyndeton*. Using commas in a list with no conjunction is *asyndeton*.

Tip: Hippos: How Big Are They?

Try a modified call and response to a read-aloud of *Hippos Are Huge!* by Jonathan London. The students repeat the title, the first line, and the last line of the book, "HIPPOS ARE HUGE!" We signal them to shout the sentence by raising our right hand throughout the read-aloud. And since the end punctuation is an exclamation mark in all three cases, we yell it. (The author is begging us to.) Some students may notice that the three versions of the sentence in the book are in all caps and the word *huge* is the largest. Ask them, "Why do you think the author did that?" Adjectives usually come before a noun, but *Hippos Are Huge!* and our chant remind writers that adjectives can follow the noun and a verb of being (*is, are, was, were, be, been, am*). In other words, adjectives are easy.

What do you notice?

Shadows, he thought, are like ink. They are shady and shifty and mysterious.

—Brianne Farley, *Ike's Incredible Ink*

How are they alike and different?

Shadows, he thought, are like ink. They are shady and shifty and mysterious.

Lies, he thought, are like slime. They are messy and sticky and troublesome.

Let's try it out.

Shadows, he thought, are like ink. They are shady and shifty and mysterious.

Lies, he thought, are like slime. They are messy and sticky and troublesome.

Shadows, he thought, are like ink. They are shady and shifty and mysterious.

What changed? What is the effect of the change?

Shadows, he thought, are like ink. They is shady and shifty and mysterious.

Shadows, he thought, are like ink. They are shady, shifty, and mysterious.

Shadows, he thought, are like ink. They are shady shifty and mysterious.

13.4   Photographic Memory: Crafting Adjectives

Standard Use descriptive adjectives.

Focus Phrase "I use adjectives only when they are needed to clarify what kind, how many, or which one."

Invitation to Notice I stared at the glossy image. Six-year-old toothless me holding Mom's hand as white waves broke on the shore behind us. A strand of dark hair blew in Mom's face, hiding what might have been a small smile.
   —Jennifer Cervantes, *Tortilla Sun*

Power Note *We intentionally used a longer piece here so we can keep the idea of adjectives spiraling upward in complexity. We don't want to use them without a need to do so. "We use adjectives only when they are needed to clarify what kind, how many, or which one." We want young writers to use adjectives selectively when a precise noun isn't able to do the work. This excerpt shows again and again that adjectives come before nouns, telling us what kind, how many, and which one. The words that function as adjectives are in bold:*

> I stared at the **glossy** image. **Six-year-old toothless** me holding **Mom's** hand as **white** waves broke on the shore behind us. A strand of **dark** hair blew in **Mom's** face, hiding what might have been a **small** smile.

Invitation to Compare and Contrast I stared at the glossy image. Six-year-old toothless me holding Mom's hand as white waves broke on the shore behind us. A strand of dark hair blew in Mom's face, hiding what might have been a small smile.

I glared at his angry face. Eight-year-old me grabbed the channel knob on the TV as my brother slapped the back of my hand. The strands of his blond bangs bounced above his hazel eyes, unable to hide his meanness.

Power Note *Don't feel like you have to discuss every adjective; rather, emphasize what the adjectives are doing for the reader and writer. Feel free to continue using the focus phrase as students engage with more complex texts, too.*

Invitation to Imitate *Imitate Independently*: Students use the models to compose their own photograph paragraph. They may use a real photo to help them freeze-frame a moment in time (see Figure 13.7). Writers use multiple adjectives across a few sentences (not all in one place in a row or string) to enhance visualization and understanding for readers as Jennifer Cervantes did in the *Tortilla Sun* excerpt.

Invitation to Celebrate As students read their paragraphs aloud, invite listeners to close their eyes and create mental images based on the adjectives. Listeners share the image that sticks with them the most after each reading. Encourage students to reflect on how conventions—such as adjectives—give writers the power of detail.

Figure 13.7 Photo imitation

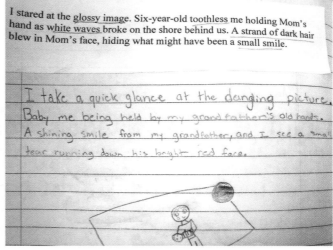

I stared at the <u>glossy image</u>. Six-year-old toothless me holding Mom's hand as <u>white waves</u> broke on the shore behind us. A strand of dark hair blew in Mom's face, hiding what might have been a <u>small smile</u>.

I take a quick glance at the dangling picture. Baby me being held by my grandfather's old hands. A shining smile from my grandfather, and I see a small tear running down his bright red face.

Figure 13.8 A fifth grader uses description to reflect on a family picture.

Invitation to Apply

Three-Sentence Memoir: Writers create an image from a freeze-frame from their lives and write a three-sentence memoir, using adjectives to give readers additional detail about the nouns. (See Figure 13.8.)

Invitation to Edit

Not-So-Fun Fact: Why did Jennifer Cervantes use hyphens in the phrase *six-year-old*? Authors always have a purpose. Cervantes is showing us that these words are one unit coming before a noun (telling the character's age). If the unit comes before a noun or is treated as a noun, hyphenate it. If it comes after a noun and is acting as an adjective, don't. For example, *I am an eleven-year-old genius* versus *I am a genius who is eleven years old.* But you would say, *I'm an eleven-year-old*, because the unit is acting as a noun. Don't fret. You can always look it up if you forget.

What did we learn about writing from Jennifer Cervantes?	
A strand of dark hair blew in Mom's face, hiding what might have been a small smile.	
What changed? What is the effect of the change?	
A strand of dark hair blew in mom's face, hiding what might have been a small smile.	*In this sentence,* Mom *is not capitalized. The pattern is to capitalize* Mom *when it acts as a mother's name. How can you tell? There is no possessive noun or pronoun in front of* Mom *to make it a common noun. A name doesn't seem as important when it is not capitalized.*
A strand of dark hair blew in Mom's face hiding what might have been a small smile.	*There is no comma to separate the sentence into its two chunks. By taking away the comma, the sentence parts run together, removing the separation of the dependent clause from the sentence.*
A strand of dark hair blew in Moms face, hiding what might have been a small smile.	*The apostrophe has been removed from* Mom's*. Because of this, the face no longer belongs to anyone, taking away the effect of a possessive noun showing whose face. Omitting the apostrophe may also cause a reader to think there is more than one Mom.*

What do you notice?

I stared at the glossy image. Six-year-old toothless me holding Mom's hand as white waves broke on the shore behind us. A strand of dark hair blew in Mom's face, hiding what might have been a small smile.

—Jennifer Cervantes, *Tortilla Sun*

How are they alike and different?

I stared at the glossy image. Six-year-old toothless me holding Mom's hand as white waves broke on the shore behind us. A strand of dark hair blew in Mom's face, hiding what might have been a small smile.

I glared at his angry face. Eight-year-old me grabbed the channel knob on the TV as my brother slapped the back of my hand. The strands of his blond bangs bounced above his hazel eyes, unable to hide his meanness.

Let's try it out.

I stared at the glossy image. Six-year-old toothless me holding Mom's hand as white waves broke on the shore behind us. A strand of dark hair blew in Mom's face, hiding what might have been a small smile.

A strand of dark hair blew in Mom's face, hiding what might have been a small smile.

What changed? What is the effect of the change?

A strand of dark hair blew in mom's face, hiding what might have been a small smile.

A strand of dark hair blew in Mom's face hiding what might have been a small smile.

A strand of dark hair blew in Moms face, hiding what might have been a small smile.

Tip: *This* and *That* Versus *These* and *Those*

This or *that*? *Those* or *these*? *That* is the question. Or is it *these* are the questions? The thing is, we don't usually spend a lot of time considering the usage of *these* words—we just use them. *That's* one of the problems with grammar instruction. Often writers and speakers do the right thing automatically, but they don't know why or (heavens to Betsy) can't label it.

We wouldn't dare suggest quibbling with first graders or fourth graders over whether a demonstrative is acting as a pronoun or an adjective. (See the Not-So-Fun Fact if you want to know how to quibble.) Yes, some standards have led a few to ask this of young writers. But the standards intend for students to use *this* or *that* as well as *these* and *those* conventionally, not use the term *demonstrative* or even *determiner*. Ever. The standard calls for first- through fifth-grade writers to know how to use these four words. When they aren't sure which one to use, this chart will help clarify it for them, if they have any questions.

	This and *That* Versus *These* and *Those*	
Determiners	What They Do	Examples
This or *That?*	Direct attention to a **singular** word or phrase. (Linked to a **singular** noun)	**This** time it was my heart that answered, a steady drumbeat inside my chest. But maybe **that** kind of magic did exist somewhere. —Natalie Lloyd, *A Snicker of Magic*
These or *Those?*	Direct attention to **plural** words or phrases. (Linked to a **plural** noun or several nouns)	In **these** last moments on the bluff, they were free. There were a lot of good and brave warriors in **those** days. —Joseph Marshall III, *In the Footsteps of Crazy Horse*

Not-So-Fun Fact: If *this* or *that* and *these* or *those* come directly before a noun, they're demonstrative adjectives. (*We don't spend a lot of time considering the usage of* ***these words***.) They're demonstrative pronouns when they're not directly in front of a noun. (***That is*** *the question.*)

Tip: In Case You Were Wondering

These is the plural form of *this*, and *those* is the plural form of *that*. *This* and *these* point to something close in space or experience, whereas *that* and *those* point to something more distant than another thing—or a specific something already mentioned.

13.5 The Describing Verb: Showing an Action or Use with -*ing* Adjectives

Standard	Use descriptive adjectives, including purpose adjectives.
Focus Phrase	"I can change a verb to an adjective by adding -*ing* to the end."
Invitation to Notice	A snake slithers through rustling leaves and climbs up into a tree. —Steve Jenkins and Robin Page, *Move!*

Power Note   *Some adjectives seem like verbs to children, such as* rustling *in* rustling leaves *or* frying *in* frying pan. *These -ing words can be used as verbs or adjectives, so it's important for writers to consider the word's purpose before they choose. In Jenkins and Page's sentence, the -ing verb (*rustling*) is describing what kind of leaves. Writers can take verbs, add -ing to the end, and place them in front of a noun, which transforms a verb into an adjective. (See Figure 13.9.)*

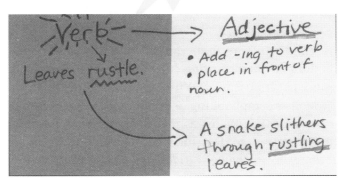

Figure 13.9 Verb to adjective

Invitation to Compare and Contrast	A snake slithers through rustling leaves and climbs up into a tree. A skier races through the glistening snow and slows at the bottom of the slope.

Power Note   Glistening *describes what the snow does in the sunlight. The snow glistens.* Glistens *is a verb. But when we use the* -ing *form of the verb and put it in front of the noun* snow, *it becomes an adjective (*glistening snow*).*

Invitation to Imitate   *Imitate Together*: Invite writers to use interactive or shared writing to compose a sentence with you and create an adjective from what would otherwise be a verb. This sentence is about a board on which you cut meat or vegetables. Add -*ing* to *cut* and you get *cutting*. Put *cutting* in front of *board* and your verb is transformed into an adjective: *cutting board*.

My mom has one cutting board for meat and one for vegetables.

Imitate Independently: Students use the models to compose their own sentences, using adjectives that are verbs transformed by adding -*ing* to them. Page does this with *rustling* leaves. It may be helpful to brainstorm a list of things students like to do or places they like to go to help create a context for transforming verbs into adjectives that tell what kind by telling readers what the noun is used for.

Invitation to Celebrate   Students share their sentences with -*ing* verbs aloud with their table groups. We listen to a few as a class. We have a little fun with the activity on the whiteboard or chart paper. We write, *The class listens.* "Help me transform

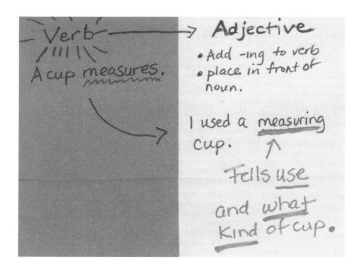

Figure 13.10
Adjectives explain use.

the verb *listens* into an adjective: *listening class, listening students.* Keep going." The students applaud. The students write. The students imitate. We keep transforming verbs into adjectives by adding *-ing* and moving them in front of the noun to show the noun's purpose or what it does. (See Figure 13.10.)

Invitation to Apply

Go on an -ing *Adjective Hunt.* An *-ing* verb can act as an adjective that explains the use of something, as in *measuring* cup. *Measuring* tells us both what kind of cup it is and what it's used for. With a partner, students pick a hobby or leisure activity, such as scrapbooking or bowling, or a place such as a kitchen, backyard, or garage. Students list as many *-ing* verbs as they can that they could work into adjectives to describe what a noun does (*steering wheel, flying machine, frying pan, mixing bowl, riding lawn mower*).

When I grow up, I will have a *swimming* pool in my backyard.

Figure 13.11
A fourth grader grapples with transforming verbs into adjectives in her writer's notebook.

Verbs to Adjectives

When I grow up, I will have a swimming pool in my backyard.

Verb	Adjective
rustle	rustling
glisten	glistening
swim	swimming
sparkle	sparkling

Basket ball:

~~dribbling~~	
running	running shoes
shooting	shooting games
dribble	dribbling drills

During basketball practice, we did dribbling drills.

Before the basket ball game, I put on my running shoes.

Invitation to Edit

What did we learn about writing from Robin Page?	
A snake slithers through rustling leaves and climbs up into a tree.	
What changed? What is the effect of the change?	
A snake slithers through rustling leaf and climbs up into a tree.	Leaves *has been changed to* leaf. *The reader's mental image is affected with this change. The sentence does not sound right, because the singular form of the noun leaves means there is only one leaf. One leaf can't rustle.*
A snake slithers through rustling leaves and climb up into a tree.	Climbs *has been changed to* climb. *The verb does not agree with the noun,* snake, *like* slithers *does. This causes the sentence to sound messy.*
A snake slithers through rustling leaves, and climbs up into a tree.	*A comma is added, separating the sentence into two parts. However, the second part of the sentence can't stand on its own. The comma is not needed.*
A snake slithers through rustle leaves and climbs up into a tree.	*The -ing ending is deleted from the adjective* rustling. *Now* rustle *is a verb, and it makes no sense where it is.*

What do you notice?

A snake slithers through rustling leaves and climbs up into a tree.

—Steve Jenkins and Robin Page, *Move!*

How are they alike and different?

A snake slithers through rustling leaves and climbs up into a tree.

A skier races through the glistening snow and slows at the bottom of the slope.

Let's try it out.

A snake slithers through rustling leaves and climbs up into a tree.

A skier races through the glistening snow and slows at the bottom of the slope.

A snake slithers through rustling leaves and climbs up into a tree.

What changed? What is the effect of the change?

A snake slithers through rustling leaf and climbs up into a tree.

A snake slithers through rustling leaves and climb up into a tree.

A snake slithers through rustle leaves and climbs up into a tree.

14

What Do Comparatives and Superlatives Do?

Young writers love superheroes, right? Do they love them *more* than American Girl dolls? What do they love the *most* about them? When you talk about relationships between people, places, and things, you often call on a comparative or superlative adjective to tell you the degree to which the things are related to each other. If you're talking about one thing, you decide if it's good or bad (adjective). If you're comparing two things, you're deciding which one is better or worse (comparative adjective). If you're comparing everything or everyone, you want to know who or what is the best or worst (superlative adjective). Figure 14.1 oversimplifies this a bit, but it's a good place to begin.

Figure 14.1
Complicated and
super simplified

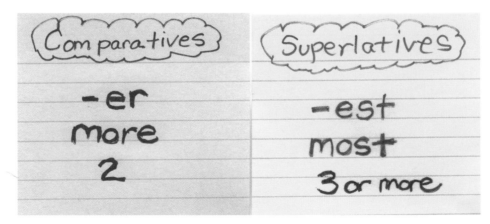

Writers don't use both the comparative and the superlative forms at the same time, though, nor do they use a suffix (comparative *-er*, superlative *-est*) with *more* or *most*. They just don't. Choosing one or the other is the pattern. We've included some general rules for clarification in Figure 14.2. We are not suggesting you transmit all this information in one sitting to young writers. It's there to help guide decisions when these issues arise. Figure 14.2 shows some guidelines we gleaned from the authoritative *Chicago Manual of Style*.

Figure 14.2
Complicated and super complicated

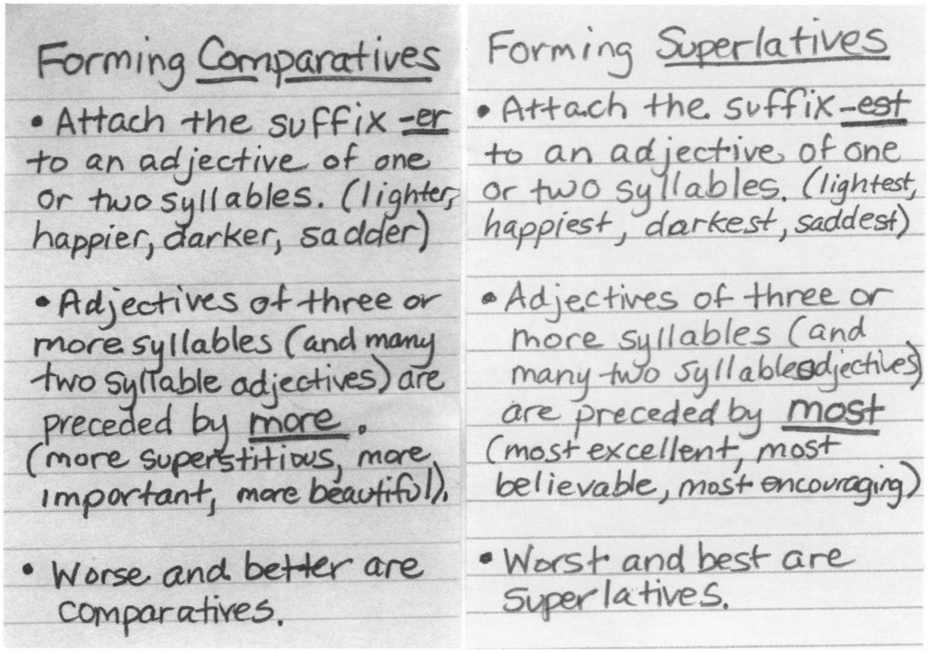
Forming Comparatives
• Attach the suffix -er to an adjective of one or two syllables. (lighter, happier, darker, sadder)
• Adjectives of three or more syllables (and many two syllable adjectives) are preceded by more. (more superstitious, more important, more beautiful).
• Worse and better are comparatives.
Forming Superlatives
• Attach the suffix -est to an adjective of one or two syllables. (lightest, happiest, darkest, saddest)
• Adjectives of three or more syllables (and many two syllable adjectives) are preceded by most (most excellent, most believable, most encouraging)
• Worst and best are superlatives.

Lesson Sets:

What Do Comparatives and Superlatives Do?

14.1 It Takes Two: Time to Compare

14.2 The Anaconda: Superlatives Are the Biggest

14.3 Youngest or Oldest: Time to Decide a Winner

14.1   It Takes Two: Time to Compare

Standard	Form and use comparatives and superlatives.
Focus Phrase	"I compare two things using *-er* or *more*. Never both."
Invitation to Notice	I wanted to be bigger, stronger, older. —Jen Bryant, *Six Dots: A Story of Young Louis Braille*

Power Note   *Share this sentence from a biography of Louis Braille, the creator of a reading system for the blind that bears his name. If you can read the entire book beforehand, that would be best. After writers' initial noticings of the sentence, ask, "Who's Louis Braille comparing himself with?" (The comparison is with his current self, so it's between two things: who he was and who he longed to be.) A student may ask why there isn't an* and *before the last item in the series. Congratulate them on noting a pattern of power. Say and write the sentence, including the conjunction* and*: I wanted to be bigger, stronger, and older. "Why do you think Jen Bryant chose to write it this way?" (The technical term for using only commas and no conjunctions is asyndeton.)*

Invitation to Compare and Contrast   I wanted to be bigger, stronger, older.
I wanted to be taller, smarter, and more thoughtful.
I wanted to be more sportsmanlike, kinder, and a better citizen.

Power Note   *This invitation to compare and contrast has three sentences to expose students to more patterns for using comparatives. We wanted to demonstrate how writers use the word* more *before adjectives of three or more syllables, as in* more sportsmanlike, more beautiful, more generous, more important, and more delicious. *We also may discuss that the more traditional pattern for a serial comma uses a coordinating conjunction such as* and *before the last item in a series.*

Invitation to Imitate   *Imitate Together*: Invite writers to use paired writing to compose a sentence. Reinforce or share some of the information about forming comparatives—how they compare two things and either use the suffix *-er* or, if the adjective has three or more syllables, place *more* in front of it.

Imitate Independently: Students use the models and information to compose their own sentences using a list of comparatives to compare two things.

Power Note   *When in doubt about the comparative form of an adjective, show writers how to look it up in a dictionary or online. It's always part of a word's definition. "When in doubt, check it out." This can be a necessary step because a few two-syllable adjectives, such as* complete, *use* more *rather than the suffix* -er *(*more complete, more careful, more boring, more common, more famous*).*

Tip: Want More Interesting Facts About Comparatives? Are You Most Curious About Superlatives?

Consider this *Chicago Manual of Style*'s final missive about irregular adjectives: "Many adjectives are irregular—there is no rule that guides their comparative and superlative forms (*good, better, best*) (*less, lesser, least*). A good dictionary will show the forms of an irregular adjective" (2010, 245).

Invitation to Celebrate

For fun, we like to play the song "Anything You Can Do, I Can Do Better." We like the original Ethel Merman and Howard Keel version as well as a wordless musical version by the Bellavista Orchestra. Music just drips with celebration, doesn't it?

Brainstorm all the different ways in which young writers can share their writing, which in comparison, will be different. Some suggestions: *louder, softer, higher, lower, faster, slower, more dramatically, breathier.* We use resources when in doubt. That's what writers do.

Invitation to Apply

At some point in the day or the next few days, student partners write a sentence in response to the content of the read-aloud using a comparative to compare two things. If writers come across a superlative, we discuss how the two forms are alike and different, anchoring ourselves in the patterns we see and discuss.

Power Note

Both comparatives and superlatives compare, but comparatives compare two things, whereas superlatives compare three or more and refer to them as the best, the worst, and so on. Point out the word super in superlative as a way to remember that, like Supergirl and Superman, superlatives are the strongest or best.

Invitation to Edit

What did we learn about writing from Jen Bryant?	
I wanted to be bigger, stronger, older.	
What changed? What is the effect of the change?	
I wanted to be bigger, stronger, and older.	The conjunction *and* is inserted before older, *making this into a more traditional pattern where commas are used in a series. Both are acceptable, but using* and *is most common.*
I wanted to be biggest, strongest, oldest.	*The comparatives are changed to superlatives, shifting the meaning from wanting to be better than he is now to wanting to be the biggest, strongest, and oldest of some group such as his brothers, his classmates, or the world.*
I wanted to be more bigger, stronger, older.	*The comparative* more *is inserted before another comparative,* bigger. *Writers use* either *more or -er, but never both.*

What do you notice?

I wanted to be bigger, stronger, older.

—Jen Bryant, *Six Dots: A Story of Young Louis Braille*

How are they alike and different?

I wanted to be bigger, stronger, older.

I wanted to be taller, smarter, and more thoughtful.

I wanted to be more sportsmanlike, kinder, and a better citizen.

Let's try it out.

I wanted to be bigger, stronger, older.

I wanted to be taller, smarter, and more thoughtful.

I wanted to be more sportsmanlike, kinder, and a better citizen.

I wanted to be bigger, stronger, older.

What changed? What is the effect of the change?

I wanted to be bigger, stronger, and older.

I wanted to be biggest, strongest, oldest.

I wanted to be more bigger, stronger, older.

14.2   The Anaconda: Superlatives Are the Biggest

Standard   Form and use superlatives.

Focus Phrase   "I compare three or more things using *-est* or *most*. Never both."

Invitation to Notice   There are many kinds of large snakes, but the anaconda is the biggest.
—Steve Jenkins, *Biggest, Strongest, Fastest*

Power Note   *The words* many kinds *and* snakes *are plural, and we can assume there are three or more. The anaconda is the super snake. This is a* superlative. *Students might be interested to know that the largest anaconda can grow to be more than twenty-five feet long and weigh more than four hundred pounds (Jenkins 1995). It's not just bigger, but the biggest.*

Invitation to Compare and Contrast   There are many kinds of large snakes, but the anaconda is the biggest.
There are many kinds of TV channels, but YouTube is the funniest.

Power Note   *The question of* TV *being an abbreviation for* television *may come up.* TV *requires no periods because it breaks the rules of common abbreviations using first and last letters, like* Mr. *for* mister. *But to be clear, in any case,* TV *in all caps without periods is the acceptable abbreviation.*

Invitation to Imitate   *Imitate Together*: Invite writers to use shared writing to compose a sentence.

There are many kinds of schools, but ours is the best.

Imitate Independently: Students use the model sentence to create their own sentences using superlatives. (See Figure 14.3.)

Figure 14.3
Fourth-grade superlative imitation

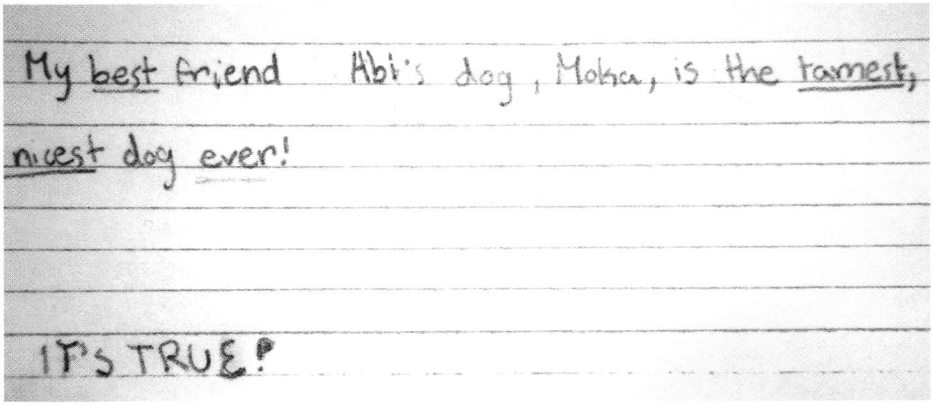

My best friend   Abi's dog, Moka, is the tamest, nicest dog ever!

IT'S TRUE!

Invitation to Celebrate   *Play Picture-Day Lineup: Tallest to Shortest*. Pretend it's picture day and line up tallest to shortest. Ask students, "Who is taller than Eric? Who is smaller than Eric?" Emphasize the relationship between whatever your comparing. Then move on to superlatives. "Who is the tallest? Who is the smallest girl?"
If you are afraid height might be a sensitive subject, use something like animal cards with lions, tigers, bears, and dogs. Distribute an animal card to

each student and ask "how many superlatives can you come up with?" Brainstorm all the possible ways in which we could show polar superlatives. *The most. The least. The best. The worst. Smallest to biggest, loudest to softest, fastest to slowest.* Also ask students to compare animal traits along the way saying things such as, "A chicken is slower than an alligator." Using both comparatives and superlatives helps students distinguish the difference.

Invitation to Apply   If we want to circle back and add comparatives to the discussion, students can generate comparative sentences about the animal cards as well:

> A rattlesnake is smaller than a python.
> A python is larger than a rattlesnake.
> An elephant is bigger than a hippo.
> A hippo is smaller than an elephant.

Invitation to Edit

What did we learn about writing from Steve Jenkins?	
There are many kinds of large snakes, but the anaconda is the biggest.	
What changed? What is the effect of the change?	
There are many kinds of large snakes, but the anaconda is the most biggest.	*The superlative* most *is inserted before another superlative,* biggest. *Writers use only one superlative, choosing between* -est *and* most; *they don't use both, or the writing will sound awkward.*
There are many kinds of large snakes, but the anaconda is the more biggest.	*The comparative* more *is inserted before a superlative. Comparatives compare two things, whereas superlatives compare three or more. Since this sentence is talking about three or more, the superlative wins. Plus, you need only one comparative or superlative. This double use confuses readers, causing them to wonder whether the sentence is referring to two things or more than two.*
There is many kinds of large snakes, but the anaconda is the biggest.	*The plural verb* are *has been replaced by the singular verb* is. *The pattern is one of subject-verb agreement in number (plural versus singular). Here, the writer needs to look after the verb to see that it's a plural subject (many kinds).*

What do you notice?

There are many kinds of large snakes, but the anaconda is the biggest.

—Steve Jenkins, *Biggest, Strongest, Fastest*

How are they alike and different?

There are many kinds of large snakes, but the anaconda is the biggest.

There are many kinds of TV channels, but YouTube is the funniest.

Let's try it out.

There are many kinds of large snakes, but the anaconda is the biggest.

There are many kinds of TV channels, but YouTube is the funniest.

There are many kinds of large snakes, but the anaconda is the biggest.

What changed? What is the effect of the change?

There are many kinds of large snakes, but the anaconda is the most biggest.

There are many kinds of large snakes, but the anaconda is the more biggest.

There is many kinds of large snakes, but the anaconda is the biggest.

14.3   Youngest or Oldest: Time to Decide a Winner

Standard	Form and use superlatives.
Focus Phrase	"I compare three or more things using -*est* or *most*. Never both."
Invitation to Notice	After the day, the month may be the oldest human unit of timekeeping. —Steve Jenkins, *Just a Second*
Power Note	*There are more than three units of time (minute, hour, day, week, month, year, decade, and so on); therefore, Jenkins uses a superlative to show which unit of time may be the oldest. Superlatives show which one is super or superior to all (three or more things).*
Invitation to Compare and Contrast	After the day, the month may be the oldest human unit of timekeeping. After cinnamon rolls, Pop-Tarts may be the tastiest breakfast choice. After cinnamon rolls, Pop-Tarts may be the most delicious breakfast choice.
Power Note	*We have three sentences here to introduce how we use either* most *or* -est, *but not both. These three sentences should help this idea float to the top. Remind students of the pattern that superlatives take the word* most *rather than the suffix* -est *when there are three syllables, and often when there are two. Use a dictionary when you're not sure. That's what writers do.*
Invitation to Imitate	*Imitate Together*: Invite writers to use interactive or shared writing to compose a sentence with you. *Imitate Independently*: Students use the model to compose their own sentences in which they use a superlative.
Invitation to Celebrate	*Hold a Superlative Contest*: Distribute slips of paper. Set a timer for two minutes to see who can list the most superlatives. The winner may wear a crown for the rest of the day.
Invitation to Apply	Have students work in pairs to write a sentence or two about your class's science and math work, using a superlative to explain a fact or opinion about the day's learning.

Invitation to Edit

What did we learn about writing from Steve Jenkins?	
After the day, the month may be the oldest human unit of timekeeping.	
What changed? What is the effect of the change?	
After the day, the month may be the most oldest human unit of timekeeping.	*The superlative* most *is inserted next to* oldest. *Writers use only one intensifier at a time—either* -est *or* most, *but not both.*
After the day the month may be the oldest human unit of timekeeping.	*The comma after the introductory element or phrase is deleted. Writers use commas to set off introductory elements. When we don't use the commas, it may make it hard for the reader to chunk the sentence.*
After the day, the Month may be the oldest human unit of timekeeping.	*The word* month *has been capitalized. Writers capitalize the name of each month, January–December, but we don't capitalize the word* month. *Similarly, we capitalize our names, but not* boys *and* girls *or* women *or* men—*or the word* names.

What do you notice?

After the day, the month may be the oldest human unit of timekeeping.
—Steve Jenkins, *Just a Second*

How are they alike and different?

After the day, the month may be the oldest human unit of timekeeping.

After cinnamon rolls, Pop-Tarts may be the tastiest breakfast choice.

After cinnamon rolls, Pop-Tarts may be the most delicious breakfast choice.

Let's try it out.

After the day, the month may be the oldest human unit of timekeeping.

After cinnamon rolls, Pop-Tarts may be the tastiest breakfast choice.

After cinnamon rolls, Pop-Tarts may be the most delicious breakfast choice.

After the day, the month may be the oldest human unit of timekeeping.

What changed? What is the effect of the change?

After the day, the month may be the most oldest human unit of timekeeping.

After the day the month may be the oldest human unit of timekeeping.

After the day, the Month may be the oldest human unit of timekeeping.

15

What Do Adverbs Do?

*L*ooking for a *really* easy way sink into grammar quicksand? Adverbs can often be explained *simply*: adverbs are all words that end in -*ly*.

Okay, *really* and *simply* do end in -*ly*, and both are adverbs. Perhaps you were taught this -*ly* rule. But what about this sentence from Nicola Davies's *Deadly! The Truth About the Most Dangerous Creatures on Earth*?

Animals with deadly poisons can be useful.

In this sentence, the word *deadly* is an adjective telling *what kind* of poison. A part of speech is defined by what it does in a particular sentence. Furthermore, some frequently used adverbs of frequency—*sometimes, always,* and *never*—don't end in -*ly*. Yet they're still adverbs. Depending on the -*ly* rule might get you through an adverb quiz, but it is better for writers and readers to understand what an adverb actually does.

To that point, adverbs *add* information to the *verb*. But beloved horror writer Stephen King warns, "The road to hell is paved with adverbs." In fact, people say all sorts of nasty things about adverbs. They're maligned as lazy writing. Annie Dillard writes, "Adverbs are a sign that you've used the wrong verb." These kinds of comments make some writers think they should *never* use an adverb. But you can't even say, "Never use adverbs!" without using the adverb *never*.

Adverbs aren't just lazy words that end in -*ly*. Writers use them *often*. Can you imagine this excerpt from Laurel Snyder's *Swan*, the biography of dancer Anna Pavlova, without the repetition of the adverb *now*? In this gorgeous picture book, Anna is awakened from her dull, dark, and cold life when she sees the ballet *Swan Lake*:

Now Anna cannot sleep. Or sit still ever. She can only sway, dip, and spin. *Now* Mama hums into her soup. *Now* the snow skitters just so at the window. *Now* the squirrels stop and watch. [Italics ours.]

Pure craft. But besides craft, adverbs serve a purpose of showing detail of *how*, *where*, and *when* something happens. Check out how adverbs in italics add detail for writers and readers in Jen Bryant's *Six Dots*:

Jen Bryant Uses Adverbs in *Six Dots: A Story of Young Louis Braille* to Answer **Questions of Detail: How? Where? When?**	
How? (Intensity, Degree, and Manner)	By the time I turned five, I was *completely* blind. I listened *closely* as he read to me from the Bible and books of poetry. As he read, I copied down the words, spelling each one *correctly*.
Where? (Location and Movement)	The Marquis, a noble lady living *nearby*, heard about me. "The code is read by touch, not by sight, so we might use it *here*, too."
When? (Time and Frequency)	*Finally*, a reply came. *Now* I knew what I had to do. Word spread *quickly*. I would *always* be held back, like that dog chained too tight. *Often*, I fell asleep a few minutes before morning. [Italics ours.]

Figure 15.1
Adverb chart

Like we discussed *already*, adverbs *add* to the *verb*, telling *how, where,* and *when*. Some budding grammarians might point out that prepositions also tell *where* and *when* in space and time. True. As we commented before, the part of speech you assign a word can change, depending on its use in a particular sentence. The reality is, we need not quibble over whether a word is acting as a preposition or an adverb. We need to tell readers where and when, and whether you use prepositions or adverbs should not be a matter of concern. But if you're still concerned, we address this in Chapter 16, "What Do Prepositions Do?"

Seriously, though, the labels don't matter. The details of where and when do; writers use either adverbs or prepositions to enhance detail, which enhances meaning.

Eventually, part of the author's craft of adverbs is to use them *sparingly*. And writers need to know that words such as *sparingly* can add a nice touch of detail to the verb by giving an explanation of *how* the adverb should be used. (As we wrote this, we were struggling to figure out whether to label *sparingly* as "how" or "when"—and then we remembered: It doesn't matter. Use does. Detail does. Clear writing does.) To clarify what adverbs can do for writers and readers, see the adverb chart in Figure 15.1.

Before and *after* can also be prepositions and subordinating conjunctions. This is one of those cases where the less said, the better. It's about use, not labeling. The bottom line: celebrate use of detail more and explain less.

Figure 15.2
Every word is doing a job, but only one is telling us how to open the door. The adverb is adding to the verb *open*, clarifying how to do it. That's not lazy; it's clear. Invite students to bring in examples of adverbs they see in the world. Is the adverb telling us how, where, or when?

Lesson Sets:

What Do Adverbs Do?

15.1   Yesterday, Today, and Tomorrow: Adverbs Remain Timely

Standard	Use adverbs of time.
Focus Phrase	"I use adverbs to tell *when* something happened, happens, or will happen."
Invitation to Notice	Today I feel silly. —Jamie Leigh Curtis, *Today I Feel Silly*

Power Note   *Read aloud* Today I Feel Silly. *Before a second reading, say to students, "Help me record all the feeling words that you notice as we read the book* Today I Feel Silly *again." Write the words they notice on a chart, which you'll use later. After you collect the feeling words, direct students' attention to the displayed sentence:* Today I feel silly. *Then, shift to another question: "What does the word* today *tell us?" If students don't answer, ask, "When is the narrator happy?" They may respond with other details from the book, but say, "That's true, but I'm just asking about the sentence displayed right now: 'Today I feel silly.'" When they answer, "Today," ask, "When is today?" They may respond, "Right now."*

"We've got a special word for right now *that we use with verbs. Do you remember what word means something is happening right now?" (Present.) "*Today *is an adverb that tells us when something happens." Write the focus phrase on the board or document camera. This gives students a moment to process the phrase as you write it: "I use adverbs to tell* when *something happened, happens, or will happen."*

Invitation to Compare and Contrast   Today I feel silly.
Yesterday, I felt sad and gloomy.

Power Note   *At some point, some bright child will notice that the focus phrase takes in the past, present, and future: "I use adverbs to tell* when *something happened, happens, or will happen." You can reply, "And we already know some words that tell us* today *is the present. What adverbs could we use for the past? The future?" (Yesterday, tomorrow.) An introductory adverb such as* today *or* yesterday *can be set off with a comma. But there is no hard-and-fast rule. Even though an adverb at the beginning of a sentence is often set off with a comma, Curtis and her editor chose not to set off* today *with a comma. We're more interested in studying the effect of a choice on readers than we are in thinking about whether it is correct. As illustrated in the imitation, the effect of using a comma after the adverb* yesterday *is different from how it would be if the comma were left out. "Which do you prefer? Why?"*

Invitation to Imitate   *Yesterday, Today, or Tomorrow*: Using the collection of feeling words from the earlier read-aloud, students illustrate themselves feeling a certain way and then write a sentence beneath their illustrations, using a time-marker such as *today, yesterday, this morning, later, last Sunday, next Wednesday,* or *now.* Charting a list of possible ways to start the sentence with a time-marker adverb will encourage students to try more of them.

Invitation to Celebrate Students orally share their own *yesterday, today,* and *tomorrow* sentences, or whatever time-marker they used—adverb or not. We celebrate because it's not about the label. The target is detailed writing that is clear and effective.

Invitation to Apply *Stem-ulate Adverb Use*: When lining up or choosing volunteers, students finish one of the following sentence stems or any that you or they might make up on the fly:

> Earlier I felt . . .
> Now I feel . . .
> When I was little, I always felt . . .

Invitation to Edit

What did we learn about writing from Jamie Leigh Curtis?	
Today I feel silly.	
What changed? What is the effect of the change?	
To day I feel silly.	*The adverb* today *is broken into two words: to day. That's not how we write it today. But believe it or not, it was done that way at one time. You might even see an older book with* to-day *in it.*
Today i feel silly.	*The pronoun I has been changed to a lowercase i. "We always capitalize the pronoun I." (Always is an adverb too!) When we don't capitalize the pronoun I, readers may miss it.*
Today I feel silly	*The period has been deleted. When sentences are missing an end mark, readers don't know where the sentence ends or how to read it. This can cause a breakdown in comprehension.*

What do you notice?

Today I feel silly.

—Jamie Leigh Curtis, *Today I Feel Silly*

How are they alike and different?

Today I feel silly.

Yesterday, I felt sad and gloomy.

Let's try it out.

Today I feel silly.

Yesterday, I felt sad and gloomy.

Today I feel silly.

What changed? What is the effect of the change?

To day I feel silly.

Today i feel silly.

Today I feel silly

15.2 *How'd You Do It? Adverbs That Show* How

Standard	Form and use adverbs. (How: degree, intensity, and manner)

Focus Phrase "I use adverbs to show *how* something happens."

Invitation to Notice Slowly, slowly, slowly, a sloth crawled along a branch of a tree.
　　　　　—Eric Carle, *"Slowly, Slowly, Slowly," Said the Sloth*

Power Note *After you read the sentence, invite noticings. Ask volunteers to "act out" the sentence. Afterward, ask the actors, "How'd you know how to move?" (Crawled and* slowly *told them how to move. Slowly added "how" to the action or verb.) If it's not noted by end of noticing time, ask, "Why do you think Carle repeated the word* slowly *three times? Why did he use a comma after each one?"*

Invitation to Compare and Contrast Slowly, slowly, slowly, a sloth crawled along a branch of a tree.
Peacefully, a fish swam around the tank.

Power Note *Sometimes we repeat a word like* slowly, *as Carle did three times in a row. But writers repeat words only for a reason, so our imitation uses* peacefully *once to cause this conversation, which deepens understanding of how a writer's choices affect readers.*

Invitation to Imitate As a class, use interactive writing to imitate Carle's sentence to describe how your class does certain routines every day. Students add *-ly*, a comma, and the sight words *we, up,* and *for.* Here are some examples:

Quietly, quietly, quietly, we lined up for lunch.
(And yes, we repeated *quietly* for a reason.)
We quickly wash our hands after we use the restroom.
(*Sometimes* we use only one adverb, even when it's important.)

Invitation to Apply *The Actors' Workshop*: Teacher and students generate sentences with adverbs that tell how something could happen. Go with actions such as "Open the door *slowly*" or "*Quickly* open the door." Then a student acts out the sentence, using the adverb to tell him or her how to do the action. Post a list labeled *Adverbs That Tell How* for students: *quickly/slowly, angrily/calmly, hastily/deliberately, noisily/silently, sloppily/neatly, carelessly/carefully.* Students point out when opposites, or antonyms, are used. (See Figure 15.3.)

Figure 15.3
Adverbs-that-tell-how chart

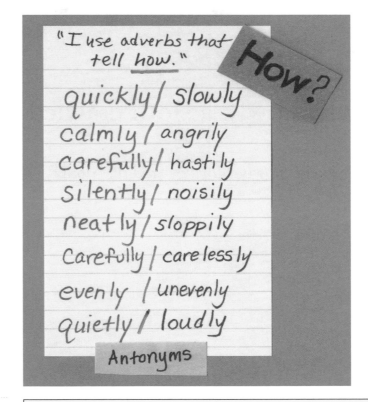

"I use adverbs that tell *how*."

How?

quickly / slowly
calmly / angrily
carefully / hastily
silently / noisily
neatly / sloppily
carefully / carelessly
evenly / unevenly
quietly / loudly

Antonyms

Invitation to Edit

What did we learn about writing from Eric Carle?	
Slowly, slowly, slowly, a sloth crawled along a branch of a tree.	
What changed? What is the effect of the change?	
Slowly, slowly, slowly, a sloth crawled along a branch off a tree.	The sight word of has been changed to off. Now the sentence sounds like the sloth fell off the tree. Of is a preposition, which is followed by a noun giving more information or detail (the branch of a tree).
Slowly slowly, slowly, a sloth crawled along a branch of a tree.	The comma between the first and second slowly has been deleted. Writers separate words written in a list and all in a row, or they run together. This affects pacing and fluency for readers.
Slowly, a sloth crawled along a branch of a tree.	Two of the slowly adverbs have been deleted. Discuss the effects of going from three to one. (This can be the beginning of talks about the author's craft for the purpose of emphasis.)

What do you notice?

Slowly, slowly, slowly, a sloth crawled along a branch of a tree.

—Eric Carle, *"Slowly, Slowly, Slowly," Said the Sloth*

How are they alike and different?

Slowly, slowly, slowly, a sloth crawled along a branch of a tree.

Peacefully, a fish swam around the tank.

Let's try it out.

Slowly, slowly, slowly, a sloth crawled along a branch of a tree.

Peacefully, a fish swam around the tank.

Slowly, slowly, slowly, a sloth crawled along a branch of a tree.

What changed? What is the effect of the change?

Slowly, slowly, slowly, a sloth crawled along a branch off a tree.

Slowly slowly, slowly, a sloth crawled along a branch of a tree.

Slowly, a sloth crawled along a branch of a tree.

15.3   Sooner or Later: Adverbs of Time

Standard   Use adverbs to modify verbs, showing time.

Focus Phrase   "I use adverbs to show *when* something happens."

Invitation to Notice   I couldn't wait to see Barry's face when I set him free. Soon we'd be romping through the fields together, just like old times.
    —Victoria Jamieson, *The Great Pet Escape*

Power Note   *The word* soon *is telling when something will happen—in the near future. This future time-marker causes the verb to change to* would. *Here it is contracted with the noun (*we'd*). The word* together *is also an adverb, telling how they'd romp—together.*

Invitation to Compare and Contrast   I couldn't wait to see Barry's face when I set him free. Soon we'd be romping through the fields together, just like old times.
    I couldn't wait to see Zaneta's face when I walked into her classroom. Later we'd be roaming the playground together, just like old times.

Power Note   *If students don't notice how apostrophes do two different things, you might stand back from the sentence and say, "Hmm. You know what I notice? There are two apostrophes in each sentence, but they don't do the same thing. Which ones are alike and which ones are different?" (Some help form posses-sives and some indicate contractions.)*

Invitation to Imitate   Use shared or interactive writing to imitate Jamieson's sentence, experiment-ing with adverbs to tell when something happened or will happen. Afterward, if you think students are ready, invite them to "try it out" in pairs.

Power Note   *When doing imitations, you might share a list of other adverbs that tell time, or refer to one you created in an earlier lesson:* now, later, soon, today, yester-day, tomorrow, before, during, after, *and the* when *phrase that starts this sentence. If appropriate, you can also make links to verb tenses:* yesterday *(past);* now, today *(present); and* tomorrow, soon, later *(future). (See Figure 15.4.)*

Invitation to Apply   *Playtime: What's the* When *Word?* Throughout the day students scour the environment around them for time words. We discuss how these time words give readers and speakers and writers a way to show when something happened, happens, or will happen. Model possibilities: "Today, we'll have recess after lunch. Oh, my! I just used a time-marker adverb. Which word was it?" Repeat the sentence, if necessary. "During our self-selecting reading time . . ." A recorder tallies each use of a time-marker, or better yet, starts a list of them.

Figure 15.4
Second graders use adverbs when writing procedural text or to help explain a sequence in a story.

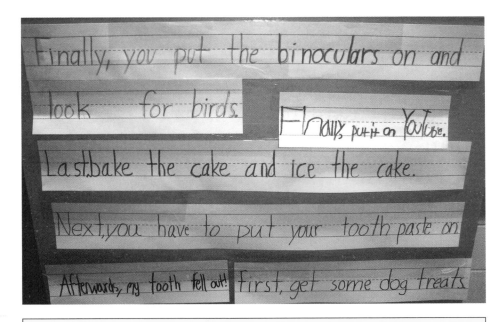

Finally, you put the binoculars on and look for birds.

Finally, put it on YouTube.

Last, bake the cake and ice the cake.

Next, you have to put your tooth paste on

Afterwards, my tooth fell out!   First, get some dog treats

Invitation to Edit

What did we learn about writing from Victoria Jamieson?	
I couldn't wait to see Barry's face when I set him free. Soon we'd be romping through the fields together, just like old times.	
What changed? What is the effect of the change?	
I couldn't wait to see Barry's face when I set him free. Soon we'd be romping through the fields, just like old times.	*The adverb* together *has been deleted, which explained how they'd be romping:* together. *It's not wrong without* together, *but* together *creates clarity.*
I couldn't wait to see Barry's face when I set him free. Later we'd be romping through the fields together, just like old times.	*The adverb* soon *has been replaced by* later, *another adverb. Both tell when. They are close in meaning, though* soon *connotes happening more promptly than* later.
I couldn't wait to see Barry's face when I set him free. Soon we'd be romping through the fields to gether, just like old times.	*The adverb* together *has been separated into two words.* Together *is one word. This irregularity may slow readers down, taking them out of the writer's message.*

What do you notice?

I couldn't wait to see Barry's face when I set him free. Soon we'd be romping through the fields together, just like old times.

—Victoria Jamieson, *The Great Pet Escape*

How are they alike and different?

I couldn't wait to see Barry's face when I set him free. Soon we'd be romping through the fields together, just like old times.

I couldn't wait to see Zaneta's face when I walked into her classroom. Later we'd be roaming the playground together, just like old times.

Let's try it out.

I couldn't wait to see Barry's face when I set him free. Soon we'd be romping through the fields together, just like old times.

I couldn't wait to see Zaneta's face when I walked into her classroom. Later we'd be roaming the playground together, just like old times.

I couldn't wait to see Barry's face when I set him free. Soon we'd be romping through the fields together, just like old times.

What changed? What is the effect of the change?

I couldn't wait to see Barry's face when I set him free. Soon we'd be romping through the fields, just like old times.

I couldn't wait to see Barry's face when I set him free. Later we'd be romping through the fields together, just like old times.

I couldn't wait to see Barry's face when I set him free. Soon we'd be romping through the fields to gether, just like old times.

15.4   Here and There: Adverbs of Place

Standard	Form and use adverbs to show where.
Focus Phrase	"I use adverbs to tell *how, where,* and *when* something happens."
Invitation to Notice	
Power Note	*Read aloud this passage from Jennifer L. Holm's* Full of Beans. *The narrator, Beans, is describing what living at his house is like:*

> Our place was shotgun-style, one and a half stories. We rented it from some shirttail cousin on my father's side. My mother said he should have paid us to live in it, because the place was full of pests. Termites. Ants. Roaches. Scorpions. But the worst pest in the joint was still in diapers.
> Buddy.
> My mother was wrestling my three-year-old baby brother into a crib in his little bedroom upstairs. He was squirming and rolling around and rubbing his eyes.

Read aloud the last sentence again. "Where is the baby brother rolling?" Crib, bedroom, and upstairs *are all acceptable answers, but if no one brings up the word* around, *ask, "Does* around *describe where he's rolling?"*

Then study Jennifer Holm's highlighted sentence with the usual invitation process.

> My mother was wrestling my three-year-old baby brother into a crib in his little bedroom upstairs.
> —Jennifer Holm, *Full of Beans*

Power Note   Upstairs *is the adverb in this sentence telling where the mother is wrestling with the narrator's three-year-old brother. "Adverbs often end in -ly, but not always." Write* always *and* often *on the board. "Often is an adverb telling how frequently adverbs end in –ly." The point is, we can tell* how, where, *or* when *with and without using -ly adverbs."*

Invitation to Compare and Contrast

> My mother was wrestling my three-year-old baby brother into a crib in his little bedroom upstairs.
> My father was telling my twelve-year-old sister to go to her room downstairs.

Power Note   *It may not be your first thought that* upstairs *and* downstairs *are adverbs. However, in both these sentences, they are adverbs of place, explaining where something is happening or where someone is going. The big deal is that they add to the verb. Holm's sentence shows where the mother is wrestling the narrator's baby brother. And in the imitation sentence,* downstairs *explains where the narrator's sister is supposed to go.*

Invitation to Imitate

For this imitation, we find it helpful to share some options writers may choose from if they like. Select and share the pairs you think are most useful or appropriate for your students:

outside/inside	*upstairs/downstairs*	*somewhere/anywhere*
there/here/nearby	*backward/forward*	*everywhere/nowhere*

Adverbs of place (*where?*) are usually placed after the main verb they modify or tell about, as they do in the two sentences we compared and contrasted.

Invitation to Celebrate

Place Off: After a student shares his or her imitation sentence, listeners raise their hands and pick out the place word in the sentence. The class agrees or disagrees by standing *up* or sitting *down*. The teacher breaks any ties.

Invitation to Apply

Rapid Revision: Students read and reread something they've written and see if they need to show where something happened. They may also add an adverb that shows how or when something happened. (See Chapter 3 for more discussions and options for Rapid Revision.)

Invitation to Edit

What did we learn about writing from Jennifer Holm?	
My mother was wrestling my three-year-old baby brother into a crib in his little bedroom upstairs.	
What changed? What is the effect of the change?	
My mother was wrestling my 3-year-old baby brother into a crib in his little bedroom upstairs.	*The word* three *is written numerically, rather than spelled out. In prose we usually write out numbers one through nine and use numerals for 10 and above, although some sources say to write out one through ninety-nine. It has no effect on meaning, but it stands out because it doesn't follow the convention we expect, and there is no reason to make it stand out.*
My mother was wrestling my three-year-old baby brother into a crib in his little bedroom.	*The adverb* upstairs *has been deleted, lessening readers' clarity of the crib's location. It's not incorrect—just less precise. The adverb* upstairs *tells us where this event happened.*
My mother was wrestling my three-year-old baby brother into a crib in his little bedroom outside.	*Who wouldn't want their crying baby brother's crib outside? But* outside *isn't where the crib is, so the meaning in terms of an accurate location is changed.*

What do you notice?

My mother was wrestling my three-year-old baby brother into a crib in his little bedroom upstairs.

—Jennifer Holm, *Full of Beans*

How are they alike and different?

My mother was wrestling my three-year-old baby brother into a crib in his little bedroom upstairs.

My father was telling my twelve-year-old sister to go to her room downstairs.

Let's try it out.

My mother was wrestling my three-year-old baby brother into a crib in his little bedroom upstairs.

My father was telling my twelve-year-old sister to go to her room downstairs.

My mother was wrestling my three-year-old baby brother into a crib in his little bedroom upstairs.

What changed? What is the effect of the change?

My mother was wrestling my 3-year-old baby brother into a crib in his little bedroom upstairs.

My mother was wrestling my three-year-old baby brother into a crib in his little bedroom.

My mother was wrestling my three-year-old baby brother into a crib in his little bedroom outside.

15.5   Give Me Details on *Where, When,* and *Why* It Happened: Relative Adverbs

Standard	Use relative adverbs.
Focus Phrase	"I use the words *why, where,* and *when* to link additional information."
Invitation to Notice	He squinted up into a nearby tree, where a couple of withered leaves still hung on, fluttering like flags. —Adina Rishe Gewirtz, *Zebra Forest*
Power Note	*Though* nearby *is often an adverb, a word that can be an adverb that is used before a noun may be considered an adjective. Even though labels don't really matter, we clarify this in case a student or small group wants to know. (Adverb:* She stood nearby. *Adjective when followed by a noun:* She hid behind a nearby tree.) *If you do discuss this with young writers, say, "The label doesn't matter. What matters is making sense and being clear. Don't worry about what part of speech* nearby *is—just use words like* nearby *when you need them, and make sure your thoughts make sense. Labels don't really matter."*
Invitation to Compare and Contrast	He squinted up into a nearby tree, where a couple of withered leaves still hung on, fluttering like flags. She peeked behind the bookcase, where dust bunnies had settled, balled up like critters.
Power Note	*The adverb clause* where the dust bunnies had settled *does the adverb's job of telling us where the dust bunnies ended up. (See the discussion of phrases and clauses in Chapter 20, "Why Do Writers Use Complex Sentences?")*
Invitation to Imitate	*Imitate Together*: Invite writers to use interactive or shared writing to compose a sentence with you that shows the location of something in the classroom or school. The sink, where we wash our hands, is an absolute mess. *Imitate Independently*: Students use the models to compose their own sentences, using a relative adverb to give the reader greater detail of where something is, when something happened, or why something occurred.
Invitation to Celebrate	Students share their imitations on Padlet or a class blog, or in a way you choose, such as a wall chart, door chart, or hall chart. (See Figure 15.5.)
Invitation to Apply	*Argue Why with an Adverb*: Students tend to easily use *where* and *when* clauses to situate us in time and space. However, our experience shows us that they have more trouble with *why*. In academic settings, using *why* as a link to an explanation will come in handy in all sorts of situations. Invite students to use the word *why* to link reasons to a proposition. (Students may need to be led through this if it is too difficult for them.)

I think the reasons why they were protesting are important.
The colonists wondered why they were taxed without any representation.
I wonder why people don't vote.

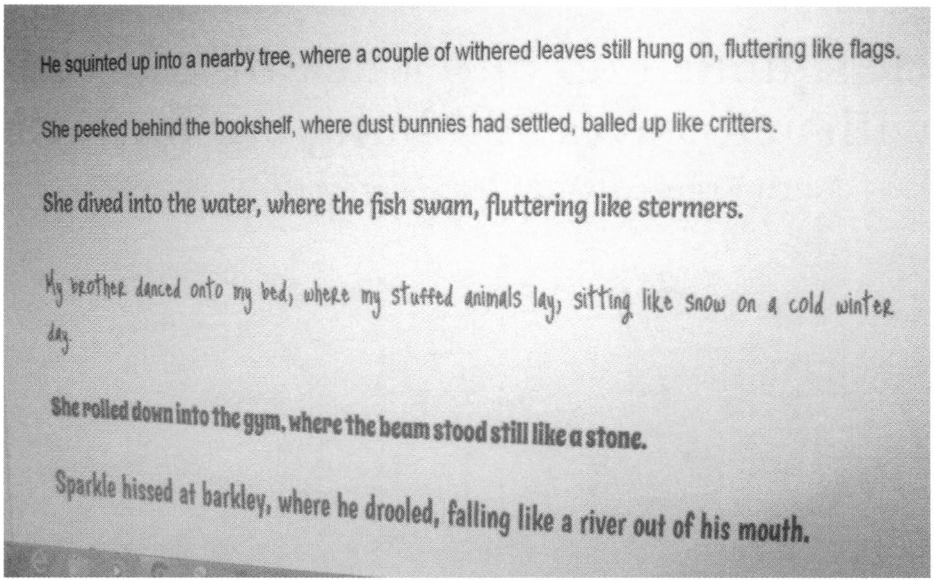

Figure 15.5
Third graders share their imitations with each other using Google Docs.

He squinted up into a nearby tree, where a couple of withered leaves still hung on, fluttering like flags.

She peeked behind the bookshelf, where dust bunnies had settled, balled up like critters.

She dived into the water, where the fish swam, fluttering like stermers.

My brother danced onto my bed, where my stuffed animals lay, sitting like snow on a cold winter day

She rolled down into the gym, where the beam stood still like a stone.

Sparkle hissed at barkley, where he drooled, falling like a river out of his mouth.

Invitation to Edit

What did we learn about writing from Adina Rishe Gewirtz?
He squinted up into a nearby tree, where a couple of withered leaves still hung on, fluttering like flags.
What changed? What is the effect of the change?

He squint up into a nearby tree, where a couple of withered leaves still hung on, fluttering like flags.	*The -ed ending has been deleted from the past-tense form of the verb* squint. *Writers pay attention to the endings of verbs because the time changes when the endings do (past, present, or future).*
He squinted up into a nearby tree, where a couple of withered leaves still hang on, fluttering like flags.	*The irregular past-tense verb* hung *has been changed to the present-tense* hang. *Writers use consistent verb tenses in sentences. Shifting tenses can confuse readers about the sequence of events and their relationship to each other.*
He squinted up into a nearby tree where a couple of withered leaves still hung on, fluttering like flags.	*The comma before* where *has been deleted. There is no pause now, causing a different effect and emphasis. The comma sets the relative clause off as a chunk of meaning for the reader.*

What do you notice?

He squinted up into a nearby tree, where a couple of withered leaves still hung on, fluttering like flags.

—Adina Rishe Gewirtz, *Zebra Forest*

How are they alike and different?

He squinted up into a nearby tree, where a couple of withered leaves still hung on, fluttering like flags.

She peeked behind the bookcase, where dust bunnies had settled, balled up like critters.

Let's try it out.

He squinted up into a nearby tree, where a couple of withered leaves still hung on, fluttering like flags.

She peeked behind the bookcase, where dust bunnies had settled, balled up like critters.

He squinted up into a nearby tree, where a couple of withered leaves still hung on, fluttering like flags.

What changed? What is the effect of the change?

He squint up into a nearby tree, where a couple of withered leaves still hung on, fluttering like flags.

He squinted up into a nearby tree, where a couple of withered leaves still hang on, fluttering like flags.

He squinted up into a nearby tree where a couple of withered leaves still hung on, fluttering like flags.

16

What Do Prepositions Do?

"Where are my keys?"

"Where is the remote?"

"Where are my glasses?"

You might ask these questions about lost items every day. To answer them, you'll need a preposition. Prepositions give details about the various locations where lost items can be. Are they . . .

- between the couch cushions?
- on the floor?
- in the pocket of my shorts in the washing machine?
- under the seat of my car?
- amid stacks of paper?

Prepositions are far more than everywhere your keys or remote can be. They are far more than everywhere a cat or squirrel can go. There are about 150 prepositions in the English language. In fact, most Americans don't know that the word *like*, in fact, sometimes functions as a preposition. Check out how Kathi Appelt and Alison McGhee craft sensory detail with *like* as a preposition in *Maybe a Fox*:

The shirt was thin and soft and smelled like cotton and coconut shampoo and Sylvie.

The words that follow a preposition (including a noun or nouns) make a prepositional phrase (a group of words that follow a preposition). Here Appelt and McGhee use the preposition *during* to show a swath of time:

It wasn't the first time Elk had come by during the day.

However, it is true that simple location and time words are the most important place for young writers to start.

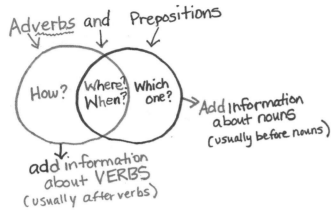

Figure 16.1
Adverbs and prepositions

The long-term goal is for students to understand that prepositions help writers add detail to their writing, answering readers' questions of where and when, grounding readers in space and time. (See Figure 16.1.) We know, we know. "I thought you said *adverbs* answer the questions where and when!" You're right; they do. So how do we know the difference between them? First of all, what matters is that writers are adding details of where and when to their writing—whatever you call the words they use to do it. But if we oversimplify things a bit, you'll easily see the overlap and the subtle differences between them. In short, **adverbs** *add* to *verbs*, and **prepositions** *show relationships* between *nouns* and other parts of speech.

Also, writers use prepositions to "tie nouns and pronouns logically to other parts of speech" (Hale 2013). Look at the award-winning picture book *Marvelous Cornelius* by Phil Bildner for an abundance of prepositions and powerful detail about the moves of the flashy New Orleans garbage man:

> Cornelius front flipped to the curb and flung the bags over his head, behind his back, between his legs, into the truck.

Can you imagine it *without* prepositions? It becomes word salad.

> Cornelius front flipped the curb and flung the bags his head, his back, his legs, the truck.

Those nouns and pronouns need their preposition connectors to tie it all together in time and space.

Prepositional phrases tell the location of characters and objects and the relationships between them. They also show the relationship of events in the space of time. A writer can anticipate a listener or reader's questions of where and when with prepositional phrases (a preposition plus a noun or a group of words following and related to the preposition): *Before school*, I had a Pop-Tart *in the cafeteria with Marquis.*

Before, during, or after your study of prepositions, read the concept-building books that connect prepositions to their linking function. We love *Over and Under the Snow; Up in the Garden, Down in the Dirt; and Over* and *Under the Pond* by Kate Messner. You might also share *In Front of My House* by Marianne Dubuc. It overflows with delightful pictures linked to prepositions in multiple relationships. Like the other books mentioned, it's a great book to set face-out for further exploration and explanation after sharing.

Lesson Sets:

What Do Prepositions Do?

16.1 A Phrase I'm Going Through: PrePOSITIONS

16.2 You Rang? When and Where?

16.3 One Prepared Pig: Which One?

16.1   A Phrase I'm Going Through: PrePOSITIONS

Standard
Use and understand prepositions and prepositional phrases.

Focus Phrase
"I use prepositions to explain where things are."

Invitation to Notice
She tucked her beak beneath her wing.
—Kate DiCamillo, *Louise, The Adventures of a Chicken*

Power Note
In the sentence from Louise, The Adventures of a Chicken, *the prepositional phrase* beneath her wing *answers the question* where. *Ask a volunteer to get beneath or on or by a few things in the classroom and have students orally compose sentences about the person's various positions. Whisper in the volunteer's ear, "Stand on the chair." After the volunteer stands on a chair, look out at your shocked class. "Who'd like to make a sentence that explains what they see now?"*

Invitation to Compare and Contrast
She tucked her beak beneath her wing.
The boy stuffed the green beans into his sleeve.

Power Note
We chose to give another preposition option here, adding into *as a choice. Soon, we will teach students a song with prepositions, so they'll have a whole menu of prepositions with which to start prepositional phrases.*

Invitation to Imitate
Imitate Together: Invite writers to use interactive or shared writing to compose a sentence with you. Here's an example:

The students tucked their books into their backpacks.

Imitate Independently: Students use model sentences to compose their own imitations, using prepositional phrases to ground their reader in time and space. "I use prepositions to explain where things are." (See Figures 16.2 and 16.3.)

Figures 16.2 and 16.3
First graders write with prepositional phrases to create a class book.

Invitation to Celebrate
Thank You for the Music: For a new celebration, we learn the preposition song and sing it to the tune of "Yankee Doodle" (see page 313 for lyrics). For assistance, search YouTube. There is no shortage of preposition songs. Memorization has its place. But don't stop at the song. The song opens a path

for young writers, giving them a menu of options for how to intentionally and purposefully use prepositions to locate their nouns (and readers) in time and space. The goal of teaching prepositions is to give students another way to integrate detail into their writing.

Invitation to Apply

Student Mentors: Students meet with a learning buddy one or two grade levels below them and teach the buddy the preposition song. The whole group sings it through a few times, and if there is time, student pairs, young and old, generate sentences that use prepositional phrases.

Invitation to Edit

What did we learn about writing from Kate DiCamillo?	
She tucked her beak beneath her wing.	
What changed? What is the effect of the change?	
She tucked here beak beneath her wing.	*The sight word* her *has been changed to* here. *Writers know that adding or leaving off one letter makes a difference. The wing belongs to* her, *not* here. *Leaving off a letter can cause confusion for readers.*
She tuck her beak beneath her wing.	*The -ed ending of the verb* tuck *has been deleted. Now it is in neither the past nor the present tense. To change to the present tense, we'd add an s to the end of* tuck. *To end in the past tense, we put back the -ed. When our verbs don't end well, neither do our sentences.*
She tucked her beak under her wing.	Beneath *has been changed to* under, *which is a synonym. Young editors notice small changes. Since this alteration doesn't change the meaning, it doesn't have much effect.*

Beginning Preposition Song (To the tune of "Yankee Doodle")

About, above, across, after
Along, among, around, at
Before, beside, between, against
Within, without, beneath, through
During, under, in, into
Over, of, off, to, toward
Up, on, near, for, from, until
By, with, behind, below, down.

Advanced Preposition Song (To the Tune of "Yankee Doodle")

With, on, for, after, at, by, in
Against, instead, of, near, between
Through, over, up, according to, around, among, beyond, (and) to

Still, within, without, upon
From, above, across, along
Toward, before, behind, below
Beneath, beside, during, under

What do you notice?

She tucked her beak beneath her wing.

—Kate DiCamillo, *Louise, The Adventures of a Chicken*

How are they alike and different?

She tucked her beak beneath her wing.

The boy stuffed the green beans into his sleeve.

Let's try it out.

She tucked her beak beneath her wing.

The boy stuffed the green beans into his sleeve.

She tucked her beak beneath her wing.

What changed? What effect does the change have?

She tucked here beak beneath her wing.

She tuck her beak beneath her wing.

She tucked her beak under her wing.

16.2 You Rang? When and Where?

Standard	Use and understand prepositions and prepositional phrases.
Focus Phrase	"I use prepositions to explain *where* and *when*."
Invitation to Notice	Late one afternoon in May, the phone at the Animal Control Center rang. —Kate DiCamillo, *Francine Poulet Meets the Ghost Raccoon*

Power Note *The prepositional phrases in this sentence are* in May *(when?) and* at the Animal Control Center *(where?). If students don't notice the prepositional phrases during their noticing time, don't forget the ol' now-you-see-it, now-you-don't game to get them to zero in on a convention.*

Late one afternoon, the phone rang.

After revealing the "prepositional phrase–less" version, ask, "How are they alike and how are they different?" This will lead the discussion to what prepositions and prepositional phrases do for writers and readers. "I use prepositions to explain where *and* when.*"*

Invitation to Compare and Contrast

Late one afternoon in May, the phone at the Animal Control Center rang.
Late one morning in math, the cell phone in my backpack rang.

Power Note *In this imitation, we chose to show another preposition pattern. Instead of* at a place, *we chose* in a type of bag or container, *like a backpack. The addition makes the conversation about how writers craft detail with prepositions richer, because students see more options for grounding a reader in time and space.*

Invitation to Imitate *Imitate Together*: Invite writers to use interactive or shared writing to compose a sentence with you.

Late one afternoon in September, bad weather made school end early.

Imitate Independently: Students use model sentences from the compare-and-contrast invitation as well as others created by the class to compose their own imitation.

Invitation to Apply *Start a Time Log*: Hang chart paper and tape a marker on a string to it. Write "Prepositional Time Log" across the top. Invite students to come up one at a time and log what happened at certain times throughout the day using all sorts of time prepositions. The challenge is to not always use the same preposition. (Share the information from the "It's About Time" tip box.) For example, "At 8:52 a.m., we returned from gym." If students forget, just walk over and model how you're adding another entry. "Let's check the time: yes, it's 12:11. I will write, 'At 12:12, the class will leave for the cafeteria.'"

Tip: It's About Time: What's the Pattern for Prepositions of Time?

Time prepositions follow patterns. Certain prepositions come before certain units of time. Writers use patterns because readers expect and are attracted to patterns. Our goal isn't to have our readers notice our preposition. They generally don't when we follow the convention. But when we don't follow the reader-writer agreement, readers may be stopped in their tracks.

- *At* is used with *noon, night, midnight*, and with times of day (*of the clock* or its contraction, *o'clock*).
- *In* is used with other parts of the day (*in the morning, in the afternoon, in the evening*); months; seasons (*in the summer*); and years (*in 2018*).
- *On* is used with days (*on Friday*).

For a meeting announcement to be clear, we follow the time patterns: *On Thursday at nine thirty in the morning, we will sing the preposition song.*

Invitation to Edit

What did we learn about writing from Kate DiCamillo?	
Late one afternoon in May, the phone at the Animal Control Center rang.	
What changed? What is the effect of the change?	
Late one afternoon in may, the phone at the Animal Control Center rang.	*The month of May is no longer capitalized. Writers always capitalize months: January–December. Always. When we don't capitalize the name of a month, our reader may not know it's a month.*
Late one afternoon on May, the phone at the Animal Control Center rang.	*The preposition in front of* May *has been changed from* in *to* on. *This sounds funny, which interrupts the flow of meaning.* • *At is used with* noon, night, *and* midnight. • *On is used with days.* • *In is used with months and seasons.*
Late one afternoon in May, the phone at the Animal Control center rang.	*The C in* center *is lowercase now. Each word in the name of the entire agency or place needs to be capitalized, as we do with* Jim Bowie Elementary.

What do you notice?

Late one afternoon in May, the phone at the Animal Control Center rang.

—Kate DiCamillo, *Francine Poulet Meets the Ghost Raccoon*

Late one afternoon, the phone rang.

How are they alike and different?

Late one afternoon in May, the phone at the Animal Control Center rang.

Late one morning in math, the cell phone in my backpack rang.

Let's try it out.

Late one afternoon in May, the phone at the Animal Control Center rang.

Late one morning in math, the cell phone in my backpack rang.

Late one afternoon in May, the phone at the Animal Control Center rang.

What changed? What is the effect of the change?

Late one afternoon in may, the phone at the Animal Control Center rang.

Late one afternoon on May, the phone at the Animal Control Center rang.

Late one afternoon in May, the phone at the Animal Control center rang.

16.3   One Prepared Pig: Which One?

Standard   Use and understand prepositions and prepositional phrases.

Focus Phrase   "I use prepositional phrases to tell *where, when,* and *which one.*"

Invitation to Notice   The pig with the umbrella was waiting for the rain.
            —Kevin Henkes, *Waiting*

Power Note   *If students do not discuss the phrase* with the umbrella, *play now-you-see-it, now-you-don't again. (The pig was waiting.) As readers, students compare each version. At some point in the discussion ask, "What is the pig waiting for? How would you know which pig the writer is talking about?" As students answer, say, "Wow! Now we need to add words to our preposition focus phrase: 'I use prepositional phrases to tell* where, when, *and* which one.'"

Invitation to Compare and Contrast   The pig with the umbrella was waiting for the rain.
            A girl with glasses was waiting for the bus.

Power Note   *In addition to repeating the focus phrase with our new addition* (which one), *emphasize how* with *phrases and* for *phrases give readers important details, answering questions such as, "Which pig? Which girl? Waiting for what?"*

Invitation to Imitate   *Imitate Together*: Invite writers to use interactive or shared writing to compose a sentence with you to experiment with prepositional phrases, including those that answer which one.

            The kid with the bicycle is riding on the sidewalk.

Imitate Independently: To explore prepositional phrases, including those that answer which one, students use model sentences as well as others created by the class to compose their own imitations.

Invitation to Celebrate   *Table Talk*: Writers share imitations with table groups. Groups start and end each celebration making a joyful noise by singing the preposition song from Lesson 16.1 as quickly as they can.

Invitation to Apply   *Rapid Revision*: Writers reread a piece of writing twice, looking for a place to add a which-one preposition. (For more information on Rapid Revision, see Chapter 3.) Students use a preposition song to help them come up with which-one words to head their descriptive prepositional phrases, revising for detail.

Invitation to Edit

What did we learn about writing from Kevin Henkes?	
The pig with the umbrella was waiting for the rain.	
What changed? What was the effect of the change?	
The pig with the umbrella is waiting for the rain.	Changing *was* to *is* puts this sentence in the present tense (technically the present progressive). The present tense makes it seem like it's happening now, which changes what the author meant.
The pig was waiting for the rain.	The prepositional phrase *with the umbrella* has been deleted. If there were other pigs, we may not know to which pig the author is referring.
The pig with an umbrella was waiting for the rain.	The article has been changed from *the* to *an*. The article *the* means a particular noun, whereas the article *a/an* means any noun. ("Let's read a book" versus "Let's read the book.")

Less Common **Prepositions** at Work

Despite everything, Audrey continued to dance.
  —Margaret Cardillo, *Just Being Audrey*

Squirrels, like all rodents, have gnawing teeth.
  —Lois Ehlert, *Nuts to You!*

I didn't say anything as Betty leaned the stick against the tree and continued up the path away from me.

When I was finished, Toby looked astonishingly unlike Toby.

There was nothing about my grandmother that frightened me, except the thought that she'd be gone soon.

I guess it was jealousy I felt at the sight of them carrying on so well and easily without me.
  —Lauren Wolk, *Wolf Hollow*

What do you notice?

The pig with the umbrella was waiting for the rain.
—Kevin Henkes, *Waiting*

The pig was waiting.

How are they alike and different?

The pig with the umbrella was waiting for the rain.

A girl with glasses was waiting for the bus.

Let's try it out.

The pig with the umbrella was waiting for the rain.

A girl with glasses was waiting for the bus.

The pig with the umbrella was waiting for the rain.

What changed? What is the effect of the change?

The pig with the umbrella is waiting for the rain.

The pig was waiting for the rain.

The pig with an umbrella was waiting for the rain.

The Power of Combining

Some things just go together: vanilla ice cream and hot apple pie, deep-dish pizza and Coke Zero, a sunny beach and a swimsuit. Like life, things in writing can be combined to make it more meaningful, enjoyable, and effective. Sometimes thoughts, words, and sentences are better expressed together. The separation of a period is sometimes too strong, becoming a wall between thoughts that are better connected for clarity, meaning, and balance.

Where do we start with our youngest writers? What patterns of combining will serve them? Perhaps you need a conjunction—coordinate or subordinate—to link ideas or show a specific relationship or transition. Perhaps writers need a comma to chunk their sentences or to keep them from running on or fragmenting. When run-on sentences appear in your students' writing, it's a sign they're ready for compound and complex sentences. They're demonstrating a need for access to how writers combine effectively; they need the patterns of combining that writers use. For instance, what writer can live without the detail stacking, packing, and efficient serial comma? We used four serial commas in the first paragraph of this section.

In this section we start with the power of conjunctions at the word level, exploring how our youngest writers can use them to more efficiently and effectively group words with *but, and,* and *or*, and how to craft other kinds of relationships with their thoughts with *when, because,* and *if.* Then we move on to the most-tested sentence pattern: the compound sentence, building on patterns we've learned so far. The serial or list comma comes next, and then finally the most complex pattern we get to in this book: the complex sentence. Since we teach complex sentences in the upper-elementary grades, 3–5, we thought it would be interesting to tell a story through wall charts to end this introduction. See "If These Walls Could Speak: Follow a Fourth-Grade Classroom's Journey Toward Complex Sentences" in which a grade 4 classroom travels the path toward complex sentences that unfold before your very eyes.

If These Walls Could Speak: Follow a Fourth-Grade Classroom's Journey Toward Complex Sentences

To help their fourth graders grasp the difference between sentences and nonsentences, as well as compound and complex ones, Whitney, Mona Macias, and their colleagues sat down and planned an interactive growing sentence wall. The plan for the wall: Immerse writers in each component, spiraling back to the focus of what it takes to make a sentence. Making a plan to teach what their students needed to know about sentences, they sketched what it would look like at the end. The sentence wall took many weeks to complete, but at the end, it was plump and overflowing with student work.

Sentence Wall

Now let's zoom in on the components of the chart, one by one.

Zooming In on the Beginning

First, Ms. Macias began with a title of the ever-evolving wall chart: "Writers Revise Sentences." We want students to know that combining and rearranging sentences is the heart of revision. Writing and revision is about conventions and craft, growth and variety, not right and wrong. There isn't one answer to this growth. That's a worksheet. There isn't one path, but it's clear this classroom cares about and is involved in the craft of growing sentences.

Writers Revise Sentences

Zooming In on Two- and Three-Word Sentences First

Ms. Macias started simply, with two- or three-word simple sentences, using the lessons found in the "The Power of Sentences: Why Do Writers and Readers Use Sentences?" (Chapters 4–8). At this point, students wrote their simple sentences on blank mailing labels. The compact size of the labels allowed all students to add their simple sentences to the wall without taking up too much space. She went for participation instead of ease of viewing, which is a valid choice. There is no right and wrong, even with wall charts.

Simple Sentence

Zooming In on Fragments

In the meantime, Ms. Macias, Whitney, and their colleagues pondered introducing their students to sentence fragments. They didn't want the children to use a mentor sentence that was a fragment, yet they wanted young writers to have an understanding of what a fragment is. In their planning meeting, they texted Jeff and he sent them the definition from Dictionary.com, which gave them three definitions for the noun: "fragment: 1. a part broken off or detached 2. an isolated, unfinished, or incomplete part 3. an odd piece, bit, or scrap." Jeff also texted the comments that fragments aren't bad; they're just part of a sentence. Suddenly the texts stopped as the teachers and Whitney discussed fragments. They had a lightbulb moment. They'd use the two- and three-word sentences they'd already created and divide them into parts, pieces, bits, fragments.

In class, Ms. Macias looked up the word with her class, using an online dictionary. Together, they crafted their own definition for a fragment and decided to represent any piece of a sentence with a puzzle piece on their wall chart. The students gathered at the wall to reread the simple sentences they had crafted days earlier. They chose just one piece of their simple sentences to write as a fragment on another mailing label to stick on the wall under "NOT a Sentence." Some chose to write just the subjects of their sentences, whereas others wrote the verb or the complete predicate, if their sentences had one. In a concrete way, using their own words, they discovered the truth about fragments. They aren't awful things. They're merely parts. And every once in a great while, you want to emphasize a part, and you can with a rare fragment. Just like writers do in the books all over your classes and libraries. *Rarely.* Not *never.* The kids quite literally made meaning with their own words.

Fragment

Compound Sentence

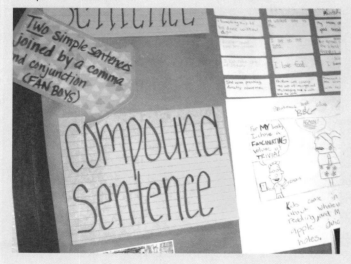

Zooming In on Compound Sentences

After a few weeks of analyzing and revising their own writing, paying attention to simple sentences and fragments, Ms. Macias introduced the compound sentence. Her writers learned that two of their simple sentences could be combined using a coordinating conjunction, or the mnemonic discussed in Chapters 17 and 18, FANBOYS (*for, and, nor, but, or, yet, so*). To add a little more than just a sentence to the wall, she encouraged her students to find or write a compound sentence about a visual they either found or created. They eased "write" on in to compound sentences. For more lesson information, see Chapter 18 in this section, "Why Do Writers Use Compound Sentences?"

Zooming In on the Run-On Sentence

"But what happens when you have many sentences but no punctuation?" Ms. Macias asked. Everybody runs on sometimes. The writer's notebooks in Ms. Macias's classroom were flooded with writing, which was great. However, run-on sentences were flooding students' prose, too, and some writing was even drowning in them. In elementary school, it's very common for students to write their ideas down without any sentence boundaries. You don't need data to tell you that. Students need some flood insurance from run-ons, like they did fragments. They need to know how to go back and look at their writing through a new lens. Once they realized the meaning of a run-on sentence and the effect it had on the meaning of their pieces, they began using more sentence boundaries. And, in part because they were being flooded with examples of working patterns such as compound sentences, they moved toward those standard patterns—not because it was wrong *not*

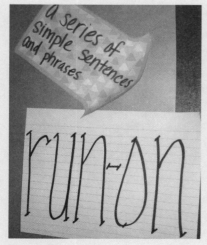

Run-on Sentences

to, but because they understood the *what*, the *why* (purpose), the *where*, and the *how* (craft). As we say again and again, "Writers read their writing twice, so readers have to read it only once."

Zooming In on Complex Sentences

Finally, when her writers were ready (or as ready as they were going to be), Ms. Macias introduced complex sentences with a simple way to remember how to craft them, use them, and even really and truly avoid sentence fragments. The AAAWWUBBIS hands, five clauses on each hand, one on each finger, are another conjunction mnemonic (common subordinating conjunctions this time), which are demonstrated in depth with lessons in Chapters 17 and 20.

Students enjoyed playing around with subordinate clauses, finding out where they might belong in a sentence, and that they could not stand alone. Knowing that clauses were just pieces of sentences, they chose to write them on puzzle pieces. For a full study of how creating complex sentences actually helps writers avoid run-ons and sentence fragments, see Chapter 20, "Why Do Writers Use Complex Sentences?"

Complex Sentences (left)
Subordinate Clauses (right)

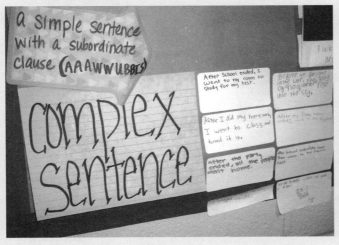 

Zooming In on the Tools That Guided the Journey to the "Great Wall"

Ms. Macias used the invitational method, described in Part 1 of this book, "Getting Started with the Patterns-of-Power Process," as well as many lessons in Part 2, "Into the Patterns-of-Power Lesson Sets."

As her literacy coach, Whitney worked with Ms. Macias and her team of fourth-grade teachers on lessons from what was in the process of becoming the *Patterns of Power*. Ms. Macias began by inviting students to notice, learn a focus phrase, compare and contrast, and imitate patterns of power. For more information on teaching the patterns-of-power process that she used, see Chapter 1, "Into Planning: What Do You Need to Do Before Teaching the Invitations?" and Chapter 2, "Into the Classroom: How Do You Teach Conventions with the Invitations Process?"

To apply their learning to writing, she invited them to go back to their writing to revise their sentences. For more on the process and application of the patterns of power, see Chapter 3, "Into Application: How Do You Ensure

Writers Apply What They Know?" Through this revision process, students gained a better understanding of sentences and the choices authors make when creating them.

Sentence (left)
NOT a Sentence (right)

The lessons in this section explore a writer's power to combine as well as how these patterns add craft and are used to achieve certain purposes, not to avoid making mistakes. But readers and writers are drawn to patterns, and there are some predominant structures writers need to know as they grow and stretch beyond fragments and run-ons. Follow the road, but don't be afraid to take detours if you or your young writers need them.

Highways are nice and paved, and they have signs telling you which way to go.
Life isn't like that at all.
—Benjamin Alire Saenz

What Do Conjunctions Do?

Conjunctions are like doors that lead into another room—a passageway or link to other words, sentence parts, and sentences.

The prefix *con-* in *con*junction is a variant of the prefix *com-*, meaning "together" or "with." And *junction* means "the act of joining or combining." That's what conjunctions do—combine and join things together. They can coordinate as the coordinating conjunctions do, acting as transitions between thoughts and words, joining and defining the relationships between or among basically equal parts. For example, Mo Willems's characters Elephant and Piggie are joined with the coordinating conjunction *and*, which connects them as a popular pair. In *A Big Guy Took My Ball!* Piggie says, "I found a big ball, *and* it was so fun!" (italics ours). Here again, Mo Willems is joining two equal parts with the conjunction *and*. This time he joined two sentences with a comma and the coordinating conjunction *and*, crafting a compound sentence.

What can conjunctions connect? If it's like the crane in Rebecca Kai Dotlich's *What Can a Crane Pick Up?* it could be anything. With its cumulative *and* as the crane just keeps picking up everything from trucks to submarines, this perfect, lively read-aloud shows the piling-up power of *and*. But lest we think the cumulative *and* is for picture books only, let's look at Newbury Medal winner Kelly Barnhill crafting the power of the cumulative *and* in *The Girl Who Drank the Moon*:

> The Elders owned the bog, too. And the orchards. And the houses. And the market squares. Even the garden plots.

Conjunctions are tools writers use to create effects that enhance the meaning of their message. Barnhill crafted the emphasis on the Elders being all powerful with a litany of fragments beginning with *And*.

Writers can join equal words, phrases, clauses, or sentences with coordinating conjunctions. The conjunction *or* in the previous sentence's list coordinates differently from *and*. How is *or* different? *Or* is a joining choice; *and* is pairing up or piling up. The other coordinating conjunctions are easy to remember with this age-old mnemonic: FANBOYS (*for, and, nor, but, or, yet, so*). (See Figure 17.1.)

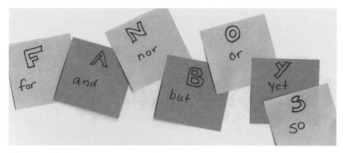

Figure 17.1
This mnemonic helps us remember coordinating conjunctions.

Figure 17.2
AAAWWUBBIS hand

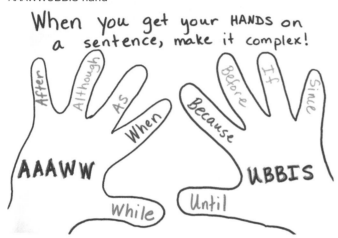

But coordinating conjunctions are not the only conjunctions in town. If subordinate conjunctions stick themselves in the front of a sentence, the sentence is transformed from independent to dependent.

> You are late. (This is an *independent clause* or sentence.)
> If you are late . . . (It's a *dependent clause* now.)

With that subordinating *if* at the helm, the clause needs to be attached to a sentence: *If you are late*, you will be counted tardy. **When any of the AAAWWUBBIS words begin a sentence**, a comma is probably on its way. AAWWUBBIS in another mnenomic for common subordinate conjunctions (*as, after, while, when, until, because, before, if, since*). (See Figure 17.2.)

Subordinating conjunctions also order ideas or sentence parts by importance. To explore what subordinating conjunctions do, let's deconstruct a sentence from Alexis O'Neill's *Recess Queen*:

> Mean Jean was Recess Queen and nobody said any different. Nobody swung until mean Jean swung. Nobody kicked until mean Jean kicked. Nobody bounced until Mean Jean bounced.

Mean Jean swung on its own is a sentence. But when a writer attaches *until* in front of the clause, it becomes dependent: *Until Mean Jean swung* leaves you hanging. It's dependent on another sentence or clause now. (*Until, if, unless,* and *as long as* each imply a condition—or that something has to happen.)

> *Until Mean Jean swung*, nobody swung.
> Nobody swung until Mean Jean swung.

Subordinating conjunctions link like coordinating conjunctions, but unlike coordinating conjunctions, subordinate clauses become dependent and less important than the independent clause (sentence) they join. The addition of the subordinating conjunction has made the clause sub-ordered, setting up an unequal relationship between the two clauses. The sentence is the top, and the subordinate clause is the lesser of the two.

Lesson Sets:

What Do Conjunctions Do?

17.1 Sticks and Stones: The Power of *And*

17.2 Coordinating Outfits: Using *And* to Combine

17.3 Feeling Squirrelly: Using *Though* to Contrast

17.4 Give Me a Reason: Using *Because* to Show Why

17.5 What a Choice: Using *Or* to Show Options

17.6 There's a Negative Correlation: Neither . . . Nor

17.1   Sticks and Stones: The Power of *And*

Standard	Use conjunctions.
Focus Phrase	"I use *and* to make pairs."

Invitation to Notice

Power Note   *Read aloud* Stick and Stone *by Beth Ferry. On the second reading, focus the discussion on the first four pages—when Stick is lonely and Stone is alone. "Alone is no fun." (If you're feeling extra dramatic, you can play the song "One" by Three Dog Night as you transition into this lesson.)*

> *It might go like this:*
> *"What happens in the story?" you ask.*
> *"Stick and Stone become friends."*
> *"That's right," you say. "One way we can put the names together is shown in the title." You hold the cover up.*
> *"Stick and Stone," several students answer.*
> *"Right," you say. "And joins a pair."*

Invitation to Compare and Contrast   *Stick and Stone*
Frog and Toad
Elephant and Piggie

Power Note   *We chose to use titles instead of sentences in this comparison to call students' attention to all the signals and craft that titles provide. For fun, students may want to generate a list of other pairs. If they stumble upon groups of three or more, based on student readiness, either move forward with a discussion on lists versus pairs or save it for when you teach about using commas in a list.*

Invitation to Imitate   *Imitate Together*: Invite writers to use interactive, shared, or paired writing to compose a sentence with you. Our task is to brainstorm as many pairs as possible from the world around us.

> Spaghetti and meatballs
> Juan and Chris (two friends in the class)
> Hamburger and French fries

Imitate Independently: Students use the model to create their own pair, using the coordinating conjunction *and*. They can illustrate their pair if they want.

Invitation to Celebrate   Create a bulletin board or wall chart and label it "The Joining Power of *And*." Post kids' pair work all over the board. As we stumble across pairs while reading in other subjects, or use them in our writing, we add them to the board. When we keep the bulletin boards alive by adding to and referring to them, they are far more useful to students as scaffolds and clarification.

Invitation to Apply   Hunt for the use of *and* throughout the day and talk about the work it's doing: creating pairs or stacking things and ideas together. (See Figure 17.3.) Students often see that commas act like *ands* too, separating and joining elements. These noticings happen when we keep our work open-ended and full of a sense of discovery.

Figure 17.3
Conjunction pairings

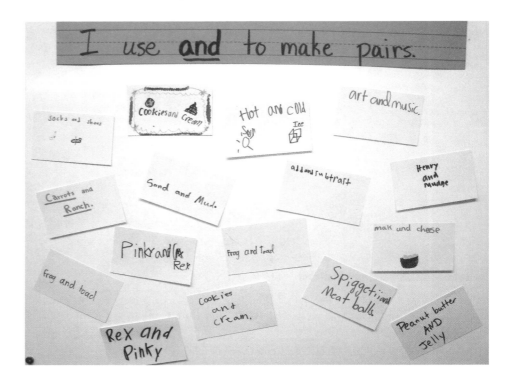

17.2   Coordinating Outfits: Using *And* to Combine

Standard	Use coordinating conjunctions.
Focus Phrase	"I use *and* to join ideas."
Invitation to Notice	Kiki Kittie mixes stripes, solids, patterns, and colors with style.
	—Charise Mericle Harper, *Fashion Kitty Versus the Fashion Queen*
Invitation to Compare and Contrast	Kiki Kittie mixes stripes, solids, patterns, and colors with style.
	Myron mixes crushed Oreos, chocolate pudding, gummy worms, and Cool Whip to make dirt cake.

Power Note   *Our focus is on how the conjunction* and *joins the mixture or list beyond pairs. Of course, commas and capitalization of proper nouns will also be recognized and discussed, spiraling them back into the mix of our instruction. When students notice the commas or capitals, ask groups to build a theory about what the commas or capital letters are doing in Harper's sentence: "What do the commas do when you read it aloud? What do the commas do when you read it with your eyes?"*

Invitation to Imitate   *Imitate Together*: Invite writers to use interactive or shared writing to compose a sentence with you.

> Yesterday in science, we mixed milk, dish soap, pepper, and food coloring to show how sunspots form.

Imitate Independently: Students use the models to compose their own sentences, using the coordinating conjunction *and* to combine or mix a list of items.

Invitation to Celebrate   Students create their own drawings of their mixtures or lists. They write their imitation sentences beneath the pictures and create a class book. Before they begin, ask, "Do you think you'll need to use commas and the word *and* in your writing?"

Invitation to Apply   With a partner, students use the conjunction *and* or *commas* as a tool to respond to something they've read, joining three or more ideas in their written response. (See Figure 17.4.)

> I think that Rose Blanche and Jenny are alike because they are both brave, they are both caring, and they both learned some thing new.
>
> | Reason 1: They are brave | e.A: "I carefully handed it to them through the pointed wire" |

Invitation to Edit

What did we learn about writing from Charise Mericle Harper?	
Kiki Kittie mixes stripes, solids, patterns, and colors with style.	
What changed? What is the effect of the change?	
Kiki Kittie mixes stripes, solids, patterns, colors with style.	*The coordinating conjunction and has been deleted. Read the sentence both with and without the and, and then discuss which one students prefer and why. Though using and before the last item in the list is the most common pattern, a writer may use only commas in a list (a technique called asyndeton).*
Kiki Kittie mixed stripes, solids, patterns, and colors with style.	*The verb mixes is changed to the past tense by adding -ed, indicating that this event occurred in the past. Verbs tell time for our reader, so the meaning that this happened in the past is being communicated.*
Kiki Kittie mixes stripes, solids patterns, and colors with style.	*The comma between solids and patterns has been deleted, making the two run together. Writers use commas between nouns to separate them in a list. When they don't follow this pattern, readers can be confused.*

What do you notice?

Kiki Kittie mixes stripes, solids, patterns, and colors with style.

—Charise Mericle Harper, *Fashion Kitty Versus the Fashion Queen*

How are they alike and different?

Kiki Kittie mixes stripes, solids, patterns, and colors with style.

Myron mixes crushed Oreos, chocolate pudding, gummy worms, and Cool Whip to make dirt cake.

Let's try it out.

Kiki Kittie mixes stripes, solids, patterns, and colors with style.

Myron mixes crushed Oreos, chocolate pudding, gummy worms, and Cool Whip to make dirt cake.

Kiki Kittie mixes stripes, solids, patterns, and colors with style.

What changed? What is the effect of the change?

Kiki Kittie mixes stripes, solids, patterns, colors with style.

Kiki Kittie mixed stripes, solids, patterns, and colors with style.

Kiki Kittie mixes stripes, solids patterns, and colors with style.

17.3   Feeling Squirrelly: Using *Though* to Contrast

Standard   Use conjunctions.

Focus Phrase   "I use *though* and *although* to show a contrast between ideas."

Invitation to Notice   Gray squirrels are tree squirrels. They love trees, though you often see them on the ground.
  —Lois Ehlert, *Nuts to You!*

Power Note   *We chose to use two sentences because we thought the word* though *made more sense that way. When students notice the* though—*even if it's just to say, "How do you say that word?"—answer their question and then ask, "What is the conjunction* though *doing in this sentence?" If students don't notice the* though, *remember the now-you-see-it, now-you-don't trick. Rewrite the sentence underneath the original, without* though, *and ask, "How are these sentences alike and different?"*

Invitation to Compare and Contrast   They love trees, though you often see them on the ground.
Kids love to read, though they often stream videos.

Power Note   *We thought the concept and spelling of* though *was complex enough that we should repeat it in the imitation. We keep emphasizing* though's *connective ability to show contrast or a shift in ideas.*

Invitation to Imitate   *Imitate Together*: Invite writers to use interactive writing to compose a sentence with you. (See Figure 17.5.)

Figure 17.5
Interactive writing with *though*

Birds love seeds, though they'll eat little bits of bread.

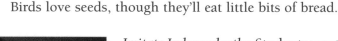

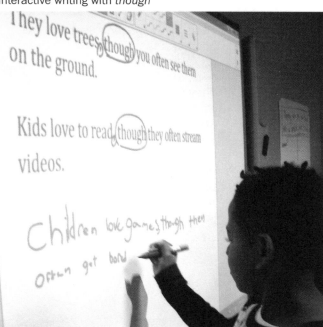

Imitate Independently: Students use the model to create their own sentences, using the subordinating conjunction *though* to contrast ideas.

Contrasting Conjunctions	
Coordinating Conjunctions	**Subordinating Conjunctions**
But
Yet	Although
Even though
Though
While

Invitation to Celebrate	Students share their sentences, turning their bodies dramatically when they read the *though* part.
Invitation to Apply	In another content area, attempt to use *though* or *although* to create a statement reflecting on the day's learning or experiences. Here are some examples: Although they start their lives as caterpillars, they become butterflies eventually. Though map pencils are cool, markers are better.
Invitation to Edit	

What did we learn about writing from Lois Ehlert?
Gray squirrels are tree squirrels. They love trees, though you often see them on the ground.

What changed? What is the effect of the change?	
Gray squirrels are tree squirrels. They love trees, although you often see them on the ground.	*The conjunction* though *has been changed to* although. *The meaning isn't changed, because both conjunctions show a contrast. They're essentially synonyms.*
Gray squirrels are tree squirrels. It love trees, though you often see them on the ground.	*The pronoun in the second sentence has been changed from* they *to* it, *from a plural pronoun to a singular pronoun. Since the antecedent (squirrels) is plural, the pattern is to match singular nouns to singular pronouns and plural nouns to plural pronouns. That's pronoun-antecedent agreement.*
Gray squirrels are tree squirrels. They love trees, though you often see they on the ground.	Them *in the second sentence has been changed to* they. *Both are plural, so they agree in number, but they do not agree in case.* They *is in the subjective case (think* subject—near the beginning of a sentence) *and* them *is in the objective case. (The object isn't the doer, but is the receiver of action or comes after a preposition. Objects are often nearer the end of the sentence; you often see them at the end.)*

What do you notice?

Gray squirrels are tree squirrels. They love trees, though you often see them on the ground.

—Lois Ehlert, *Nuts to You!*

How are they alike and different?

They love trees, though you often see them on the ground.

Kids love to read, though they often stream videos.

Let's try it out.

They love trees, though you often see them on the ground.

Kids love to read, though they often stream videos.

Gray squirrels are tree squirrels. They love trees, though you often see them on the ground.

What changed? What is the effect of the change?

Gray squirrels are tree squirrels. They love trees, although you often see them on the ground.

Gray squirrels are tree squirrels. It love trees, though you often see them on the ground.

Gray squirrels are tree squirrels. They love trees, though you often see they on the ground.

17.4   Give Me a Reason: Using *Because* to Show Why

Standard	Use conjunctions.
Focus Phrase	"I use *because* to show how one thing causes another."
Invitation to Notice	One morning Mr. Squirrel woke up because the moon had fallen onto his tree. —Sebastian Meschenmoser, *Mr. Squirrel and the Moon*
Power Note	*If students ask why there isn't a comma after* morning, *read it aloud with and without the comma. "Why do you think he chose not to use a comma?" Perhaps Meschenmoser thought the pause unnecessary. It certainly changes the energy a bit. Every choice a writer makes has an effect.*
Invitation to Compare and Contrast	One morning Mr. Squirrel woke up because the moon had fallen onto his tree. Every morning, I wake up because my brother makes noise.
Power Note	*Students may need help understanding that for something to have a cause, it has to have happened. Highlight this fact in the sentences if students don't note it. We chose to use the comma after the imitation sentence's opener to show that it's okay, even preferable at times. Students will notice the difference in tense as well as the irregular verb* wake/woke *and how verbs place actions in time.*
Invitation to Imitate	*Imitate Together*: Invite writers to use paired writing to compose a sentence. Every afternoon, we perk up because we have recess. *Imitate Independently*: Students use the model to create their own sentences, using the subordinating conjunction *because* to show why the subject of their sentence does something (a cause/effect relationship).
Invitation to Celebrate	*Timing Is Everything.* Students share their sentences. When students finish reading their sentences aloud, we ask, "Which event happened first?" Once we have the answer, we follow up with, "How do we know?"
Invitation to Apply	*Defend Your Thinking.* When answering questions, students use the word *because* to further explain their answer. ("*I think Zack felt embarrassed because he tried to disappear.*") (See Figure 17.6.)

Tip: *Because* You Need a Conjunction to Show Cause/Effect Relationships

To teach the concept of *because*, we love reading aloud the brief and deft *Because of an Acorn* by Lola and Adam Schaefer. The cause/effect relationship of everything in the universe comes to light in the simple text: one cause is linked to one effect, and then that effect causes the next effect, link upon link.

Figure 17.6
A second grader supports her thinking with text evidence using the conjunction *because*.

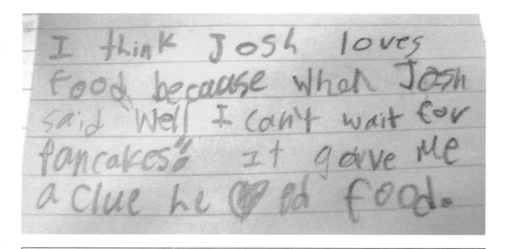

I think Josh loves food because when Josh said "Well I can't wait for pancakes!" It gave me a clue he ♡ ed food.

Invitation to Edit

What did we learn about writing from Sebastian Meschenmoser?	
One morning Mr. Squirrel woke up because the moon had fallen onto his tree.	
What changed? What is the effect of the change?	
One morning Mr. Squirrel woke up when the moon had fallen onto his tree.	*The subordinating conjunction* because, *which shows a cause/effect relationship, has been changed to* when. When *shows a time relationship. Which one is better? Why? (The moon falling caused Mr. Squirrel to wake up.)*
One morning Mr. Squirrel woke up because the moon had falled onto his tree.	*The past-perfect verb phrase* had fallen *has been changed to a nonstandard form,* had falled. *The past-perfect shows an action in the past of the past. Here, the moon fell before Mr. Squirrel woke. Therefore to show that the moon had fallen first, the author used the form* had fallen.
One morning Mr Squirrel woke up because the moon had fallen onto his tree.	*The period after the abbreviation of the title* mister *has been deleted. The pattern is to put a period after abbreviations, such as Mr., Dr., and Ms., to show that the titles have been shortened.*

Cause-and-Effect-or-Why Conjunctions	
Coordinating Conjunctions	**Subordinating Conjunctions**
So For	Because If Siince

What do you notice?

One morning Mr. Squirrel woke up because the moon had fallen onto his tree.

—Sebastian Meschenmoser, *Mr. Squirrel and the Moon*

How are they alike and different?

One morning Mr. Squirrel woke up because the moon had fallen onto his tree.

Every morning, I wake up because my brother makes noise.

Let's try it out.

One morning Mr. Squirrel woke up because the moon had fallen onto his tree.

Every morning, I wake up because my brother makes noise.

One morning Mr. Squirrel woke up because the moon had fallen onto his tree.

What changed? What is the effect of the change?

One morning Mr. Squirrel woke up when the moon had fallen onto his tree.

One morning Mr. Squirrel woke up because the moon had falled onto his tree.

One morning Mr Squirrel woke up because the moon had fallen onto his tree.

17.5   What a Choice: Using *Or* to Show Options

Standard   Use conjunctions.

Focus Phrase   "I use *or* to show choices."

Invitation to Notice   I hate dodgeball more than math homework, Brussels sprouts, or chin-ups.
— Jeff Anderson, *Zack Delacruz: Just My Luck*

Power Note   *Though a serial comma is used here, it's not the only focus of the sentence, but it can and should be part of the discussion, either to preteach the use of this convention or to reinforce previous learning. Brussels is capitalized because the delightful vegetable comes from Belgium. It's capitalized as an adjective because its origin is a proper noun—a country.*

Invitation to Compare and Contrast   I hate dodgeball more than math homework, Brussels sprouts, or chin-ups. I love pizza more than French fries, Big Red, and bubble gum.

Power Note   *French comes from the proper noun France, deepening the concept of Brussels. Hate, love, like—the verb doesn't matter. Students need choice. If a student asks, "Can I change the verb to despise?" we like to reply with, "Why don't you try it and see what happens?"*
"Can I put four things I love?"
"Well, lists are three or more items, so what do you think?"

Invitation to Imitate   *Imitate Together*: Invite writers to use paired writing to compose a sentence.

Imitate Independently: Students use the model to compose their own sentences, using the coordinating conjunction *or* to show choices or options in a list.

Invitation to Celebrate   Students share their sentences with the class, reading them twice. We always clap for every writer. Celebration and audience connects our writing community and honors the risk and hard work of writing.

Invitation to Apply   *Student-Choice Rewards*: Students generate sentences in which they describe three choices of what they like to get or what they would like to do for a reward. As a side benefit, it will give you a look into what they value.

Invitation to Edit

What did we learn about writing from Jeff Anderson?	
I hate dodgeball more than math homework, Brussels sprouts, or chin-ups.	
What changed? What is the effect of the change?	
I hate dodgeball more than Math homework, Brussels sprouts, or chin-ups.	*The subject* math *has been capitalized. School subjects aren't capitalized in prose, unless they are a language such as English or Spanish or Chinese. Languages and nationalities are capitalized because they come from proper nouns.*
I hate dodgeball more than math homework Brussels sprouts, or chin-ups.	*The comma after* math homework *has been deleted, making it run together with* Brussels sprouts. Brussels sprouts *may feel like homework, but they're two separate things. Commas separate and connect the things Zack hates.*
I hate dodgeball more than math homework, Brussels sprouts, or chinups.	*The hyphen from* chin-ups *was deleted.* Chin-ups *needs a hyphen. Certain words need to be hyphenated. When unsure, look in a dictionary for the conventional pattern.*

Tip: Correlative Conjunctions **Either** Come in Pairs **or** They're Not Correlative Conjunctions

The truth is, *neither* you *nor* I really want to talk about correlative conjunctions, but *either* you *or* I will have to sooner or later, because standard writers think small children need to learn about them.

> Genius is neither learned nor acquired.
> —Patricia Polacco, *Junkyard Wonders*

N-O spells *no*. Everyone knows the negative two-letter word *no* starts with the letter *n*. Knowing this can help you decide which set of correlative conjunctions to use—*either . . . or*, or *neither . . . nor*. Patricia Palacco chose to use the *neither . . . nor* pair because *no one* learns or acquires genius, and *neither . . . nor* both start with *n*, like *no*. Not that you've ever called them correlative conjunctions, but we can *either* know their names *or* use them correctly. I say drop the abstract name and just call them what they are: *neither . . . nor* and *either . . . or*.

Although the coordinating conjunction *or* is one of the most common conjunctions, you have to use it with *either* only if you want to pair it. Never use *neither* with *or*. Neither word requires the other, but when they're used together, they must match, like in Patricia MacLachlan's sentence in *The Poet's Dog*:

> Being a writer is not easy, you know. It is, now that I think of it, either full of sorrow or full of joy.

Here's the skinny on correlative conjunctions:

- To tell which pair to use, think about the second word in each pair: *nor* versus *or*.
- *Or* means a choice, *either* one *or* the other, a choice between two.
- If it's not a choice—it's *no* to both—use *neither . . . nor*.
- The negative correlative conjunctions *neither . . . nor* hang out together—both start with the letter *n*, like the word *no*.

What do you notice?

I hate dodgeball more than math homework, Brussels sprouts, or chin-ups.
—Jeff Anderson, *Zack Delacruz: Just My Luck*

How are they alike and different?

I hate dodgeball more than math homework, Brussels sprouts, or chin-ups.

I love pizza more than French fries, Big Red, and bubble gum.

Let's try it out.

I hate dodgeball more than math homework, Brussels sprouts, or chin-ups.

I love pizza more than French fries, Big Red, and bubble gum.

I hate dodgeball more than math homework, Brussels sprouts, or chin-ups.

What changed? What effect does the change have?

I hate dodgeball more than Math homework, Brussels sprouts, or chin-ups.

I hate dodgeball more than math homework Brussels sprouts, or chin-ups.

I hate dodgeball more than math homework, Brussels sprouts, or chinups.

17.6   There's a Negative Correlation: Neither . . . Nor

Standard	Use correlative conjunctions.
Focus Phrase	"I show that two things didn't happen with *neither . . . nor.*"
Invitation to Notice	Neither Peter nor Harold slept at all. —Philip C. Stead, *Lenny and Lucy*
Power Note	*After students share their noticings, ask, "What does this sentence mean?" (Peter and Harold didn't sleep.) "How do you know?" Discuss how* neither *and* nor *start with* n *and both mean* no *or the negative. Emphasize that the two* n's *will always go together, if paired (*neither . . . nor*).*
Invitation to Compare and Contrast	Neither Peter nor Harold slept at all. Neither Gerald nor Piggie turned in their homework.
Power Note	*After the students share how the two sentences are alike and different, ask,* *"Did Gerald do his homework? How do you know? Did Piggie do his home-* *work? How do you know?" Discuss. "I show that two things didn't happen with* neither . . . nor.*"*
Invitation to Imitate	*Imitate Together*: Invite writers to help you write a sentence using *neither* and *nor* to show that two things didn't happen.

Invitation to Edit

What did we learn about writing from Philip C. Stead?	
Neither Peter nor Harold slept at all.	
What changed? What is the effect of the change?	
Neither Peter or Harold slept at all.	*The conjunction* nor *has been changed to* or. Neither *always go with* nor, *never with* or. Or *has the effect of showing choice, whereas* neither *and* nor *both mean something didn't/won't happen.* "I show that two things didn't happen with *neither . . . nor."*
Neither Peter nor Harold sleeped at all.	*The irregular verb* slept *has been changed to nonstandard* sleeped. *The irregular past-tense pattern of* sleep *is* slept. *The change causes readers to be confused.*
Either Peter nor Harold slept at all.	Neither *has been changed to* Either. Either *implies a choice.* "What does the sentence mean now? What does it say?" *Discuss.* "I show two things didn't happen with *neither . . . nor."*

What do you notice?

Neither Peter nor Harold slept at all.

—Philip C. Stead, *Lenny and Lucy*

How are they alike and different?

Neither Peter nor Harold slept at all.

Neither Gerald nor Piggie turned in their homework.

Let's try it out.

Neither Peter nor Harold slept at all.

Neither Gerald nor Piggie turned in their homework.

Neither Peter nor Harold slept at all.

What changed? What is the effect of the change?

Neither Peter or Harold slept at all.

Neither Peter nor Harold sleeped at all.

Either Peter nor Harold slept at all.

18

Why Do Writers Use Compound Sentences?

Compound sentences are made when two or more sentences are joined together with a comma and a coordinating conjunction (FANBOYS). The mnemonic FANBOYS defines the relationship between the sentences. Consider Adina Rishe Gewirtz's compound sentence from *Zebra Forest*:

I could hear the desperation in his voice, **and** my stomach went liquidy. [Bold ours.]

This is a compound sentence. On both sides of the *comma* and the *coordinating conjunction* is a sentence, each with its own subject (*I/stomach*) and verb (*hear/went*). Gewirtz chose to combine the two, but she could have chosen to write them as two separate sentences:

I could hear the desperation in his voice.
My stomach went liquidy.

Gewirtz chose the coordinating conjunction *and* to join the sentences; the link denotes combination rather than contrast (which would have been expressed with *but* or *yet*), choice (*or*), or cause and effect (*so/for*).

Don't Be Tricked by the Compound Predator

The main nemesis standing in the way of students learning compound sentences is a compound predicate. We like to call them compound predators because one of the subjects was eaten. But that wasn't enough for the compound predator: it also ate the comma. Let's make it real simple. *Birds fly. Birds chirp.* Two sentences become one; however, the subject is not repeated on both sides of the conjunction *and*. There isn't a comma either: *Birds chirp and fly.* Even though the sentence has an *and* as well as two verbs, there is only one subject on one side of the *and*. You need both a comma and an *and* to join two sentences. (See Figure 18.1.)

Figure 18.1
Birds fly and chirp

With simple sentences, it's easier to see the compound predator, but longer sentences prove more difficult. Consider this sentence from Natalie Lloyd's *A Snicker of Magic*:

Mama slowed the van and leaned her arm across me.

Note that the sentence has one subject (*Mama*) and two actions (*slowed/leaned*). There isn't a comma between the two actions, but there is the coordinating conjunction *and*. In addition to there not being a comma, there's no subject on the right side of the coordinating conjunction. Thus, this is a compound predicate, or one subject with two actions. To make this sentence compound, the writer could add a second subject like this: *Mama slowed the van, and she leaned her arm across me.* Here a few more compound predicates from Dan Gemeinhart's *The Honest Truth*:

I unzipped the duffel bag and spread it open.
I pulled the money out of the pocket of my blue jacket and handed it to him.

In each of Gemeinhart's sentences, the single subject is *I*. No comma before the *and*. No subject to the right of the *and*. No compound sentence. To close, we look at a compound sentence (a subject and verb on both sides of the comma and coordinating conjunction) from Jennifer Nielsen's *The Scourge*:

Few things were worth the risk to my life, but the juicy vinefruit was one of them.

Lesson Sets:

What Do Compound Sentences Do?

Tip: The Story of a Compound Sentence

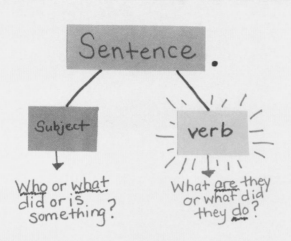

Figure 18.2 The sentence

In the beginning, there was a sentence. How do you know if a string of words is a sentence or not? That's a good question. As you already know, a sentence needs at least two things—a subject and a verb. A subject answers the question "Who or what does or is something?" A verb answers the question "What are they or what did they do?" (See Figure 18.2.)

And writers love sentences. They love stacking them up, one on top of the other, telling stories or explaining their thinking. Dear reader, writers love sentences so much that they sometimes choose to combine them. Look at the sentence from Jen Bryant's *Six Dots* in Figure 18.3.

I was a curious child, and my eyes studied everything.

Figure 18.3 Bryant's sentence

It's a sentence, right? A good one, in fact. It starts with a capital letter and ends with a period. But let's check to see if it passes muster as a sentence. Does it have a subject and a verb? (See Figure 18.4.)

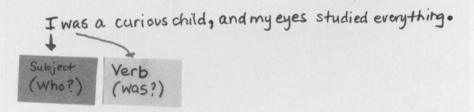

Figure 18.4 Subject and verb

Yes, it does have a subject and a verb, but are you noticing something? Take a look to the right of the comma. A little farther. To the right of the *and*. Do you see another sentence—another subject and another verb sitting on the right side of the *comma* and the *and*? (See Figure 18.5.)

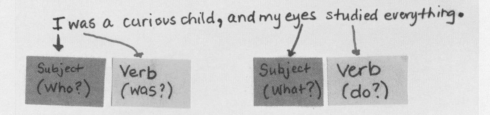

Figure 18.5 Subject + verb X 2

Indeed there are two sentences joined with a *comma* and an *and*. In the past, when you put two words together, such as *basket* and *ball*, and made the word *basketball*, what did you call that? A compound word. That's right. Guess what you call

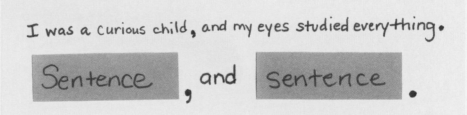

Figure 18.6 Compound sentence

it when you join two sentences with a comma and an *and*? A compound sentence. Here is a graphic to help you see what the compound sentence looks like without the words. This is just its structure, plain and simple. Compound sentences are an important pattern of power that you'll use for the rest of your life. (See Figure 18.6.)

(continued)

If you ever tire of joining two sentences with a comma and an *and*, there are other choices. These words are called coordinating conjunctions. I know. It's a real mouthful. Call them FANBOYS. It's easier to say and easier to remember. In fact, each letter of the FANBOYS stands for one of the coordinating conjunctions. See the picture. Be careful, though: each of the FANBOYS has a specific job to do when it connects two related sentences after a comma. The FANBOYS tell you the relationship between the two sentences. Which of the FANBOYS do you think you'll use the most? In writing, the three most common are *but, and,* and *or*, but that just spells BOA, so . . . (see Figure 18.7).

That's enough for now. Whenever you find yourself with two sentences that go together, instead of using a period, try using a comma and one of the FANBOYS to join two sentences. You'll be glad you did.

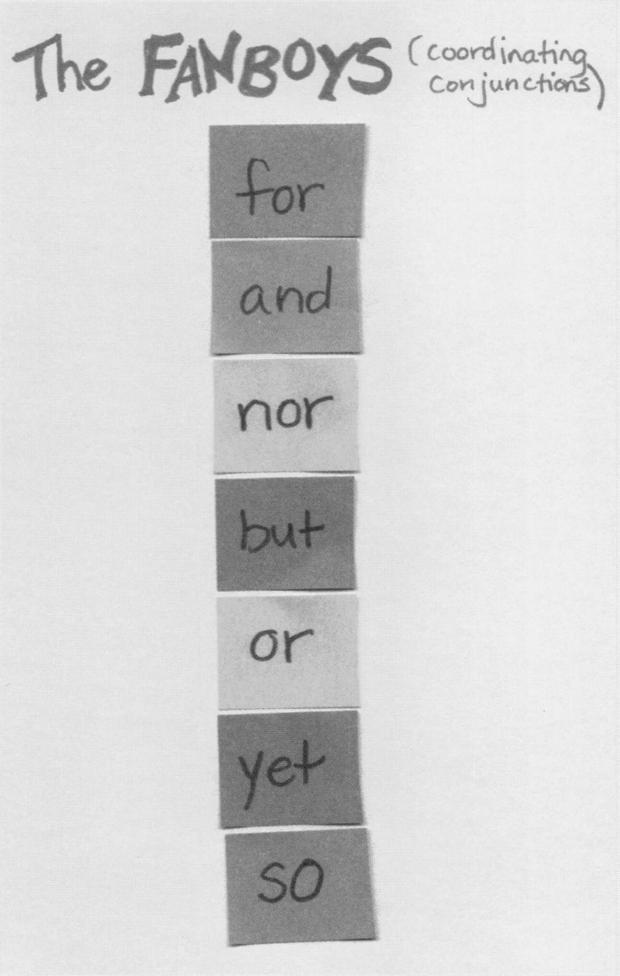

The **FANBOYS** (coordinating conjunctions)

for
and
nor
but
or
yet
so

Figure 18.7 FANBOYS

18.1   Curious and Studied: Combining Sentences

Standard	Use coordinating conjunctions and a comma to produce compound sentences.
Focus Phrase	"I use a comma and an *and* to join two sentences."
Invitation to Notice: Day 1	I was a curious child. My eyes studied everything.
Power Note	*This invitation begins with a different purpose. Go through the normal noticing, honoring, naming, and extending, but at the end of the exploration ask, "Do you think these two sentences are related?" As you discuss possibilities, students work in pairs to make these two sentences into one. Allow for all experiments. We are all about options. Have students share their creations.*
Invitation to Notice: Day 2	*I was a curious child, and my eyes studied everything.* —Jen Bryant, *Six Dots: A Story of Young Louis Braille*
Power Note	*"This is the pattern the author chose. Let's explore what we notice in Bryant's sentences." Students or you note that there are two sentences. (Go through the sentence test for each side of the compound sentence. Who or what does or is something? What are they or what do they do? See the tip box "The Story of a Compound Sentence.")*
Invitation to Compare and Contrast	I was a curious child, and my eyes studied everything. I was an active child, and my body never stopped moving.
Power Note	*Highlight that there is both a subject and a verb on both the left and the right side of the comma and coordinating conjunction. Repeat this with every compound sentence you look at. It's that important.*
Invitation to Imitate	*Imitate Together*: Invite writers to use interactive paired writing to compose a sentence.

Figure 18.8 (left)
Simple sentences
Figure 18.9 (right)
Compound sentences with *and*

Imitate Independently: Students use the model to create their own sentences, using the coordinating conjunction *and* to combine two sentences. (See Figures 18.8 and 18.9.)

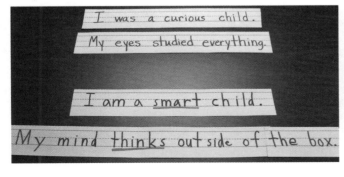

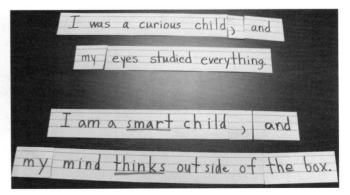

Invitation to Celebrate Volunteers read their imitation sentences aloud. This is the best celebration of all—having an audience for which writers can write.

Invitation to Apply *Are You Feeling This?* With a partner, writers compose a compound sentence about a character's feelings in a book they're reading. They help each other describe the feelings so that they each understand them. Partners also ensure a subject and verb is on both sides of the comma and one of the FANBOYS. Remind them to always check that subjects and verbs agree in number and person.

Invitation to Edit

What did we learn about writing from Jen Bryant?	
I was a curious child, and my eyes studied everything.	
What changed? What is the effect of the change?	
I was a curious child, my eyes studied everything.	*The conjunction and has been deleted. This is a comma splice. To match the compound sentence pattern, it needs to have both a comma and a coordinating conjunction.*
I was a curious child and my eyes studied everything.	*The comma has been deleted. Ask students to read the sentence aloud with the comma and without it. Discuss how the effect is different. To match the compound sentence pattern, it needs to have both a comma and a coordinating conjunction.*
I was a curious child, and my eyes study everything.	*The verb studied has been changed to the present tense. Since the first half of the sentence is in the past tense, the second half needs to be in the past tense to be consistent.*

What do you notice?

I was a curious child, and my eyes studied everything.

—Jen Bryant, *Six Dots: A Story of Young Louis Braille*

How are they alike and different?

I was a curious child, and my eyes studied everything.

I was an active child, and my body never stopped moving.

Let's try it out.

I was a curious child, and my eyes studied everything.

I was an active child, and my body never stopped moving.

I was a curious child, and my eyes studied everything.

What changed? What is the effect of the change?

I was a curious child, my eyes studied everything.

I was a curious child and my eyes studied everything.

I was a curious child, and my eyes study everything.

18.2   Hearing Voices: Compound Sentences 101

Standard Use coordinating conjunctions and a comma to produce compound sentences.

Focus Phrase "I use a comma and an *and* to join two sentences."

Invitation to Notice Her voice was high, and her words jumped around like grasshoppers.
—William Alexander, *Goblin Secrets*

Power Note *Within students' noticings, highlight the elements of the two sentences, which are joined by a comma and one of the FANBOYS. Usually in a compound sentence, the parts are closer to the same length, but the essential ingredients are there and Alexander's writing is fun, so we decided to study it. It's a perfect opportunity to show the craft of comparison, namely with similes, giving readers a deeper understanding of the sound of the voice. We don't think of voices as being compared to grasshoppers, but that's the thing: Alexander is being fresh. Hot like an oven is technically a simile, but the craft lies in coming up with something true that no one else would think of.*

Invitation to Compare and Contrast Her voice was high, and her words jumped around like grasshoppers.
His voice was gravelly, and his words bubbled like black soda.

Power Note *Highlight that both sentences have a subject and a verb on both the left and the right side of the comma and coordinating conjunction.*

Invitation to Imitate *Imitate Together*: Invite writers to use interactive or shared writing to compose a sentence with you.

Their voices were musical, and their words floated into the rafters like moving clouds.

Imitate Independently: Students use the model to create their own sentences, using the coordinating conjunction *and* to combine two sentences about sounds.

Invitation to Celebrate Students share their responses with the class. We clap after each student shares. If we run out of time, we collect the responses and display them with the focus phrase on the door or in any available space. We celebrate writing.

Invitation to Apply Have students work with partners to write a compound sentence about a character's feeling in a book they're reading.

Invitation to Edit

What did we learn about writing from William Alexander?	
Her voice was high, and her words jumped around like grasshoppers.	
What changed? What is the effect of the change?	
Her voice was high and jumped around like grasshoppers.	*The comma before and has been deleted, and there is no subject on the right-hand side of the and. This sentence is a compound predicate, not a compound sentence. It needs a subject on both sides to match the compound sentence pattern.*
Her voice was high, her words jumped around like grasshoppers.	*The and after the comma has been deleted. "I use a comma and an and to join two sentences." The effect is a comma splice or run-on sentence.*
Her voice was high, and her words jump around like grasshoppers.	*The -ed ending is deleted from the verb jumped, making the tense inconsistent with the first half of the sentence. This can disorient the reader in time.*

What do you notice?

Her voice was high, and her words jumped around like grasshoppers.

—William Alexander, *Goblin Secrets*

How are they alike and different?

Her voice was high, and her words jumped around like grasshoppers.

His voice was gravelly, and his words bubbled like black soda.

Let's try it out.

Her voice was high, and her words jumped around like grasshoppers.

His voice was gravelly, and his words bubbled like black soda.

Her voice was high, and her words jumped around like grasshoppers.

What changed? What is the effect of the change?

Her voice was high and jumped around like grasshoppers.

Her voice was high, her words jumped around like grasshoppers.

Her voice was high, and her words jump around like grasshoppers.

Additional sentences for study:
He sifted words through his head like fine dust through his hands, and he caught what he could.

    —William Alexander, *Goblin Secrets*

Wind whistles through last year's plants, and mud sucks at my rain boots.

    —Kate Messner, *Up in the Garden, Down in the Dirt*

18.3 The Draw of a Compound Sentence: Coordinating Contrast

Standard	Use coordinating conjunctions and a comma to produce compound sentences.
Focus Phrase	"I use a comma and *but* to join two contrasting sentences."
Invitation to Notice	She once tried to draw me a Darth Vader, but it ended up looking like some weird mushroom-shaped robot. —R. J. Palacio, *Wonder*
Invitation to Compare and Contrast	She once tried to draw me a Darth Vader, but it ended up looking like some weird mushroom-shaped robot. José once tried to draw a chicken for me, but it ended up looking like some weird stain-shaped blob with claws.
Power Note	*Make sure to focus on all it took to join the two sentences (a subject and verb on each side). "I use a comma and one of the FANBOYS, in this case, but, to join two sentences."*
Invitation to Imitate	*Imitate Together*: Invite writers to use interactive, shared, or paired writing to compose a sentence with you. Regina once tried to draw a map to her house for me, but it ended up looking like a smeared tic-tac-toe board. *Imitate Independently*: Students use the model to create their own sentences, using the coordinating conjunction *but* to join and show contrast between two ideas. (See Figures 18.10 and 18.11.)

Figure 18.10 (left)
Compound with *but*
Figure 18.11 (right)
Compound with *but*

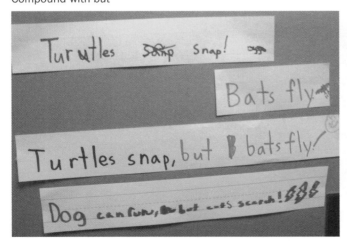

Invitation to Celebrate   *Compound Sentence Art*: Students create a drawing for a partner. After exchanging drawings, they ask what the drawing is supposed to look like and say what it actually looks like. Students write a compound sentence expressing these thoughts on the drawing.

Invitation to Apply   Students write a compound sentence to summarize each subject—math, social studies, science—as it wraps up throughout the day.

Invitation to Edit

What did we learn about writing from R. J. Palacio?	
She once tried to draw me a Darth Vader, but it ended up looking like some weird mushroom-shaped robot.	
What changed? What is the effect of the change?	
She once tried to draw me a Darth Vader but it ended up looking like some weird mushroom-shaped robot.	*The comma before* but *has been deleted.* "I use a comma and *but* to join two contrasting sentences."
She once tried to draw me a Darth Vader, it ended up looking like some weird mushroom-shaped robot.	*The conjunction* but *has been deleted.* "I use a comma and *but* to join two contrasting sentences."
She once try to draw me a Darth Vader, but it ended up looking like some weird mushroom-shaped robot.	*The verb* tried *has been shifted to the present-tense* try. *This makes the tenses inconsistent, and it doesn't make sense.*

What do you notice?

She once tried to draw me a Darth Vader, but it ended up looking like some weird mushroom-shaped robot.

—R. J. Palacio, *Wonder*

How are they alike and different?

She once tried to draw me a Darth Vader, but it ended up looking like some weird mushroom-shaped robot.

José once tried to draw a chicken for me, but it ended up looking like some weird stain-shaped blob with claws.

Let's try it out.

She once tried to draw me a Darth Vader, but it ended up looking like some weird mushroom-shaped robot.

José once tried to draw a chicken for me, but it ended up looking like some weird stain-shaped blob with claws.

She once tried to draw me a Darth Vader, but it ended up looking like some weird mushroom-shaped robot.

What changed? What is the effect of the change?

She once tried to draw me a Darth Vader but it ended up looking like some weird mushroom-shaped robot.

She once tried to draw me a Darth Vader, it ended up looking like some weird mushroom-shaped robot.

She once try to draw me a Darth Vader, but it ended up looking like some weird mushroom-shaped robot.

If your kids need another go, here some other possibilities for additional model sentences:

He had words in his head, but they didn't always make it to his mouth.
—Kevin Henkes, *The Year of Billy Miller*

Audrey knew she looked different, but it didn't matter much to her.
—Margaret Cardillo, *Just Being Audrey*

Amos had a lot to do at the zoo, but he always made time to visit his good friends.
—Philip Stead, *A Sick Day for Amos McGee*

He tried to swallow, but his throat was dry.
—William Alexander, *Goblin Secrets*

His voice was honey, but his face was a glowing ember.
—Kelly Barnhill, *The Girl Who Drank the Moon*

You wouldn't want to try it, but you can stand a baseball bat straight up inside a hippo's mouth.
—Jonathan London, *Hippos Are Huge!*

Lonnie would have loved a workshop of his own, but there just wasn't room.
—Chris Barton, *Whoosh! Lonnie Johnson's Super-Soaking Stream of Inventions*

Buckley and his mama lived in a small wooden house by the sea. They didn't have much, but they always had each other.
—Jessixa Bagley, *Boats for Papa*

18.4   *So . . . . :* What Compound Sentences Cause and Effect

Standard   Use coordinating conjunctions and a comma to produce compound sentences.

Focus Phrase   "I use a comma and *so* to join two sentences with a cause/effect relationship."

Invitation to Notice   I once dreamed the sun and moon were my mom and dad, so maybe my name should be Star Boy.
       —Sherman Alexie, *Thunder Boy Jr.*

Power Note   *In Sherman Alexie's* Thunder Boy Jr. *the narrator argues for a name other than Thunder Boy Jr., which he admits he hates. Alexie uses the pattern* I once _____, so my name should be _____ *repeatedly, demonstrating the cause/effect meaning indicated by the coordinating conjunction. Start the lesson by sharing Alexie's picture book. The next day start with a new invitation to notice.*

Invitation to Compare and Contrast   I once dreamed the sun and moon were my mom and dad, so maybe my name should be Star Boy.
I once fantasized my parents were from *Modern Family*, so maybe my name should be Luke.

Power Note   *The focus is on all it took to join the two sentences—the cause/effect relationship of the coordinating conjunction or FANBOYS, the fact that there must be a subject and verb on each side of the sentence, and the fact that the comma comes before the coordinating conjunction, as well as the need to join sentences with both.*

Invitation to Imitate   *Imitate Together*: Invite writers to use interactive, shared, or paired writing to compose a sentence with you. (See Figure 18.12.)

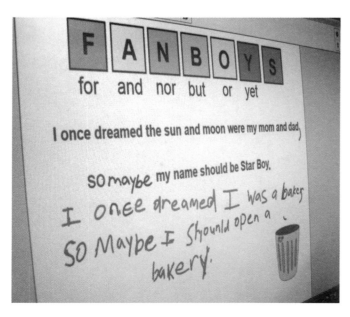

Imitate Independently: Students use the model to create their own sentences, using the coordinating conjunction *so* to join and show a cause/effect relationship. (See Figures 18.13 and 18.14.)

Figure 18.12
This fourth-grade class manipulated the mentor sentence as simple sentences, using the interactive whiteboard to create a compound sentence, and then wrote another one together.

Figure 18.13
Simple sentences

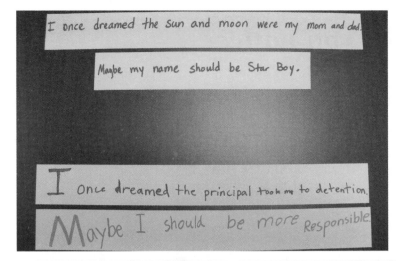

Figure 18.14
This fourth-grade partnership worked together to create a compound sentence using the mentor as a model.

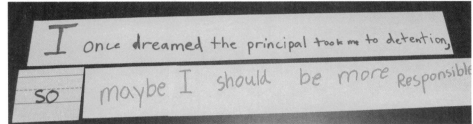

Invitation to Celebrate　Students share their sentences with the class.

Invitation to Apply　Have students write a compound sentence using the coordinating conjunction *so* that shows something that has happened or that they have learned this year. If kids are into books, you could create a class book and call it *So What? Cause and Effect Just Got Real.*

Invitation to Edit

What did we learn about writing from Sherman Alexie?	
I once dreamed the sun and moon were my mom and dad, so maybe my name should be Star Boy.	
What changed? What is the effect of the change?	
I once dreamed the sun and moon was my mom and dad, so maybe my name should be Star Boy.	*The verb* were *has been changed to* was. *Because the sentence refers to both the sun AND the moon, a writer must use the plural verb* were.
I once dreamed the sun and moon were my Mom and dad, so maybe my name should be Star Boy.	Mom *is capitalized. When* Mom *or* Dad *are proceeded by* my, your, *or any other possessive, they are not capitalized.*
I once dreamed the sun and moon were my mom and dad, maybe my name should be Star Boy.	*The coordinating conjunction* so *has been deleted.* "I use a comma and *so* to join two sentences with a cause/effect relationship."

What do you notice?

I once dreamed the sun and moon were my mom and dad, so maybe my name should be Star Boy.

—Sherman Alexie, *Thunder Boy Jr.*

How are they alike and different?

I once dreamed the sun and moon were my mom and dad, so maybe my name should be Star Boy.

I once fantasized my parents were from *Modern Family*, so maybe my name should be Luke.

Let's try it out.

I once dreamed the sun and moon were my mom and dad, so maybe my name should be Star Boy.

I once fantasized my parents were from *Modern Family*, so maybe my name should be Luke.

I once dreamed the sun and moon were my mom and dad, so maybe my name should be Star Boy.

What changed? What is the effect of the change?

I once dreamed the sun and moon was my mom and dad, so maybe my name should be Star Boy.

I once dreamed the sun and moon were my Mom and dad, so maybe my name should be Star Boy.

I once dreamed the sun and moon were my mom and dad, maybe my name should be Star Boy.

18.5   *Driving Miss Crazy*: The Choice *Or* Gives

Standard   Use coordinating conjunctions and a comma to produce compound sentences.

Focus Phrase   "I use a comma and *or* to join sentences to present choices."

Invitation to Notice   Louisiana's grandmother did not believe in stop signs, or she did not see them, or maybe she did not think they applied to her.
　　　　—Kate DiCamillo, *Raymie Nightingale*

Power Note   *Though we usually talk about a compound sentence as joining two sentences, it can be more. For example, Kate DiCamillo combined three independent clauses or sentences here. All are joined by the coordinating conjunction or, which indicates there is a choice in each sentence.*

Invitation to Compare and Contrast   Louisiana's grandmother did not believe in stop signs, or she did not see them, or maybe she did not think they applied to her.
Terry's grandfather did not believe in kindness, or he did not know what kindness was, or maybe he did not think it applied to him.

Power Note   *Because of the change from female to male in the imitation sentence, we have a chance to spiral back to pronoun antecedent agreement. Comparing the pronouns used for signs and kindness gives us more opportunities, widening our discussion to agreement in number.*

Invitation to Imitate   *Imitate Together*: Invite writers to use interactive, shared, or paired writing to compose a sentence with you that gives three choices about something someone does not obey.

Imitate Independently: Students use the model to create their own sentences, using the coordinating conjunction *or* to join and present choices.

Invitation to Celebrate   Students share their sentences, raising a hand every time they hear the conjunction *or* read aloud. The trick is that they must alternate hands every time.

Invitation to Apply   Students write compound sentences using the coordinating conjunction *or* to show choices. (See Figure 18.15.) They can write a sentence with three choices, or they can write one with two. See what we did there?

Figure 18.15
Writer's notebook: compound sentences

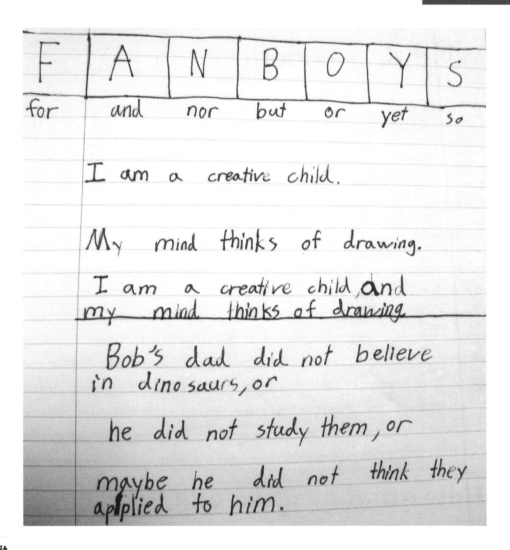

Invitation to Edit

What did we learn about writing from Kate DiCamillo?	
Louisiana's grandmother did not believe in stop signs, or she did not see them, or maybe she did not think they applied to her.	
What changed? What is the effect of the change?	
Louisiana's Grandmother did not believe in stop signs, or she did not see them, or maybe she did not think they applied to her.	*The noun* grandmother *was changed to* Grandmother. *Mom, Dad, Grandmother, and Grandfather are not capitalized when they're preceded by a possessive. Possessive pronouns or possessive nouns knock the capital to lowercase when they precede the kinship name.*
Louisiana's grandmother did not believe in stop signs or she did not see them, or maybe she did not think they applied to her.	*The comma between* signs *and* or *was deleted. This takes out part of the separation writers provide when joining independent clauses. "I use a comma and* or *to join sentences to present choices."*
Louisianas grandmother did not believe in stop signs, or she did not see them, or maybe she did not think they applied to her.	*The possessive apostrophe was deleted, which makes Louisiana become multiple Louisianas, and neither is showing possession as intended by the author.*

What do you notice?

Louisiana's grandmother did not believe in stop signs, or she did not see them, or maybe she did not think they applied to her.

—Kate DiCamillo, *Raymie Nightingale*

How are they alike and different?

Louisiana's grandmother did not believe in stop signs, or she did not see them, or maybe she did not think they applied to her.

Terry's grandfather did not believe in kindness, or he did not know what kindness was, or maybe he did not think it applied to him.

Let's try it out.

Louisiana's grandmother did not believe in stop signs, or she did not see them, or maybe she did not think they applied to her.

Terry's grandfather did not believe in kindness, or he did not know what kindness was, or maybe he did not think it applied to him.

Louisiana's grandmother did not believe in stop signs, or she did not see them, or maybe she did not think they applied to her.

What changed? What is the effect of the change?

Louisiana's Grandmother did not believe in stop signs, or she did not see them, or maybe she did not think they applied to her.

Louisiana's grandmother did not believe in stop signs or she did not see them, or maybe she did not think they applied to her.

Louisianas grandmother did not believe in stop signs, or she did not see them, or maybe she did not think they applied to her.

19

Why Do Writers Use the Serial Comma?

A h, the simplicity of the serial comma. When we are children, lists are one of the first ways we learn to combine things—things to buy when we're shopping, things to do or remember. We don't have to ask for only one thing for breakfast or have only one reason to be able to get a dog. A pair is nice, but when we have three or more, only the serial or list comma will do.

A list of specific nouns can help a reader see something. *We want a Jolly Rancher, green apple bubble gum, and a sack of gummy worms.* Is your mouth watering? We could've written *We want candy* to little effect. However, when we pulled out the big guns of specific nouns in a list, we created a mouth-gusher sentence—a list of items.

A list of actions also helps us boss our little brothers or sisters around: *I want you to rake the shag carpet, collect all the dishes from around the house, and tell Mom I'm the one who did it.* As a matter of author's craft, it's important that all the verbs be in the same tense. That's called parallelism, and it's part of lists' beauty.

Science writers like lists as much as fiction writers. Check out Dianna Hutts Aston's *A Rock Is Lively*. It's chock-full of lists:

A rock is mixed up. All rocks are made of a mix of ingredients called minerals. Just as a batter of flour, butter, and sugar makes a cookie, a batter of minerals makes a rock. The recipe for a rock might include minerals like aluminum, copper, diamond, fluorite, gold, gypsum, lead, nickel, platinum, quartz, silver, sulfur, tin, topaz, and turquoise.

That's *way* more than three, but the rule of thumb for lists is three *or more* items or actions. As a matter of craft, more isn't always better. The ear loves three, but occasionally a longer list can be used for effect.

Lists are a way to pack specific nouns and examples into one sentence. Lists give writers a way to link actions. Yes, authors separate the items in the list, but the whole purpose of the comma is to both separate and connect. Punctuation talks to the reader.

A period says, "Stop."

A comma says, "But wait, there's more."

Lesson Sets:

What Does the Serial Comma Do?

19.1   Catalogue a Frog: Items in a List

Standard	Use commas to separate single words in a series.
Focus Phrase	"I use commas to separate words in a list."
Invitation to Notice	Frogs can be red, yellow, or orange. —Elizabeth Carney, *Frogs!*
Power Note	*We highly recommend reading aloud* Frogs *by Elizabeth Carney before this lesson. When students say they notice the commas, we have them collaborate with their table group on what the commas are doing in this sentence when they read them aloud or read them with their eyes. Share theories.*
Invitation to Compare and Contrast	Frogs can be red, yellow, or orange. Frogs can hop, splash, and croak.
Power Note	*Often we name separate items (nouns) in a list, but Carney's sentence shows us we can make a list of adjectives (colors), and our imitation shows we can also list verbs (actions frogs can do). "What do you think we need to remember when we put actions or verbs in a list?"*
Invitation to Imitate	*Imitate Together*: Invite writers to use interactive or shared writing to compose a sentence with you.

Dogs can be friendly, mean, or playful.

Imitate Independently: Students use the model sentences to create their own sentences, using commas to separate words in a list—adjectives, verbs, or otherwise. (See Figure 19.1.)

Figure 19.1
Listing imitation on process sheet

Imitate
Give it a go!

There were candy canes, ginger bread mans, and lollipops in the Nutcracker.

Celebrate

Power Note   *In general, it's best if list items are parallel—all verbs, all nouns, or all adjectives. In other words, the words in lists need to match as much as they can.*

> Positive Parallelism: Though this quote is not exactly a list, it is three sentences in a row in which repetition is used to affect emphasis—the repetition of *nothing*, all verbs in the present tense, and ending with the same prepositional phrase (*except your _____s*).
>
> > Nothing binds you except your thoughts. Nothing limits you except your fears. And nothing controls you except your beliefs.
> > > –Marianne Williamson
>
> We like to think of parallelism as matching in tense, but it's more than that, as Williamson shows.

Invitation to Celebrate   Students share their sentences with classmates aloud or by posting them online. Celebrating is sharing with an audience, large or small. Sometimes we may read our sentence only to a partner or to our table group. But sharing is crucial.

Invitation to Apply   Frogs usually live in wet places. They like rivers, lakes, and ponds.
   —Elizabeth Carney, *Frogs!*

Animal Hunt: Put students in groups of three. Have them investigate an animal and write one to three sentences about what they learn, using at least one list.

Invitation to Edit

What did we learn about writing from Elizabeth Carney?	
Frogs usually live in wet places. They like rivers, lakes, and ponds.	
What changed? What is the effect of the change?	
Frogs usually live in wet places. They like rivers lakes, and ponds.	*The comma between* rivers *and* lakes *has been deleted. This affects the meaning because now it looks like there might be a lake called Rivers Lake.* "I use commas to separate words in a list."
Frogs usually live in wet places. They like rivers, lake, and ponds.	*The -s is deleted from* lakes, *making it singular. This affects the meaning because it looks like the author is talking about only one lake.*
Frogs usually live in wet places they like rivers, lakes, and ponds.	*The period after* places *has been deleted, creating a run-on sentence. Run-on sentences make it hard for readers to follow our ideas because the sentences become all mixed up without boundaries like end marks.*

What do you notice?

Frogs can be red, yellow, or orange.

—Elizabeth Carney, *Frogs!*

How are they alike and different?

Frogs can be red, yellow, or orange.

Frogs can hop, splash, and croak.

Let's try it out.

Frogs can be red, yellow, or orange.

Frogs can hop, splash, and croak.

Frogs usually live in wet places. They like rivers, lakes, and ponds.

What changed? What is the effect of the change?

Frogs usually live in wet places. They like rivers lakes, and ponds.

Frogs usually live in wet places. They like rivers, lake, and ponds.

Frogs usually live in wet places they like rivers, lakes, and ponds.

19.2   Whatever Rings Your Smell: Items in a List

Standard	Use commas in a series.
Focus Phrase	"I use commas to separate three or more items in a list."
Invitation to Notice	Summer always smelled like heat, the ocean, and the spines of old books. —Patricia MacLachlan, *Edward's Eyes*
Power Note	*Mixtures of smells always make for powerful writing, and the list comma works well, as MacLachlan shows. "What are the commas doing in this sentence?" Let children build a theory of what the commas do when they read the sentence aloud and when they read it silently. "How many items does it take to make a list? What are the items in this sentence? How do you know?"*
Invitation to Compare and Contrast	Summer always smelled like heat, the ocean, and the spines of old books. Winter smells like coolness, a pile of leaves, and the smoke of burning fires.
Power Note	*After they talk about how the sentences are alike and different, students may be interested to know that of all our senses, smell has the strongest link to readers' memories. "What's a smell that triggers a memory for you? Pay attention to smells today and tonight, because we're going to write our own lists tomorrow."*
Invitation to Imitate	Students write their own sentences, using commas to separate and connect three smells they associate with a place, a person, or a season.
Invitation to Celebrate	*If You Smelt It, You Dealt It*: Students share their sentences, filling the room with smells and memories. (See Figure 19.2.)

Figure 19.2
Smells list celebration

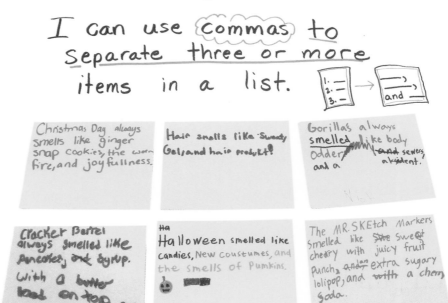

Invitation to Apply   The whole place smelled of fish, riverweed, and tar.
—William Alexander, *Goblin Secrets*

Smells of . . . Have students return to a piece of writing and find a place to add smells. Add a list of smells, in fact.

Invitation to Edit

What did we learn about writing from Patricia MacLachlan?	
Summer always smelled like heat, the ocean, and the spines of old books.	
What changed? What is the effect of the change?	
Summer always smelled of heat, the ocean, and the spines of old books.	The preposition *like* has been changed to *of*. Discuss the effects of the different prepositions. "Does the meaning change? What do you think? Why?"
Summer always smelled like heat the ocean, and the spines of old books.	The comma after *heat* has been deleted. "I use commas to separate three or more items in a list. When we don't follow the serial comma pattern, our meaning might get fuzzy."
Summer smelled like heat, the ocean, and the spines of old books.	The adverb *always* has been deleted, removing how often the writer felt summer smelled that way—all the time. "How does deleting the word *always* affect the sentence?"

What do you notice?

Summer always smelled like heat, the ocean, and the spines of old books.

—Patricia MacLachlan, *Edward's Eyes*

How are they alike and different?

Summer always smelled like heat, the ocean, and the spines of old books.

Winter smells like coolness, a pile of leaves, and the smoke of burning fires.

Let's try it out.

Summer always smelled like heat, the ocean, and the spines of old books.

Winter smells like coolness, a pile of leaves, and the smoke of burning fires.

Summer always smelled like heat, the ocean, and the spines of old books.

What changed? What is the effect of the change?

Summer always smelled of heat, the ocean, and the spines of old books.

Summer always smelled like heat the ocean, and the spines of old books.

Summer smelled like heat, the ocean, and the spines of old books.

19.3　Sisters, Brothers, or Friends: A Series of Things They Do

Standard　Use commas to separate items and actions in a series.

Focus Phrase　"I use commas to separate three or more actions."

Invitation to Notice　Regina could be bossy, selfish, and annoying. Her grades gave my parents unrealistic expectations about mine. She always hogged the closet, took too long in the bathroom, and nagged me about cleaning up my half of the room. But I was going to miss her.
　　—Wendy Wan-Long Shang, *The Great Wall of Lucy Wu*

Invitation to Compare and Contrast　Regina could be bossy, selfish, and annoying. Her grades gave my parents unrealistic expectations about mine. She always hogged the closet, took too long in the bathroom, and nagged me about cleaning up my half of the room. But I was going to miss her.

Ben could be mean, hurtful, and frightening. His grades gave my dad unrealistic expectations about mine. He always hogged desserts, stank up the bathroom, and pushed my face into the grass. I never got a chance to miss him.

Invitation to Imitate　She always hogged the closet, took too long in the bathroom, and nagged me about cleaning up my half of the room. But I was going to miss her.

He always hogged desserts, stank up the bathroom, and pushed my face into the grass. I never got a chance to miss him.

Invitation to Celebrate　*Celebration As Experimentation, Exploration, and Play*: Sometimes the celebration is just using the convention to explore our own thinking. It's a celebration because it's fun to try new things, share, and succeed. (See Figure 19.3.)

Invitation to Apply　*Math Makes a List*: Student pairs list a series of three or more actions taken to solve a math problem.

Figure 19.3

A third-grade writer plays around with listing actions and using commas in his writer's notebook. Notice the last sentence is actually a compound sentence. Be sure to value risk taking.

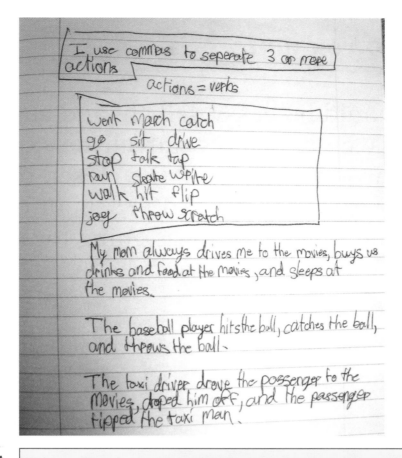

Invitation to Edit

What did we learn about writing from Wendy Wan-Long Shang?	
She always hogged the closet, took too long in the bathroom, and nagged me about cleaning up my half of the room.	
What changed? What is the effect of the change?	
She always hogged the closet, took to long in the bathroom, and nagged me about cleaning up my half of the room.	*The adverb* too *has been changed to one of its homophones, the preposition* to. *The two words mean different things and would confuse readers.*
She always hogged the closet took too long in the bathroom, and nagged me about cleaning up my half of the room.	*The comma after the action* hogged the closet *has been deleted, making the action* took too long *run together with* closet. *This missing comma causes misunderstanding. "I use commas to separate three or more actions."*
She always hogged the closet, takes too long in the bathroom, and nagged me about cleaning up my half of the room.	*The past-tense irregular verb* took *is changed to the present-tense* takes. *The verbs in all three actions need to be in the same tense or readers will stumble.*

What do you notice?

Regina could be bossy, selfish, and annoying. Her grades gave my parents unrealistic expectations about mine. She always hogged the closet, took too long in the bathroom, and nagged me about cleaning up my half of the room. But I was going to miss her.

—Wendy Wan-Long Shang, *The Great Wall of Lucy Wu*

How are they alike and different?

Regina could be bossy, selfish, and annoying. Her grades gave my parents unrealistic expectations about mine. She always hogged the closet, took too long in the bathroom, and nagged me about cleaning up my half of the room. But I was going to miss her.

Ben could be mean, hurtful, and frightening. His grades gave my dad unrealistic expectations about mine. He always hogged desserts, stank up the bathroom, and pushed my face into the grass. I never got a chance to miss him.

Let's try it out.

She always hogged the closet, took too long in the bathroom, and nagged me about cleaning up my half of the room. But I was going to miss her.

He always hogged desserts, stank up the bathroom, and pushed my face into the grass. I never got a chance to miss him.

She always hogged the closet, took too long in the bathroom, and nagged me about cleaning up my half of the room.

What changed? What is the effect of the change?

She always hogged the closet, took to long in the bathroom, and nagged me about cleaning up my half of the room.

She always hogged the closet took too long in the bathroom, and nagged me about cleaning up my half of the room.

She always hogged the closet, takes too long in the bathroom, and nagged me about cleaning up my half of the room.

Lists to Study

Dressing Up Your Nouns in a List

He wore a torn beige shirt, thick slacks, and heavy shoes.
    —Adina Rishe Gewirtz, *Zebra Forest*

Open a Package of Prepositional Phrases

A few weeks later, a package arrived. Inside, Horace found colored pencils, a pair of brushes, and a box of paints.
    —Jen Bryant, *A Splash of Red: The Life and Art of Horace Pippin*

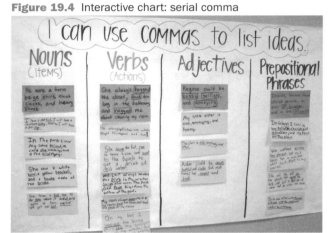

Figure 19.4 Interactive chart: serial comma

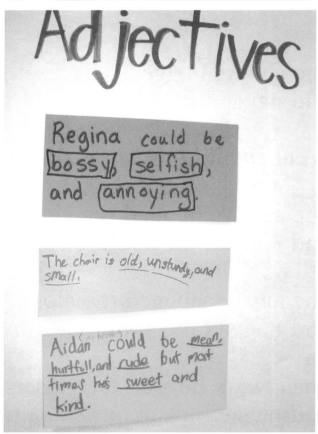

Figure 19.5 Interactive chart close-up: prepositional phrases   **Figure 19.6** Interactive chart close-up: adjectives

20

Why Do Writers Use Complex Sentences?

Complex sentences give writers and readers a way to gather ideas together without the separation of a period. In technical terms, complex sentences contain an independent clause and one or more dependent or subordinate clauses, which can be placed anywhere in a sentence—as an opener, an interrupter, or a closer—and are usually set off with commas. Figure 20.1 shows the three basic patterns.

Figure 20.1
Sentence patterns

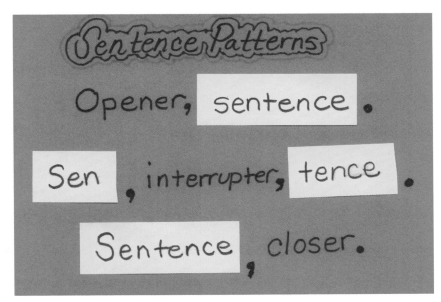

In the end, the most important thing isn't whether we quibble over the definition of *clauses* or *phrases* as much as we understand that some sentence parts that can't stand on their own are set off with a comma or commas. To illustrate, let's look at Karen Romano Young's complex sentences from *Hundred Percent*:

Since the second bell hadn't rung yet, he just went, without taking the wooden bathroom pass.

The second bell hadn't rung yet is a sentence on its own; however, when we add the word *since* to the front of the sentence, it becomes a dependent clause. Simply said, it's not a sentence on its own.

> *Since the second bell hadn't rung yet . . .*

Now the clause is a fragment, only part of a sentence, leaving the reader hanging, waiting until the idea is completed by a sentence attached with a comma. In other words, this dependent or subordinate clause needs to be attached to a sentence to form both a complete and complex sentence. *He just went* fits the bill:

> Since the second bell hadn't rung yet, *he just went.*

Opener, sentence.

Young didn't stop there; she added a *prepositional phrase* to the end, leading off with the preposition *without*.

> Since the second bell hadn't rung yet, he just went, *without taking the wooden bathroom pass.*

Opener, sentence, closer.

Whether they're phrases or clauses, fragments (pieces of sentences that are not whole) often need to be set off with commas. In case you're wondering, Young's example, which we've been looking at closely, is a complex sentence with or without the prepositional phrase at the end. What matters is that if sentence parts or fragments need to be set off with a comma or commas, we do that. (See Figures 20.1 and 20.2A and B.)

Figures 20.2 A and B
Student sentences

Because of the rain, I had to stay inside.

Although I am sike, I had to go to school.

Lesson Sets:

What Do Complex Sentences Do?

Tip: Term Up the Complex Sentences: For Teachers' Eyes Only

The point of teaching grammar is not to transfer all the terms to students' brains. However, as we teachers start discussing complex sentences, there are some terms we need to define with some accuracy. This is a bit oversimplified but more than enough to teach elementary school grammar. You'll decide how much or how little to share with your young writers. Rule of thumb: Less is more.

- A **clause** has both a noun and a verb.
- A **dependent** or **subordinate clause** (these two terms are often used synonymously) has both a noun and verb, but can't stand on its own because it is headed by a subordinating conjunction.
- An **independent clause** is a sentence. Often if you take away a subordinating conjunction at the beginning, you'll be left with a sentence (independent clause).

This color-coded visual with an example may help make it more digestible:

Complex Sentences	
A **complex sentence** is composed of an independent clause and a **subordinate** or dependent clause.	As her mom drives away, Dahlia grabs my arm and pulls me through the automatic glass doors.
An independent clause is a sentence that can stand on its own, containing at least **one** noun **and one** verb.	As her mom drives away, Dahlia grabs my arm and pulls me through the automatic glass doors.
A subordinate or dependent clause also has a noun and a verb, but it begins with a **subordinating conjunction** and can't stand on its own.	As her mom drives away, Dahlia grabs my arm and pulls me through the automatic glass doors.

The Difference Between Phrases and Clauses	
A **phrase** is a group of words containing either a noun or a verb, but not both.	As her mom drives away, Dahlia grabs my arm and pulls me **through the automatic glass** doors. = a prepositional phrase
A **clause** contains at least one noun and one verb.	As her mom drives away = **a subordinate or** dependent clause. Dahlia grabs my arm and pulls me through the automatic glass doors = **an independent clause**.

When you get your HANDS on a sentence, make it complex!

AAAWW — After, Although, As, When, While

UBBIS — Before, If, Since, Because, Until

Figure 20.3
Both AAAWWUBBIS hands

One easy way for elementary students to use complex sentences is to introduce the AAAWWUBBIS mnemonic first mentioned in Chapter 17, "What Do Conjunctions Do?" (See Figure 20.3.)

The mnemonic takes the first letter of several common subordinate conjunctions to create a nonsense word that can be whooped nice and loud. When a subordinating conjunction heads a clause, it is dependent. It needs to be hooked up with an independent clause or sentence. Here's a chart with the AAAWWUBBIS mnemonic for often-used subordinating conjunctions:

In the chart, the subordinating conjunction is the first word of the sentence. When subordinating conjunctions are the first word, you usually need a comma. If you don't have a comma, you may need one or you may have a fragment. If the AAAWWUBBIS isn't the first word of the sentence, more

AAAWWUBBIS: The Subordinating Conjunctions	
After	After we hung up, I went back to my room and laid on the Cinderella pillows and felt sorry for myself. —Barbara O'Connor, *Wish*
Although	Although rain is good, too much of it is dangerous. —Penelope Arlon (DK Book), *Water*
As	As he walked away, Winky shouted, "Always a pleasure doing business with you, Beans!" —Jennifer Holm, *Full of Beans*
When	When the wind blew, the bear was happy. —Kevin Henkes, *Waiting*
While	While Nicole and her mom argued, I sat thinking in the backseat. —Victoria Jamieson, *Roller Girl*
Until	Until one night she takes the stage . . . Anna becomes a glimmer, a grace. —Laurel Snyder, *Swan: The Life and Dance of Anna Pavlova*
Because	Because I am a dog with a good nose and fine ears, I can hear that he is not breathing easily. —Patricia MacLachlan, *The Poet's Dog*
Before	Before I had time to stack too many worries, we pulled into the bus station. —Barbara O'Connor, *Wish*
If	If Chinese school was going to ruin my life, it was going to ruin everybody's life. —Wendy Wan-Long Shang, *The Great Wall of Lucy Wu*
Since	Since she didn't have any friends aside from her dog, Orville, she would spend hours tinkering with things from the yard. —Steve Breen, *Violet the Pilot*

often than not it doesn't need a comma. Check out this sentence from Kate Beasley's *Gertie's Leap to Greatness*:

> She was one of those people who acted nicer **when** the teacher wasn't watching.

Sometimes authors will put a comma before a subordinate conjunction in the middle of a sentence, if they think it needs more of a pause. Here's another sentence from *Gertie's Leap to Greatness* in which Beasley uses a comma before the same subordinate conjunction when it occurs in the middle of a sentence:

> Gertie was sandwiched between her two best friends, holding a new pencil, and thinking she'd accomplish her mission in record time, **when** something poked the back of her neck.

Author's purpose and craft have the final word. Does it need a comma or not? Meaning and effect dictate the answer.

20.1 *If* You Give a Writer a Model: The Conditional Subordinate

Standard	Use conjunctions.
	Produce complex sentences.
	Use a comma to separate an introductory element from the rest of the sentence.
Focus Phrase	"When I start a sentence with *if*, I'll probably need a comma."
Invitation to Notice	If you take a mouse to school, he'll ask for your lunchbox.
	—Laura Numeroff, *If You Take a Mouse to School*
Power Note	*Our focus is on the* if *construction, sometimes called the conditional mood or here an inferred if/then structure. It also shows a cause/effect relationship between the opener and the sentence. We may also highlight the possessive pronoun* your *if students don't.*
Invitation to Compare and Contrast	If you take a mouse to school, he'll ask for your lunchbox.
	If you take a mermaid to school, she'll ask for a tub of water.
Power Note	*"When I start a sentence with* if*, I'll probably need a comma." Highlight the use of the contraction for* will *in each sentence, reviewing the way in which we reduce* he will *to* he'll *(a squish mark showing where letters were squeezed out), as discussed in Chapter 9, "What Do Apostrophes Do?"*
Invitation to Imitate	*Imitate Together:* Invite writers to use interactive, shared, or paired writing to compose a sentence with you.
	If you take a bunny to your garden, he'll eat your carrots.
	Imitate Independently: Students use the models to compose their own sentences, using the subordinating conjunction *if* to craft their if/then statement. The *then* may be implied, as it is in the model sentences.
Invitation to Celebrate	Students share their sentences aloud. For fun at the comma, writers snap their head to the side and hold it there as they read the rest of the sentence. (See Figure 20.4.)
Invitation to Apply	Students pair up and think about possibilities or conditions for if/then statements. Remind them that the *then* can be understood. They can choose a topic like Ways to Be Kind, Ways to Get What You Want, or Ways to Get into Trouble.
	If you _____, _____. (Example: *If you ask nicely, people listen to you more.*)
	If school _____, _____.(Example: *If school ended early, I'd go to the playground.*)
	If _____, _____.

Figure 20.4
First-grade imitation of Numeroff's model

Power Note *Encourage kids to reread sentences once they're completed, making sure they make sense. "Writers read their writing twice, so their readers have to read only once."*

Invitation to Edit

What did we learn about writing from Laura Numeroff?	
If you take a mouse to school, he'll ask for your lunchbox.	
What changed? What is the effect of the change?	
If you take a mouse to school, he will ask for your lunchbox.	*The contraction* he'll *is written out as* he will. *Both versions have the same meaning; the contraction is more conversational.*
If you take a mouse to school he'll ask for your lunchbox.	*The comma after the introductory element has been deleted. This change loses the pause and separation between sentence parts. "When I start a sentence with* if, *I'll probably need a comma." It also makes the cause/effect connection less strong.*
If you take a Mouse to school, he'll ask for your lunchbox.	*The common noun* mouse *is capitalized.* Mouse *is not his name. "Writers capitalize names." When* mouse *is capitalized, it looks like a name.*

What do you notice?

If you take a mouse to school, he'll ask for your lunchbox.

> —Laura Numeroff, *If You Take a Mouse to School*

How are they alike and different?

If you take a mouse to school, he'll ask for your lunchbox.

If you take a mermaid to school, she'll ask for a tub of water.

Let's try it out.

If you take a mouse to school, he'll ask for your lunchbox.

If you take a mermaid to school, she'll ask for a tub of water.

If you take a mouse to school, he'll ask for your lunchbox.

What changed? What is the effect of the change?

If you take a mouse to school, he will ask for your lunchbox.

If you take a mouse to school he'll ask for your lunchbox.

If you take a Mouse to school, he'll ask for your lunchbox.

20.2 AAAWWUBBIS: From Garbage to Treasure

Standard	Use subordinating conjunctions. Use complex sentences. Use a comma to separate an introductory element from the rest of the sentence.
Focus Phrase	"When I start a sentence with *when*, I'll probably need a comma."
Invitation to Notice	When we turned the corner, I found the magic wand on a pile of garbage. —Victoria Kann, *Emeraldalicious*
Power Note	*Ask students, "What do you notice?" If they don't note this, ask, "How many sentences do we have here?" Rewrite the dependent clause as a sentence.* 　　*We turned a corner.* 　　*When we turned a corner.* *"Which one's a sentence and which one's a fragment (only a piece of a sentence)? Turn and talk about what you and your partner think." Discuss with students how the word* when *at the start of a sentence is a comma causer. Repeat the focus phrase: "When I start a sentence with* when*, I'll probably need a comma."*
Invitation to Compare and Contrast	When we turned the corner, I found the magic wand on a pile of garbage. When I turned the corner, I found a tablet on a pile of laundry.
Power Note	*As students note how the sentences are alike and different, continue to repeat the focus phrase, "When I start a sentence with when, I'll probably need a comma." If they notice prepositions and other parts of speech, that's great, but don't mark up the sentence so that it looks like it's been diagrammed.*
Invitation to Imitate	*Imitate Together*: Invite writers to use interactive or shared writing to compose a sentence with you. 　　When we came around the corner, we found a new student waiting at 　　the door. *Imitate Independently*: Students use the model to create their own *when* sentences, using the subordinating conjunction *when* as the first word to craft their imitations. (See Figure 20.5.)
Invitation to Celebrate	Students share their when sentences aloud, saying the word comma aloud, even though we don't normally do that.
Invitation to Apply	In pairs, students think about their reading today. Students write three *when* statements about their reading.

Figure 20.5
Student imitation: *when*

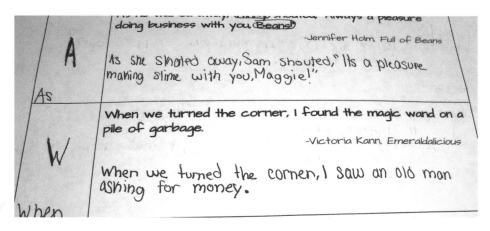

doing business with you, Beans!
—Jennifer Holm, *Full of Beans*

A
As she shouted away, Sam shouted, "It's a pleasure making slime with you, Maggie!"

W
When we turned the corner, I found the magic wand on a pile of garbage.
—Victoria Kann, *Emeraldalicious*

When we turned the corner, I saw an old man asking for money.

Power Note   *Encourage writers to reread and make sure sentences make sense. "Writers read their writing twice, so their readers have to read only once."*

Invitation to Edit

What did we learn about writing from Victoria Kann?	
When we turned the corner, I found the magic wand on a pile of garbage.	
What changed? What is the effect of the change?	
When we turned the corner, I found the magic wand on a pill of garbage.	*The word* pile *is misspelled as* pill, *which could confuse readers. Generate several words that use the v–c–e pattern.*
When we turned the corner I found the magic wand on a pile of garbage.	*The comma after the introductory element is deleted, causing the sentence to run together and lose emphasis of the separation between its two parts. "When I start a sentence with when, I'll probably need a comma."*
When we turn the corner, I found the magic wand on a pile of garbage.	*The -ed is deleted from the verb* turn, *changing its tense to present. Writers use tense consistently.*

What do you notice?

When we turned the corner, I found the magic wand on a pile of garbage.

—Victoria Kann, *Emeraldalicious*

How are they alike and different?

When we turned the corner, I found the magic wand on a pile of garbage.

When I turned the corner, I found a tablet on a pile of laundry.

Let's try it out.

When we turned the corner, I found the magic wand on a pile of garbage.

When I turned the corner, I found a tablet on a pile of laundry.

When we turned the corner, I found the magic wand on a pile of garbage.

What changed? What is the effect of the change?

When we turned the corner, I found the magic wand on a pill of garbage.

When we turned the corner I found the magic wand on a pile of garbage.

When we turn the corner, I found the magic wand on a pile of garbage.

Extra When Sentences for Further Study

When I saw the station up ahead, I ducked around a corner and crouched down in an alley.
> —Dan Gemeinhart, *The Honest Truth*

When her parents saw Jeanne, their faces went white as wool.
> —Adam Gidwitz, *The Inquisitor's Tale*

When she stopped singing, the baby wailed.
> —Pam Muñoz Ryan, *Echo*

The Reason Why the Focus Phrase Says "Usually"

If it wouldn't confuse things for your students, study this sentence from a recent Newbery Honor Book.

When things got really bad I could go away inside my head.
> —Kimberly Brubaker Bradley, *The War That Saved My Life*

Ask, "Why do you think this author chose to omit the comma after the opener?" Discuss author's purpose and craft. (Perhaps she didn't want the separation the comma caused, or she didn't want the reader to slow down in that space.)

20.3 Robot AAAWWUBBIS: As You Know

Standard	Use conjunctions. Use complex sentences.
Focus Phrases	"When I start a sentence with *as*, I'll probably need a comma."
Invitation to Notice	As you might know, robots don't really feel emotions. —Peter Brown, *The Wild Robot*
Power Note	*After students share what they note about Brown's sentence, ask, "What does the word* as *do in this sentence?"*
Invitation to Compare and Contrast	As you might know, robots don't really feel emotions. As you know, teachers don't really appreciate being interrupted.
Power Note	*After students compare and contrast the two sentences, ask, "What effect does the choice of using/not using* might *have?"*
Invitation to Imitate	*Imitate Together*: Use shared writing for the kids to have an opportunity to express something they don't appreciate. As you might know, students don't appreciate waiting for the teacher to pick them up after lunch. *Imitate Individually*: Continue the theme of what others know we appreciate or things we know or wish others knew.
Invitation to Celebrate	Students read aloud their sentences in a read-around. One person starts, and writers read their sentence one after the other. At the end, we cheer for each other for exactly thirty seconds and then go silent.
Invitation to Apply	*Passive-Aggressive Notes*: Students write passive-aggressive notes to someone who needs one. (See Figures 20.6 A, B, and C.) Not every fifth grader gets the whole passive-aggressive thing. Some are downright direct. As you may already know, it's a delightful and practical application of the complex sentence, either way. That's not the point. Many students used a variation on the "As-you . . ." opener to start their expository-explanatory essays. Here are a few gems from some fifth graders: Dear Gum Chewer, As you are probably aware, everyone hates it when you stick your gum under the table. Sincerely, Ruined Soccer Shorts

Dear Reader,

As you are aware, you love to read and you read all the time. Please pay more attention ✖✚in class.

Sincerely,
Your Teacher

Dear Barkers,

As you are probably aware, I am scared to go to your house, and I hate when you have to chase me.

sincerely,
Mailman

Dear Rival,
As you might know, ~~Evelore~~ All of Us in Martial arts do not appreciate your ~~distracting~~ distracting Others in Jiu-Jitsu

You probably do not care at all, but Personally it's really annoying to me. I'd appriciate it if You stopped.

Sincerely,
Karate Kid

Figures 20.6 A, B, and C
Fifth graders enjoy writing passive-aggressive notes.

Dear Houseguest,
As you know, many people sit on the toilet seat after you're finished. You might put it back down when you're finished.

Yours truly,
A Concerned Restroom User

Here are a few possible stems or starters to help students get to know sentences that start with the subordinate conjunction *as* (AAAWWUBBIS).

As you might know, _____
As you remember, _____.
As _____, _____.

Invitation to Edit

What did we learn about writing from Peter Brown?	
As you might know, robots don't really feel emotions.	
What changed? What is the effect of the change?	
As you might know robots don't really feel emotions.	The comma helps set off the introductory element with a pause. "When I start a sentence with *as*, I'll probably need a comma." *When the* comma *is missing, the sentence runs together, causing confusion.*
As you might know, robots do not really feel emotions.	The contraction don't *is written out as* do not, *which sounds more formal. Both mean the same thing, but the contraction is less formal.*
As you might know. Robots don't really feel emotions.	*The comma is replaced with a period, which causes a sentence fragment: As you might know. Sentence fragments (or pieces of sentences) can be used only rarely. Too many make writing appear careless and choppy. "When I start a sentence with as, I'll probably need a comma."*

What do you notice?

As you might know, robots don't really feel emotions.
—Peter Brown, *The Wild Robot*

How are they alike and different?

As you might know, robots don't really feel emotions.

As you know, teachers don't really appreciate being interrupted.

Let's try it out.

As you might know, robots don't really feel emotions.

As you know, teachers don't really appreciate being interrupted.

As you might know, robots don't really feel emotions.

What changed? What is the effect of the change?

As you might know robots don't really feel emotions.

As you might know, robots do not really feel emotions.

As you might know. Robots don't really feel emotions.

20.4 Before You Lose Your Nerve: AAAWWUBBIS Continued

Standard	Use conjunctions. Use complex sentences.
Focus Phrase	"When I start a sentence with an *AAAWWUBBIS word*, I'll probably need a comma."
Invitation to Notice	Before she lost her nerve, she stepped over the invisible line and onto the trail. —Kathi Appelt and Alison McGhee, *Maybe a Fox*
Power Note	*We have been building toward the mnemonic AAAWWUBBIS, and now it's time to reveal all the letters and their corresponding subordinating conjunctions. Discuss which side of the comma has the sentence (right) and why it's a sentence and the other side (left) isn't. "What makes the left side of the sentence a dependent clause as an introductory element?"* *Like the word after, before can be a preposition. (After school and before lunch are prepositional phrases.) It doesn't really matter if it's a preposition or subordinating conjunction. What matters is that we put a comma after an introductory element if we need one.*
Invitation to Compare and Contrast	Before she lost her nerve, she stepped over the invisible line and onto the trail. Before she lost her nerve, Anna stepped onto the balance beam and into the competition.
Power Note	*Students may note the different prepositions (onto and over) and their different effects but similar functions. Repeat the focus phrase often: "When I start a sentence with an AAAWWUBBIS word, I'll probably need a comma."*
Invitation to Imitate	*Imitate Together*: Use shared writing to express something students think takes a lot of nerve to do. Discuss why we do something like dive off a diving board instead of waiting and suffering. While I waited for the first day of middle school, a gymnastics meet was held in my stomach. After I finished my first lap, I knew it was really as bad as I thought. *Imitate Individually*: Continue the theme of "You've Got a lot of Nerve." Students choose from the full menu of AAAWWUBBIS words to start their sentences with. "Just make sure, if your sentence starts with an AA . . ." and they'll finish the focus phrase for you. (See Figure 20.7.)
Invitation to Celebrate	Students read aloud their sentences in a read-around. One person starts, and the whole room reads their AAAWWUBBIS sentence. We cheer for each other for exactly fifteen seconds and then go silent. The actual times are of course insignificant, but randomizing them keeps them fresh.

Figure 20.7
This writer imitates sentences with AAAWWUBBIS words on a processing sheet provided by the teacher.

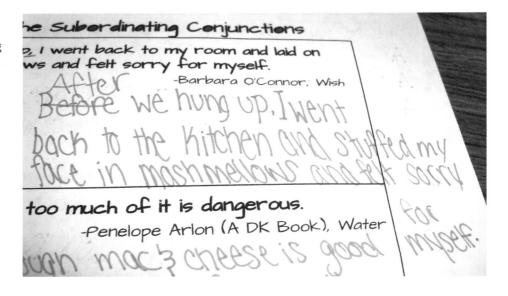

Invitation to Apply   *Conquering Fear: You've Got A Lot of Nerve.* Students write a couple of paragraphs about conquering a fear, using as many AAAWWUBBIS words as they can.

Invitation to Edit

What did we learn about writing from Kathi Appelt and Alison McGhee?	
Before she lost her nerve, she stepped over the invisible line and onto the trail.	
What changed? What is the effect of the change?	
Before she lost her nerve. She stepped over the invisible line and onto the trail.	*The comma is replaced with a period, creating a sentence fragment:* Before she lost her nerve. "When I start a sentence with an AAAWWUBBIS, I'll probably need a comma."
Before she lost her nerve, she stepped over the invisible line and into the trail.	*The preposition* onto *has been changed to* into, *which sounds funny because we walk* on *a trail, drive* on *a highway, or ride our bike* on *a street or bridge. When our prepositions don't follow the pattern readers expect, it causes a breakdown in understanding or fluency.*
Before she lost her nerve she stepped over the invisible line and onto the trail.	*The comma helps set off the introductory element with a pause.* "When I start a sentence with as, I'll probably need a comma." *When the comma is missing, the sentence has no boundaries and it's harder to read.*

What do you notice?

Before she lost her nerve, she stepped over the invisible line and onto the trail.

—Kathi Appelt and Alison McGhee, *Maybe a Fox*

How are they alike and different?

Before she lost her nerve, she stepped over the invisible line and onto the trail.

Before she lost her nerve, Anna stepped onto the balance beam and into the competition.

Let's try it out.

Before she lost her nerve, she stepped over the invisible line and onto the trail.

Before she lost her nerve, Anna stepped onto the balance beam and into the competition.

Before she lost her nerve, she stepped over the invisible line and onto the trail.

What changed? What is the effect of the change?

Before she lost her nerve. She stepped over the invisible line and onto the trail.

Before she lost her nerve, she stepped over the invisible line and into the trail.

Before she lost her nerve she stepped over the invisible line and onto the trail.

20.5 Plenty of Raisins for No Comma: When the AAAWWUBBIS Isn't First

Standard	Produce complex sentences.
Focus Phrase	"When an AAAWWUBBIS word isn't the first word in the sentence, I probably won't need a comma."
Invitation to Notice	Gertie stared at Junior until his voice dried up like a raisin. 　　—Kate Beasley, *Gertie's Leap to Greatness*
Power Note	*Talk about the effect of putting a comma after Junior. Read it both ways. "Which do you prefer? Why?" Don't be shy about sharing your reasoning as well. You're modeling how to think about author's purpose and craft. "Every choice we make has an effect."*
Invitation to Compare and Contrast	Gertie stared at Junior until his voice dried up like a raisin. José stared at Zack until his mouth dried up like a desert.
Power Note	*Repeat the focus phrase as appropriate: "When an AAAWWUBBIS word isn't the first word in the sentence, I probably won't need a comma." If students find an example of a comma before an AAAWWUBBIS word, invite them to share it. Discuss why the author might have crafted his or her sentence that way.*
Invitation to Imitate	*Imitate Together*: Use shared writing to express something happening "until" something else happens. Use the AAAWWUBBIS word in the middle of a sentence.
	Michael and DuShell were happy they had a sub until he yelled at them to sit down.
	Imitate Individually: Students choose any AAAWWUBBIS word to connect ideas in the middle of the sentence. (See Figure 20.8.)
Invitation to Celebrate	Students read aloud their sentences, sharing them twice. The rest of the students clap. "Did anyone write a sentence with a different AAAWWUBBIS word?"
Invitation to Apply	*AAAWWUBBIS Transitions*: Use Rapid Revision (See Chapter 3 for more detail) on a piece of current writing. Look for places to use AAAWWUBBIS words to combine or connect ideas, realizing each of the conjunctions has a different meaning and therefore a different effect.

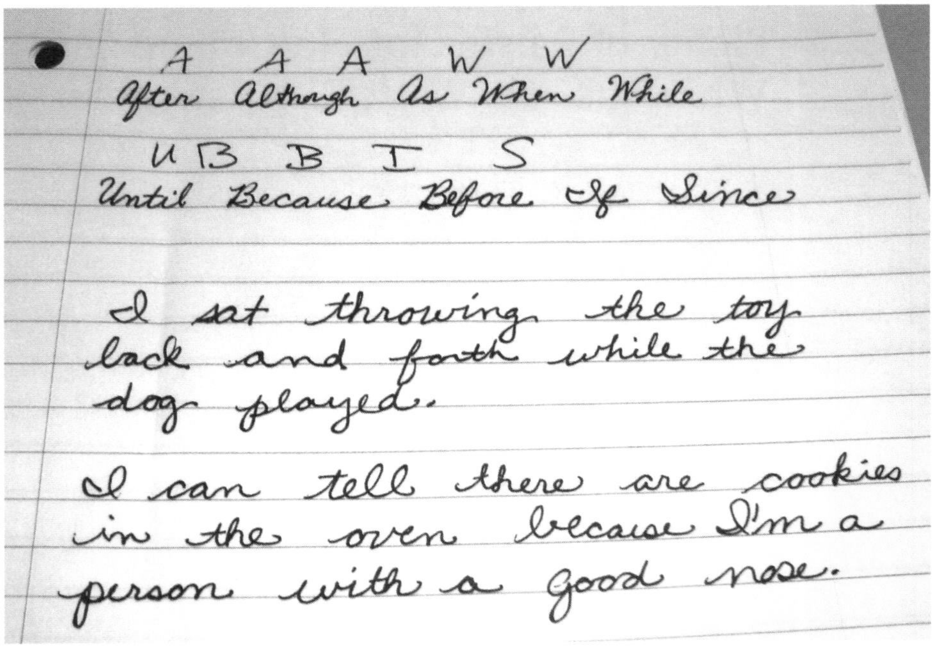

Figure 20.8
AAAWWUBBIS in the middle of a
sentence

Invitation to Edit

What did we learn about writing from Kate Beasley?	
Gertie stared at Junior until his voice dried up like a raisin.	
What changed? What is the effect of the change?	
Gertie stared at Junior, until his voice dried up like a raisin.	*A comma is added before* until. *"How does it affect the way we read the sentence?" Read it aloud both ways and discuss. Sometimes writers do place a comma before a subordinating conjunction in the middle of sentence. But it's more likely to not have the comma, unless there's a reason.*
Gertie stared at junior until his voice dried up like a raisin.	*Junior's name is not capitalized. "Writers capitalize names." When writers don't capitalize a name, our readers may think it isn't a name.*
Gertie stared at Junior until his voice dried up as if it were a raisin.	*The preposition* like *has been replaced with* as if it were. *They have the same meaning, but how does the wording affect the sentence?*

What do you notice?

Gertie stared at Junior until his voice dried up like a raisin.

—Kate Beasley, *Gertie's Leap to Greatness*

How are they alike and different?

Gertie stared at Junior until his voice dried up like a raisin.

José stared at Zack until his mouth dried up like a desert.

Let's try it out.

Gertie stared at Junior until his voice dried up like a raisin.

José stared at Zack until his mouth dried up like a desert.

Gertie stared at Junior until his voice dried up like a raisin.

What changed? What is the effect of the change?

Gertie stared at Junior, until his voice dried up like a raisin.

Gertie stared at junior until his voice dried up like a raisin.

Gertie stared at Junior until his voice dried up as if it were a raisin.

What Do Relative Pronouns Do?

Think pronouns are nothing more than a substitute that links nouns with a few stand-in words? Well, move over, boredom, and hello, relative pronouns—the relative you want to stay awhile. These nifty friends do the work of connecting in number and in person, but they also glue clauses of wonderful description to your worn sentence patterns.

Yes, relative pronouns are simple, and most of us use them quite handily without ever knowing their names. But to get to know your relative pronouns, here's a starter list:

who, whose, whom, which, that

These words link up descriptive clauses that are sometimes called adjective clauses.

20.6 *That Which* Made Me Sick: What Relative Pronouns Clause

Standard Use relative pronouns to link descriptive information to nouns.

Focus Phrase "I use relative pronouns to identify my nouns with additional details."

Invitation to Notice She sat straight up, which instantly made her feel sick.
—Christina Soontornvat, *The Changelings*

He coughed and sneezed so often that he carried a handkerchief in one paw at all times.
—Kate DiCamillo, *The Tale of Despereaux*

Power Note *Students choose one of the mentor sentences to study. We discuss both. If* that *and* which *don't come up on the first day, return to the sentences and ask, "What are* that *and* which *doing in each of these sentences?" We'd hope to explain that* that *and* which *link more information to sentences. We'd also talk about the differences between* that *and* which*. Which requires a comma before it, and* that *abhors commas and needs them not.*

Invitation to Compare and Contrast He coughed and sneezed so often that he carried a handkerchief in one paw at all times.
The dog wheezed and coughed so often that no one would pet him anymore.

She sat straight up, which instantly made her feel sick.

Ella leapt up from her desk, which instantly made everybody look at her.

Invitation to Imitate *Imitate Together*: Invite writers to use interactive, shared, or paired writing to compose a sentence with you. (See Figure 20.9 A and B.)

Imitate Independently: Students use the model to create their own sentences, choosing to imitate the *that* or *which* sentence.

I use relative pronouns to identify my nouns with additional details.

She sat straight up, which instantly made her feel sick.

He coughed and sneezed so often that he carried a handkerchief in one paw at all times.

She twirled and spun so much that she got dizzy.

Figures 20.9A and B Fifth graders work together to imitate the sentence, using a relative pronoun.

Invitation to Celebrate

Which *Versus* That: Students choose a *which* or *that* sentence to imitate. On one side of the room write the word *which* on one big sheet of paper and make a comma on another. Tape the comma up before the *which*. For the other side of the room, write the word *that* on a big sheet like you did with *which*. Then make a comma with an international *no* sign over it (a red circle surrounding the comma with a line through it). Hang those on the wall opposite the *which* sheet. Students line up on different sides of the room, corresponding to the *which* or *that* side. (See Figure 20.10.)

Figure 20.10
Which versus *that*

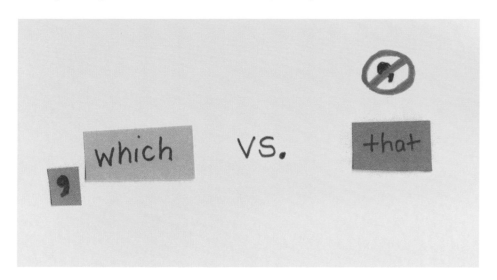

Invitation to Apply

Keeping Score: For the rest of the day, writers keep score of how many times they come across *that* or *which*. Make a T-chart and have kids add a hash mark each time.

Invitation to Edit

What did we learn about writing from Christina Soontornvat?	
She sat straight up, which instantly made her feel sick.	
What changed? What is the effect of the change?	
She sat straight up which instantly made her feel sick.	*There is no comma before the which relative clause. When the relative pronoun which heads a relative clause, it is set off with a comma. The comma goes before the which. When we don't follow the pattern, we may make our readers have to stop and reread.*
She sat straight up, which instantly made him feel sick.	*Her has been changed to him. Although this would be possible, we know it wasn't the writer's original meaning. This version shows that a male is sickened by the way she sat up.*
She sat straight up, instantly made her feel sick.	*The which has been deleted. We need a comma and which to link information to the sentence. When we don't, we have a run-on sentence, which makes writing more difficult to understand.*

What do you notice?

She sat straight up, which instantly made her feel sick.

—Christina Soontornvat, *The Changelings*

He coughed and sneezed so often that he carried a handkerchief in one paw at all times.

—Kate DiCamillo, *The Tale of Despereaux*

How are they alike and different?

He coughed and sneezed so often that he carried a handkerchief in one paw at all times.

The dog wheezed and coughed so often that no one would pet him anymore.

She sat straight up, which instantly made her feel sick.

Ella leapt up from her desk, which instantly made everybody look at her.

Let's try it out.

He coughed and sneezed so often that he carried a handkerchief in one paw at all times.

The dog wheezed and coughed so often that no one would pet him anymore.

She sat straight up, which instantly made her feel sick.

Ella leapt up from her desk, which instantly made everybody look at her.

She sat straight up, which instantly made her feel sick.

What changed? What is the effect of the change?

She sat straight up which instantly made her feel sick.

She sat straight up, which instantly made him feel sick.

She sat straight up, instantly made her feel sick.

Tip: Imposter Complex Sentences: Don't Be a Phrase!

Don't go too deep in the grammar weeds with young writers. Decide what matters most, and on an as-needed basis, share as little as possible. Remember the maxim: Less is more. However, as teachers, we need to understand a bit more to make those decisions. What often seems like a complex sentence isn't. You decide whether it matters to your students. Now that that's settled, recall that complex sentences need at least two clauses. And when you start a sentence with a clause, you're usually going to set it off with a comma. But you will set off a phrase at the beginning as well. Sometimes an independent clause with a phrase set off with a comma is called a complex sentence when it's not. But who cares? It's the same pattern, isn't it? Set-off introductory elements?

> Curled up like a comma, everybody paused.
> –Linda Oatman High, *One Amazing Elephant*

That's why we prefer using terms like *opener* or *introductory element*, because it doesn't matter if it's an introductory clause, phrase, or word. It's set off with a comma. The imposters are mainly made up of participial phrases and prepositional phrases. The point is, we set them off with a comma quite often. This is true with openers and closers, as first described in Jeff's *Mechanically Inclined* (2005). In *The Poet's Dog*, Patricia MacLachlan chose to use the participial phrase as a closer, but either way the author chooses, the phrase is set off with a comma. (See Figures 20.11 and 20.12.)

Figure 20.11   **Figure 20.12**

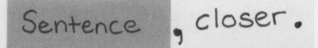

Struggling through snow and wind, we reached the clearing.

We reached the clearing, struggling through snow and wind.

We're finding more and more that the argument that closers are more common than openers in strong writing is true. The answer is to try the word or phrase as both an opener and closer and see which one has the effect you want to convey to your reader. It really doesn't matter if they're words, phrases, or clauses that are set off with commas. The point is not identification, but use. To close out this tip box, we wanted to show you how Newbery Medal–winning author Kelly Barnhill used openers and closers in her writing. Enjoy.

More Sentence *Closers* That Are Still Simple Sentences from Kelly Barnhill's Newbery Medal–Winning *The Girl Who Drank The Moon*	
The thought of it weighed upon Gherland's heart, like a stone.	The closer *like a stone* is a prepositional phrase set off with a comma. We love the pause it creates. That's author's craft and purpose.
Gherland checked his mirror again, touching up his rouge.	This closer is headed with a participle or *-ing* verb, making it a participial phrase. The craft of a participle is that it shows ongoing movement, adding life to the written word.
The Elders stared at her, open-mouthed.	*Openmouthed* is an adjective set off with a comma, acting as a closer. It's not even a phrase, so we know this is still a simple sentence. The adjective could go in the position of the opener, but it wouldn't have the same effect.
The mother made a guttural sound, deep in her chest, like an angry bear.	This sentence has two closers set off with two commas. Sure, they're prepositional phrases. Does it matter that *deep* is an adjective? We don't think so. Worrying over such things will squelch risk taking. The question is, "Does it work?"

More Openers That Are Still Simple Sentences, Also from *The Girl Who Drank the Moon*	
In the center of her forehead, she had a birthmark in the shape of a crescent moon.	This sentence opens with a prepositional phrase, crafted to locate where the birthmark is on the baby's face.
Normally, no one broke the rules.	An adverb opens this sentence. Just a word, not even a phrase. Simple sentence. Move it to the end and see if you like the effect. Barnhill has so few sentences with openers leading into them that it has a nice effect in the context of her novel.

Conclusion
Look Up!

Before you forget . . . look up.

The sky has always been above you,
is above you now,
and will always be above you.

Count on it.
It is what you will always know.
—Rebecca Kai Dotlich, *The Knowing Book*

... look up.

Illustration from *The Knowing Book*

We often begin our *Patterns of Power* workshops with Rebecca Kai Dotlich's *The Knowing Book*, which is beautifully illustrated by Matthew Cordell. Not because she moves through the tenses so deftly, not because it's so poetic and profound, not even because the pictures are so full of childlike wonder.

Nope.

We read it because the author invites us to remember the truth. And as educators in a busy whirlwind of ever-increasing change and pressure, we need to be reminded of the truth, to recalibrate to the truth, to take a breath and reflect on the truth. In this book, we focus on inviting young writers into the world of conventions in hopes that they will uncover the patterns of power that will be their key to open expression and understanding. The truth about conventions is that they are where reading and writing meet. Put simply, the conventions are where meaning is activated.

In the pages of *The Knowing Book*, Dotlich reminds us to always listen, sit, explore, and reflect, and that no matter what we do, it always leads us back home. In the world of conventions, home is writing. Writing is where the conventions of language live, creating meaning and effect. What truth are we telegraphing to young writers about the conventions? How are we shaping their attitudes, their beliefs, their associations?

What we say and do, and what we don't say and don't do, shapes our young writers' minds. This shaping affects their reading and writing lives, their perceptions of reading and writing and conventions, their perceptions of themselves as writers. In the end, our words and actions create the environment that will decide whether students will consider themselves part of "the literacy club" (Smith 1987). Through a tool used often in this work, we imitate Dotlich's pattern to say it another way:

Before you forget . . . look up!

Writing has always been the point,
is the point now,
and will always be the point.

Count on it.
It will always be so.

> Whatever you think you can do or believe you do, begin it—for action has magic grace and power in it.
>   —Goethe

So, when you or your colleagues become stuck in the sticky tar of grammar's abstractness, and it all seems like senselessness and haphazard triviality, remember the truth: every choice a writer makes has an effect. Every choice. There is a purpose behind every move. Every move has meaning and either guides our reader closer to our message or takes them further away from it.

Before you think grammar is about the labels, about right and wrong, about memorization of definitions, or sentence diagramming, look up. Look up to where writing thrives. Writing thrives in exploration of thought and experimentation of effect. Writing moves. Writing holds detail, telling us what thoughts go with others and what thoughts need to be contrasted. Writing is about voices and music. Writing is about words of meaning strung together in ways that show their relationship with each other.

The conventions of language do all these things.

The path we set down in this book is only a beginning. Don't be afraid to experiment and explore. What we have set down is our truth. The power of discovery is activated by conventions. We discover meaning through conventions. We discover effect through conventions. And conventions' patterns keep naturally unfolding in complexity, curiosity, and beauty. In turning toward writing and composing meaning with conventions, we fall in love with the wonder of the written word, without fear, without paralytic doubt.

We are free. We hope this is what your students—and you—will always know.

Write well and flourish,

J and W

The conclusion of *Patterns of Power* calls for us to look up. The day this manuscript was turned over to Stenhouse Publishers, Jeff looked up at the pergola and saw the first wisteria blooms of the year. Growth is an ongoing pattern just like the plants that populate our lives. Always look up. Mistakes are often merely evidence of growth. And you and your students will forever discover something new—about text, about craft, and about yourselves.

This turning toward what you deeply love saves you.
—Rumi

Professional Bibliography

Anderson, Jeff, and Deborah Dean. 2015. *Revision Decisions: Talking Through Sentences and Beyond.* Portland, ME: Stenhouse.

———. 2007. *Everyday Editing: Inviting Students to Develop Skill and Craft in Writer's Workshop.* Portland, ME: Stenhouse.

———. 2005. *Mechanically Inclined: Building Grammar Usage and Style into Writer's Workshop.* Portland, ME: Stenhouse.

Avery, Carol. 2002. *. . . And with a Light Touch: Learning About Reading, Writing, and Teaching with First Graders.* 2nd ed. Portsmouth, NH: Heinemann.

Barnhouse, Dorothy. 2014. *Reading Front and Center: Helping All Students Engage with Complex Text.* Portland, ME: Stenhouse.

Carol, Joyce Armstrong, and Edward E. Wilson. 2007. *Acts of Teaching: How to Teach Writing: A Text, A Reader, A Narrative.* 2nd ed. Westport, CT: Libraries Unlimited.

Chambers, Aidan. 1985. *Book Talk: Occasional Writing on Literature and Children.* New York: Bodley Head Children's Books.

Cunningham, Patricia. 2016. *Phonics They Use.* New York: Pearson.

Dean, Ceri B., Elizabeth Ross Hubbell, Howard Pitler, and B. J. Stone. 2012. *Classroom Instruction That Works: Research-Based Strategies for Increasing Student Achievement.* 2nd ed. Alexandria, VA: Association for Supervision and Curriculum Development.

Dillard, Annie. 1989. *The Writing Life.* New York: HarperCollins.

Eagleman, David. 2011. *Incognito: The Secret Lives of the Brain.* New York: Vintage Books.

Garner, Betty K. 2007. *Getting to Got It! Helping Struggling Students Learn How to Learn.* Alexandria, VA: Association for Supervision and Curriculum Development.

Graham, Steve, and Delores Perin. 2007. *Writing Next: Effective Strategies to Improve Writing of Adolescents in Middle and High School*—A Report to Carnegie Corporation of New York. Washington DC: Alliance for Education

Hale, Constance. 2013. *Sin and Syntax: How to Craft Wicked Good Prose.* New York: Three Rivers.

———. 2012. *Vex, Hex, Smash, Smooch: Let Verbs Power Your Writing.* New York: W. W. Norton.

King, Stephen. 2000. *On Writing*. New York: Scribner.

Kurtz, Adam J. 2016. *Pick Me Up*. New York: Penguin.

O'Conner, Patricia T. 2016. *Woe Is I Jr.: The Younger Grammarphobe's Guide to Better English in Plain English*. New York: Puffin.

Oxford English Dictionary, 2nd ed. (CD-ROM, version 4.0). 2009. Oxford, UK: Oxford University Press.

Smith, Frank. 1987. *Joining the Literacy Club: Further Essays into Education*. Portsmouth, NH: Heinemann.

Strunk, William, and E. B. White. 2000. *Elements of Style*. New York: Allyn & Bacon.

Thompson, Terry. 2015. *The Construction Zone: Building Scaffolds for Readers and Writers*. Portland, ME: Stenhouse.

University of Chicago Press. 2010. *The Chicago Manual of Style*. 16th ed. Chicago, IL: University of Chicago Press.

Walsh, Bill. 2013. *Yes, I Could Care Less: How to Be a Language Snob Without Being a Jerk*. New York: St. Martin's Griffin.

Winter, Caroline. 2008. "Me, Myself and I." New *York Times Magazine*, August 3.

Children's Literature Bibliography

Albee, Sarah. 2014. *Bugged: How Insects Changed History*. New York: Bloomsbury.

Alexander, William. 2013. *Goblin Secrets*. New York: Simon and Schuster.

Alexie, Sherman. 2016. *Thunder Boy Jr.* New York: Little, Brown.

Anderson, Jeff. 2016. *Zack Delacruz: Just My Luck*. New York: Sterling.

———. 2015. *Zack Delacruz: Me and My Big Mouth*. New York: Sterling.

Appelt, Kathi, and Alison McGhee. 2016. *Maybe a Fox*. New York: Atheneum Books for Young Readers.

Arlon, Penelope. 2006. *DK Eye Know: Water*. New York: DK Children.

Aston, Dianna Hutts. 2012. *A Rock Is Lively*. San Francisco, CA: Chronicle.

Bagley, Jessixa. 2015. *Boats for Papa*. New York: Roaring Book Press.

Baker, Liza. 2001. *I Love You Because You're You*. New York: Scholastic.

Barnhill, Kelly. 2016. *The Girl Who Drank the Moon*. Chapel Hill, NC: Algonquin.

Barton, Chris. 2016. *Whoosh! Lonnie Johnson's Super-Soaking Stream of Inventions*. Watertown, MA: Charlesbridge.

Beasley, Kate. 2016. *Gertie's Leap to Greatness*. New York: Farrar Straus and Giroux.

Berenstain, Stan, and Jan Berenstain. 2011. *The Berenstain Bears: Jobs Around Town*. Grand Rapids, MI: Zonderkids.

Berne, Jennifer. 2015. *Manfish: A Story of Jacques Cousteau*. San Francisco, CA: Chronicle.

Bildner, Phil. 2015. *Marvelous Cornelius*. San Francisco, CA: Chronicle.

Bradley, Kimberly Brubaker. 2015. *The War that Saved My Life*. New York: Puffin.

Bragg, Georgia. 2014. *How They Choked: Failures, Flops, and Flaws of the Awfully Famous*. New York: Bloomsbury.

Breen, Steve. 2008. *Violet the Pilot*. New York: Dial.

Bridwell, Norman. 2010. *Clifford the Big Red Dog*. New York: Scholastic.

Brinkloe, Julie. 1985. *Fireflies*. New York: Simon & Schuster.

Brown, Marc. 1997. *D.W. the Picky Eater*. New York: Little, Brown.

Brown, Peter. 2016. *The Wild Robot*. New York: Little, Brown.

Bruel, Nick. 2006. *Who Is Melvin Bubble?* New York: Roaring Book Press.

Bryant, Jen. 2016 *Six Dots: A Story of Young Louis Braille*. New York: Random House.

———. 2014. *The Right Word: Roget and His Thesaurus*. Grand Rapids, MI: Eerdmans.

———. 2013. *A Splash of Red: The Life and Art of Horace Pippin.* New York: Random House.

Burleigh, Robert. 2011. *Night Flight: Amelia Earhart Crosses the Atlantic.* New York: Simon and Schuster.

Burnham, Molly B. 2015. *Teddy Mars: Almost a World Record Breaker.* New York: HarperCollins.

Byrd, Robert. 2012. *Electric Ben: The Amazing Life and Times of Benjamin Franklin.* New York: Penguin.

Cardillo, Margaret. 2011. *Just Being Audrey.* New York: HarperCollins.

Carle, Eric. 2007. *"Slowly, Slowly, Slowly," Said the Sloth.* New York: Penguin.

———. 1988. *The Mixed-Up Chameleon.* New York: HarperCollins.

Carney, Elizabeth. 2009. *National Geographic Readers: Frogs!* Washington, DC: National Geographic Society.

Cervantes, Jennifer. 2014. *Tortilla Sun.* San Francisco, CA: Chronicle.

Choi, Yangsook. 2001. *The Name Jar.* New York: Random House.

Choldenko, Gennifer. 2011. *No Passengers Beyond This Point.* New York: Penguin.

Codell, Esme Raji. 2003. *Sahara Special.* New York: Hyperion Books for Children.

Curato, Mike. 2015. *Little Elliot, Big Family.* New York: Henry Holt.

Curtis, Christopher Paul. 2000. *The Watsons Go to Birmingham–1963.* New York: Laurel Leaf.

Curtis, Jamie Leigh. 1998. *Today I Feel Silly.* New York: HarperCollins.

Davies, Nicola. 2013. *Deadly! The Truth About the Most Dangerous Creatures on Earth.* Somerville, MA: Candlewick.

Daywalt, Drew. 2015. *The Day the Crayons Came Home.* New York: Penguin.

———. 2013. *The Day the Crayons Quit.* New York: Penguin.

de la Peña, Matt. 2015. *Last Stop on Market Street.* New York: Penguin.

dePaola, Tomie. 2006. *Now One Foot, Now the Other.* New York: Puffin.

DiCamillo, Kate. 2016. *Raymie Nightingale.* Somerville, MA: Candlewick.

———. 2015. *Francine Poulet Meets the Ghost Raccoon.* Somerville, MA: Candlewick.

———. 2013. *Flora and Ulysses.* Somerville, MA: Candlewick.

———. 2008. *Louise, The Adventures of a Chicken.* New York: HarperCollins.

———. 2007. *The Tale of Despereaux.* Somerville, MA: Candlewick.

———. 2006. *Mercy Watson Goes for a Ride.* Somerville, MA: Candlewick.

———. 2005. *Mercy Watson to the Rescue.* Somerville, MA: Candlewick.

Dotlich, Rebecca Kai. 2016. *The Knowing Book.* Honesdale, PA: Boyds Mills.

———. 2012. *What Can a Crane Pick Up?* New York: Random House.

Draper, Sharon M. 2015. *Stella by Starlight.* New York: Atheneum.

Dubuc, Marianne. 2010. *In Front of My House.* New York: Kids Can Press.

Ehlert, Lois. 2004. *Nuts to You!* New York: Houghton Mifflin Harcourt.

Fanous, Samuel. 2015. *A Barrel of Monkeys: A Compendium of Collective Nouns for Animals.* Oxford, UK: Bodleian Library.

Farley, Brianne. 2013. *Ike's Incredible Ink.* Somerville, MA: Candlewick.

Ferry, Beth. 2015. *Stick and Stone.* New York: Houghton Mifflin Harcourt.

Fleming, Candace. 2012. *Oh, No!* New York: Random House.

Freedman, Russell. 2005. *Children of the Great Depression.* New York: Houghton Mifflin.

Gemeinhart, Dan. 2015. *The Honest Truth.* New York: Scholastic.

Gewirtz, Adina Rishe. 2013. *Zebra Forest.* Somerville, MA: Candlewick.

Gidwitz, Adam. 2016. *The Inquisitor's Tale.* New York: Dutton.

Grimes, Nikki. 2010. *Dyamonde Daniel: Make Way for Dyamonde Daniel.* New York: Penguin.

Gutman, Dan. 2006. *The Million Dollar Shot.* New York: Hyperion Books for Children.

Harper, Charise Mericle. 2007. *Fashion Kitty Versus the Fashion Queen.* New York: Hyperion Books for Children.

Harris, Michael C. 2016. *What Is the Declaration of Independence?* New York: Penguin.

Henkes, Kevin. 2015. *Waiting.* New York: Greenwillow.

———. 2013. *Penny and Her Marble.* New York: Greenwillow.

———. 2013. *The Year of Billy Miller.* New York: Harper Collins.

———. 2008. *Chrysanthemum.* New York: Mulberry.

———. 2000. *Wemberly Worried.* New York: Greenwillow.

Hiaasen, Carl. 2012. *Scat.* New York: Yearling.

High, Linda Oatman. 2017. *One Amazing Elephant.* New York: HarperCollins.

Holm, Jennifer L. 2016. *Full of Beans.* New York: Random House.

Jamieson, Victoria. 2016. *The Great Pet Escape.* New York: Henry Holt.

———. 2015. *Roller Girl.* New York: Penguin.

Jenkins, Steve. 2011. *Just a Second.* New York: Houghton Mifflin Harcourt.

———. 1995. *Biggest, Strongest, Fastest.* New York: Houghton Mifflin Harcourt.

Jenkins, Steve, and Robin Page. 2006. *Move!* New York: Houghton Mifflin Harcourt.

Kann, Victoria. 2013. *Emeraldalicious.* New York: Harper Collins.

Keating, Jess. 2014. *How to Outrun a Crocodile When Your Shoes Are Untied.* Naperville, IL: Sourcebooks.

Krull, Kathleen. 2006. *Giants of Science: Isaac Newton.* New York: Puffin.

Leedy, Loreen. 2013. *Seeing Symmetry.* New York: Holiday House.

Litwin, Eric. 2011. *Pete the Cat: Rocking in My School Shoes.* New York: HarperCollins.

Lloyd, Natalie. 2014. *A Snicker of Magic.* New York: Scholastic.

London, Jonathan. 2015. *Hippos Are Huge!* New York: Candlewick.

MacLachlan, Patricia. 2016. *The Poet's Dog.* New York: HarperCollins.

———. 2007. *Edward's Eyes.* New York: Atheneum.

Marshall, Joseph, III. 2015. *In the Footsteps of Crazy Horse.* New York: Abrams.

McCall, Guadalupe Garcia. 2011. *Under the Mesquite.* New York: Lee and Low.

McClements, George. 2008. *Night of the Veggie Monster.* New York: Bloomsbury.

McDonald, Megan. 2016. *Judy Moody and the Bucket List.* New York: Candlewick.

———. 2003. *Judy Moody Predicts the Future.* New York: Candlewick.

McDonnell, Patrick. 2011. *Me . . . Jane.* New York: Little, Brown.

Meltzer, Brad. 2014a. *Ordinary People Change the World: I Am Albert Einstein.* New York: Dial.

———. 2014b. *Ordinary People Change the World: I Am Amelia Earhart.* New York: Dial.

Meschenmoser, Sebastian. 2015. *Mr. Squirrel and the Moon.* New York: NorthSouth Books.

Messner, Kate. 2017. *Over and Under the Pond.* San Francisco, CA: Chronicle.

———. 2015. *Up in the Garden and Down in the Dirt.* San Francisco, CA: Chronicle.

———. 2014. *Over and Under the Snow.* San Francisco, CA: Chronicle.

Nielsen, Jennifer A. 2016. *The Scourge.* New York: Scholastic.

Numeroff, Laura. 2002. *If You Take a Mouse to School.* New York: Harper Collins.

O'Connor, Barbara. 2016. *Wish.* New York: Farrar Straus Giroux Books for Young Readers.

O'Neill, Alexis. 2002. *The Recess Queen.* New York: Scholastic.

O'Shei, Tim. 2007. *Left for Dead! Lincoln Hall's Story of Survival.* Mankato, MN: Capstone.

Osborne, Mary Pope. 2000. *Magic Tree House: Revolutionary War on Wednesday.* New York: Random House.

Palacio, R. J. 2012. *Wonder.* New York: Random House.

Pallotta, Jerry. 2016. Who Would Win? Series. New York: Scholastic.

Park, Linda Sue. 2011. *A Long Walk to Water.* New York: Houghton Mifflin Harcourt.

Pearle, Ida. 2015. *The Moon Is Going to Addy's House.* New York: Dial.

Pennypacker, Sara. 2016. *Pax.* New York: HarperCollins.

———. 2015. *Meet the Dullards.* New York: HarperCollins.

———. 2006. *Clementine.* New York: Hyperion Books for Children.

Polacco, Patricia. 2010. *Junkyard Wonders.* New York: Philomel.

———. 1997. *Thunder Cake.* New York: Putnam Berkley Group.

Polonsky, Ami. 2016. *Threads.* New York: Disney-Hyperion.

Reynolds, Aaron. 2015. *Nerdy Birdy.* New York: Roaring Brook.

Rosenthal, Betsy R. 2015. *An Ambush of Tigers: A Wild Gathering of Collective Nouns.* Minneapolis, MN: Millbrook.

Ryan, Pam Muñoz. 2015. *Echo.* New York: Scholastic.

Santat, Dan. 2016. *Are We There Yet?* New York: Little, Brown.

———. 2014. *The Adventures of Beekle: The Unimaginary Friend.* New York: Little, Brown.

Sayre, April Pulley. 2016. *Squirrels Leap, Squirrels Sleep.* New York: Henry Holt.

Schaefer, Lola M. 2014. *Swamp Chomp.* New York: Holiday House.

———. 2013. *Lifetime: The Amazing Numbers in Animal Lives.* San Francisco, CA: Chronicle.

———. 2006. *An Island Grows.* New York: Greenwillow.

Schaefer, Lola M., and Adam Schaefer. 2016. *Because of an Acorn.* San Francisco, CA: Chronicle.

Schmidt, Gary D. 2013. *Lizzie Bright and the Buckminster Boy.* New York: Houghton Mifflin Harcourt.

Sendak, Maurice. 2012. *Where the Wild Things Are.* New York: HarperCollins.

Shang, Wendy Wan-Long. 2011. *The Great Wall of Lucy Wu.* New York: Scholastic.

Sherry, Maureen. 2010. *Walls Within Walls.* New York: HarperCollins.

Snyder, Laurel. 2015. *Swan: The Life and Dance of Anna Pavlova.* San Francisco, CA: Chronicle.

Soontornvat, Christina. 2016. *The Changelings.* Naperville, IL: Sourcebooks.

Spires, Ashley. 2014. *The Most Magnificent Thing.* Tonawanda, NY: Kids Can Press.

Stead, Philip. 2010. *A Sick Day for Amos McGee.* New York: Macmillan.

Stead, Philip C. 2015. *Lenny and Lucy.* New York: Roaring Brook.

Stead, Rebecca. 2009. *When You Reach Me.* New York: Random House.

Sweet, Melissa. 2016. *Some Writer: The Story of E. B. White.* New York: Houghton Mifflin Harcourt.

Time for Kids. 2016. *Time for Kids Big Book of Why: 1,001 Facts Kids Want to Know.* New York: Time.

Tonatiuh, Duncan. 2014. *Separate Is Never Equal: Sylvia Mendez and Her Family's Fight for Desegregation.* New York: Abrams.

Weeks, Sarah, and Gita Varadarajan. 2016. *Save Me a Seat.* New York: Scholastic.

Wenzel, Brendan. 2016. *They All Saw a Cat.* San Francisco, CA: Chronicle.

Wild, Margaret. 2006. *Fox.* La Jolla, CA: Kane/Miller.

Willems, Mo. 2013. *A Big Guy Took My Ball!* New York: Hyperion Books for Children.

———. 2008. *The Pigeon Wants a Puppy!* New York: Hyperion Books for Children.

———. 2007. *There Is a Bird on Your Head! (An Elephant and Piggie Book).* New York: Hyperion Books for Children.

———. 2004. *Knuffle Bunny.* New York: Hyperion Books for Children.

Williams-Garcia, Rita. 2011. *One Crazy Summer.* New York: HarperCollins.

Wolk, Lauren. 2016. *Wolf Hollow.* New York: Dutton.

Wright, Anna. 2015. *A Tower of Giraffes: Animals in Groups.* Watertown, MA: Charlesbridge.

Yee, Wong Herbert. 2005. *Upstairs Mouse, Downstairs Mouse.* New York: Houghton Mifflin Harcourt.

Young, Karen Romano. 2016. *Hundred Percent.* San Francisco, CA: Chronicle.

Index